# euro

## impact
## & reality

business risks and
practical responses to the
challenge of the euro

CHRIS CHARLTON

FINANCIAL TIMES
PITMAN PUBLISHING

**FINANCIAL TIMES**

# MANAGEMENT

LONDON · SAN FRANCISCO
KUALA LUMPUR · JOHANNESBURG

*Financial Times Management delivers the knowledge,
skills and understanding that enable students,
managers and organizations to achieve their ambitions,
whatever their needs, wherever they are.*

London Office:
128 Long Acre, London WC2E 9AN
Tel: +44 (0)171 447 2000
Fax: +44 (0)171 240 5771
Website: www.ftmanagement.com

*A Division of Financial Times Professional Limited*

First published in Great Britain in 1999

ISBN 0 273 63877 7

*British Library Cataloguing in Publication Data*
A CIP catalogue record for this book can be obtained from the British Library.

10 9 8 7 6 5 4 3 2 1

Typeset by Northern Phototypesetting Co. Ltd, Bolton
Printed and bound in Great Britain by Biddles Ltd, Guildford & King's Lynn

*The Publishers' policy is to use paper manufactured from sustainable forests.*

# About the author

Since graduating from Cambridge University, Chris has worked extensively in line and project management within the financial services and consultancy industries, delivering a wide range of projects from major strategic change to tactical and operational systems enhancements.

Chris now works as an independent consultant to businesses experiencing significant change including preparations for Economic and Monetary Union, integrating mergers and acquisitions, and other business development initiatives.

Chris would be delighted to receive any comments or feedback about the book or the euro by e-mail at: chrischarlton@namaste.co.uk

# Acknowledgements

Combining the pressures and demands of writing a book with full-time consulting takes a considerable toll on the amount of time you have to spend with the ones you love. My greatest thanks, therefore, must go to Freya, who has been a wonderful source of continuous support and understanding.

I am also deeply grateful for the combined input of many colleagues and clients, past and present, who have contributed to the development of this book in a multitude of ways. Whether formulating ideas, researching new material or reviewing passages of text, their help has been invaluable.

Finally my thanks to Financial Times Pitman Publishing and the production team who have been first class throughout. In particular to Richard Stagg, who has guided the book from conception to reality.

Responding to the introduction of the euro represents an unprecedented challenge to business, not just in the global financial markets, but across all sectors of the economy.

**Euro – impact and reality** looks at the practical issues and risks that organizations are facing, notably in conjunction with other major programmes, such as Year 2000 and integrating mergers and acquisitions, at the same time as running business as usual. Having analyzed these issues and the lessons learned from other significant conversions and change programmes, it recommends the best practice management actions, tools and techniques drawn from the author's experience of EMU assignments and research. These are designed to give you and your business a greater chance of immediate and lasting euro success.

# Contents

# Introduction

Do you realize that the euro will create opportunities both for business development and greater efficiency for enterprises in inner countries? In effect, the size of the domestic market will increase significantly, with a particular impact on those enterprises which do not currently engage in import/export activities. Do you realize that you will still need to prepare for the introduction of the euro even if your country is not joining Economic and Monetary Union (EMU)? This is because your competitors, purchasers or suppliers may be introducing the euro and you may be forced to do so too.

Eventually all organizations operating in Europe or in European currencies will make the transition to the euro. The impact is most immediate and far-reaching in the financial services sector but it will also stimulate significant competitive realignment in other sectors. Indeed, leading companies are already deriving competitive advantage from their investment in early preparations. However, the majority of companies are only beginning to understand the impact of the euro, in particular the complexity of managing such a significant shift in the environment in which they operate.

> **the majority of companies are only beginning to understand the impact of the euro**

The euro is just another currency. Or is it? In fact, there is no precedent for a project of this scale and complexity. Nor is there likely to be. That it has taken so long to convince the majority of managers about the seriousness of the issue is ample demonstration of the impact of uncertainty on a project.

There is no project that has been, is currently, or is likely to be more complex and demanding on organizations, particularly those operating in the financial markets, than the introduction of the euro. There are a number of reasons for this:

- *Scope* – how many projects span every single department of the organization?
- *Hierarchy* – how many projects encompass every level of the organization, from strategic decision-making to the detail of operational and system code changes?

- *Critical path* – how many projects are constrained by an externally-imposed fixed completion date?
- *Uncertainty* – how many projects are shrouded in such debate and uncertainty, from whether it will actually happen or not, to the creation of new market conventions?
- *Timing* – how many projects of this scale and uncertainty are imposed one year before another major programme, such as Year 2000, now recognized as a critical issue for organizations worldwide?

How many projects combine all of the above five attributes simultaneously?

Businesses operating across borders will be significantly affected. Any major change in currency and trading arrangements will have a considerable impact on your business activities in general, and on the management of your accounting, fiscal, treasury and other financial functions – and on the systems which support them – in particular. To a lesser degree the impact on businesses trading domestically will be similar and will be driven by trading partners' requirements and domestic participation within EMU. The businesses that are affected immediately, other than the financial services sector include:

> every individual, company or organization that uses the former national currencies of participating countries will be affected in some way, even if their 'home' country does not enter EMU

- exporters and importers to/from the euro zone – likely to come under pressure to quote/deal in the euro;
- multinationals operating in the euro zone – they will have to deal with the euro; and
- firms in supply chains that incorporate organizations that will use the euro.

Every individual, company or organization that uses the former national currencies of participating countries will be affected in some way, even if their 'home' country does not enter EMU. Companies trading with partners in the euro-zone are likely to have to deal in euros.

Several large European companies such as Siemens and Philips intend to switch to accounting in the euro in 1999 and moves by big businesses such as these could force smaller ones to follow suit. European Governments have agreed that there will be 'no compulsion' and 'no prohibition' in the use of the euro between 1999 and 2002, but if one business partner wants to use the new currency, and the other does not, commercial 'clout' will probably dictate the outcome.

Organizations outside the EMU area also need to take the euro changeover into account for a number of reasons. They include the following.

> there are a huge number of detailed and specific tasks to carry out to ensure that you are adequately prepared for the euro

- An organization outside the EMU area that has dealings in one of the participating currency units may have to convert amounts in these national currency units to euro or other national currency units.

- Organizations that have subsidiaries in the EMU area need to ensure that those subsidiaries are preparing themselves adequately for the euro changeover.

- The euro changeover will usually require that changes are made to information systems. Multinationals that use the same information systems for all their operations may have to upgrade information systems located both inside and outside the EMU area in order to maintain compatibility.

Many institutions domiciled outside Europe, and indeed many within, have to date largely ignored the issue, perhaps to concentrate on the Year 2000 compliance project. These firms will have to be made aware of the inevitable implications that the launch of the euro will have on the way they conduct business in continental Europe.

The legal and commercial implications of EMU, which remove many of the trading barriers for competitive businesses, will bring their own pressure to bear. The only businesses which might escape those pressures are those which sell a product that is bought by a local market only, have no ambition to sell outside that market, and are unlikely to face competition from outside players. In today's competitive and pan-global industries, those businesses are surely few and far between.

As organizations have woken up to the scale of the problem, it has caused all kinds of reactions. Some examples include: nearly pulling out of a quarter billion dollar acquisition after recognizing the lack of EMU preparation in the target (10 weeks into the integration process); the strategic business withdrawal from Europe; the resignation of a leading investment bank's EMU programme director; and the postponement of a major system replacement (18 months into the implementation). The massive expansion of consultancy firms' fee revenue is testimony to the fact that organizations have looked for experienced external help or, in many cases, simply to fill the gaps in resourcing requirements.

Some organizations have also woken up to the opportunities. The acceleration in merger and acquisition activity, which only compounds the difficulties, has been breathtaking in recent years and this is set to increase. The creation of groups of exceptional size and the desire to expand into what have traditionally been domestic markets has and will continue to create projects of monumental proportions.

Can organizations really find the time and resources to cope with the euro, Year 2000, a major integration, as well as run business as usual? This is a huge agenda that will stretch the capacity, skill-sets and sustainability of the resources of an organization to the limit. Do senior managers really have access to the information that allows them to judge whether their organizations can simultaneously implement projects of this scale, two of which have inescapably fixed deadlines?

The scale of official assistance is enormous. However, the vast quantities of information that has been pouring out from thousands of sources has created a serious case of information overload. Not just overload, but also inconsistencies, ambiguities, gaps and conflicts. This is because there is not a standard set of euro requirements which organizations can implement. But even in the case of Year 2000 where requirements are more fixed, there are still many issues. The German banking *EMU Bible* was an attempt at standardization, but even this 600-page document was by no means complete, and by no means consistent with the other European countries' implementation strategies.

> which web site, which market body, which official organization, which consultancy, which document, which company has the holy grail – all known EMU requirements?

Organizations that straddle European countries have to determine which paths to follow and the impact of such non-standardization on their business. Which web site, which market body, which official organization, which consultancy, which document, which company has the holy grail – all known EMU requirements? Unfortunately, none exist for two main reasons:

- Firstly, gathering and managing all sources of information is practically impossible and even those information vendors that compile as much documentation into one place as possible rarely sift the documents to prevent duplication for the reader. Ultimately, it is for the reader to determine what is new information and what is just a re-hash of old documents. Knowledge management has become critical to saving time and resource.

- Secondly, organizations have to decide what they want to do. There are few absolutely prescriptive answers to many questions posed by the euro. Many require strategic, operational and tactical decision-making, and this takes time. Co-operation has become critical to survival as the interdependencies between organizations has become all too apparent.

Whilst your major competitor is also your major counterparty or client, it is difficult to drive competitive advantage from what is also your source of revenue because if failure results, everyone is a loser. If, for example, you removed the inter-bank element from financial market statistics, how much do you think revenue and profit figures would fall? In the region of 50% for an average bank perhaps.

Being at the forefront of the changeover, financial institutions must be prepared for the introduction of the euro before other businesses and as such should be much further ahead. Their most immediate challenge has been preparing for 'Big Bang' conversion at the end of 1998. However, when you analyze the risks of introducing the euro using a bottom-up approach (i.e., can we actually do this?), the euro possibly represents the greatest single risk to the operational stability of the global financial markets that we have ever seen. We are all, in one way or another, dependent upon the financial markets – as private investors, taxpayers and business managers. At the very least, we should be aware of the changes taking place and how financial institutions and governments have been preparing themselves.

Whilst the principal objective of *euro – impact and reality* is to be a working assistant to the manager, some searching questions are asked. What are the implications for the credibility of the euro? What are the other options? What are the implications of going ahead in full knowledge of the level of risk? What should Europe's regulators do to respond to the general lack of preparation?

Due to the exceptional demand for euro-knowledgeable resources, there is currently exceptional demand for external help, but where does the experience come from? Either first-hand experience, which is applicable to the minority, or from second-hand experience that is taught and learned. I hope that this book will go some way to filling the gap in practical knowledge and experience of this issue.

This is a practitioner's guide to the issues, problems and risks of introducing the euro. Already there is a mass of publications relating to the debate surrounding the macroeconomics, the politics and the future of the financial markets in a new 'euro-zone'. The aim of this book is to provide managers from all organizations with valuable practical insights, tools and techniques to cope with the most significant economic event in 20th century history. Indeed, there is no issue in Europe, particularly in the financial markets, that will supersede the introduction of the euro for a considerable time to come.

> this is a practitioner's guide... to provide managers from all organizations with valuable practical insights, tools and techniques to cope with the most significant economic event in 20th century history

The book draws on my practical experiences of managing the introduction of the euro. This comes from over two years' full-time consulting on ten major global EMU programmes for some of the leading players in the financial markets (including US, European and Japanese institutions). I also draw on the shared experiences of a large number of clients and colleagues to provide a spread of opinion and experience from within the financial markets, industry and consulting.

The book is aimed at managers at all levels in organizations that are involved in, or have responsibility for, euro-related projects. Whilst many companies (and the media) have focused on the initial launch of the euro, the reality is that euro preparations will continue for some considerable years to come. In many cases, until the euro becomes notes and coins in the hands of the general public, many will continue to be unaware of its significance and impact.

> whilst many companies (and the media) have focused on the initial launch of the euro, the reality is that euro preparations will continue for some considerable years to come

The book is therefore aimed both at those companies that have already started their euro projects and those that have yet to begin. As company managers, we should be well-prepared, and I hope that this book contributes to your preparation.

There are two key sections to the book.

# SECTION I: IMPACT OF THE EURO

Chapter 1 is a quick guide to the introduction of the euro – a reminder for many – including the timetable, legal framework, the macro-economic arguments and the changing nature of the financial markets. It also highlights some of the key terminology and 'euro jargon'. Whilst it is not intended to be a thorough and expansive discussion, at the end of the chapter you should be able to demonstrate to your colleagues a succint understanding of the key elements of the debate surrounding Economic and Monetary Union.

Chapter 2 looks at the business issues, organized around the factors that influence competitive strategy – stakeholders, competitors, customers and supply chain. If you fail to analyze the impact of the euro on your business, you could be exposing yourself unnecessarily to your competitors. Some companies, at best, have employed a minimalist survival strategy. For these companies, this has just postponed a more thorough strategic process.

Chapter 3 highlights the information technology issues, including the types of systems that are impacted and how they are affected, as well as key IT management issues. Many euro projects have been focused on the IT issues causing undue pressure on IT departments who have been asked to provide all the answers – this simply does not work.

Conversion is analyzed in detail in Chapter 4 with a distinct emphasis on financial markets. It has a chapter all of its own as it has represented the most complex, demanding and riskiest task of all. It is also the most burdensome on an organization's resources. The key issues are higlighted as are the risks and management issues. If you have no interest in the financial markets or financial instruments, simply scan through this chapter. However, it raises some important concerns which are of relevance to all of us.

The final part of the chapter looks at the implications of the state of EMU preparations for the euro and the financial markets. What happens in January 1999 when 10% of *every* (not just one or two) financial market participants' conversion routine fails? What happens when each of these 10% failures is different from all others? What happens

> even the experienced euro-hands should at least cast their eyes across the checklists provided in each chapter

when this does not get resolved for two, three, even six weeks into 1999? What does this do to the liquidity and credibility of the euro? How successful will the ECB be in meeting its objectives in the first half of 1999? The aggregated view across the financial markets in this scenario is hugely significant, but more importantly, real. Look at the demise of Barings to see how easy it is to bring a bank down.

For those of you unfamiliar with all the impacts, Chapters 2 to 4 provide a useful summary of the issues. Even the experienced euro-hands should at least cast their eyes across the checklists provided in each chapter – it's not difficult to miss something out! Indeed, as issues continue to arise and change, a key characteristic of the euro, these checklists may soon be out-of-date. Ultimately, it is the manager's job to ensure he or she has to hand the most up-to-date information available – I hope I can reduce the number of references you require.

In addition to the direct impacts, I look at the major management issues that organizations have been facing, including the following main areas: information and awareness, organization structure, resourcing and competing priorities, including Year 2000 and integrating mergers and acquisitions.

Many organizations have fallen foul of one or more of these management issues as far as their euro projects are concerned. Each issue in isolation has caused lengthy delays in projects (up to 18 months in some cases), increased costs and loss of business. All organizations will face some combination of these issues when preparing for the euro and should at least be aware of them; better still, should be able to deal with them successfully.

Understanding the impact of the euro is critical to survival. But overcoming the management issues and complexities of implementing the change it can lead to is possibly the secret of long-term strategic success. The management actions, tools and techniques to help you do this are discussed in Section II.

Before turning to Section II, however, answer the questionnaire in Chapter 5. It will give you an indication as to the current state of your preparations. You can then benchmark your own preparations against the processes outlined in Section II.

# SECTION II: BEST PRACTICE MANAGEMENT ACTIONS, TOOLS AND TECHNIQUES

Combining practical experience from real-world EMU assignments, lengthy research and consulting experience, the author recommends the best practice management actions, tools and techniques designed to give organizations a greater chance of immediate and lasting euro success.

When striving to achieve the goals and objectives of the project, programme or organization, there is a vast array of management tools and techniques which can be used to assist the manager in his or her work. Many of these simply aid management by providing relevant information to enable improved decision-making and more effective control. I don't wish to look at the detailed specifics of most of these tools and techniques, many of which you will already be familiar, but rather highlight the key elements and how to utilize some of the best ones for the peculiarities and complexities of the euro.

> **it is important to avoid the danger of using sophisticated techniques for their own sake when simpler methods might be just as satisfactory, or using inappropriate tools that add to your problems rather than alleviate them**

It is important to avoid the danger of using sophisticated techniques for their own sake when simpler methods might be just as satisfactory, or using inappropriate tools that add to your problems rather than alleviate them. In particular, they do not replace the most important tool of all – the manager's decision-making processor – the brain. Our brains have enough to cope with without overloading them with jargon and complexity – keeping it simple will always give you a greater chance of success.

This section is split into the three essential components of a strategic process suitable for responding to a change such as the euro: analysis, planning and most importantly, implementation. Throughout, I also recommend related management actions and 'handy hints' to assist managers in implementing some of these solutions and avoiding some of the more common mistakes that I have seen on a large number of euro projects. These 'handy hints' include recommendations for impact assessment, conversion, risk management, resourcing, management structure, communications and business strategy.

Chapter 6 looks at business strategy and various techniques you can use to conduct a strategic analysis and impact assessment. In addition I have included a section on knowledge management, a technique which has become critical to managing the volume and changing nature of euro information.

Chapter 7 identifies the key components of your strategic plan, including objectives, organization and business line strategy, conversion strategy, communication strategy, management structure, resourcing and management controls. The section on conversion strategy identifies the key decisions, processes and alternatives that you have in making a successful transition to the euro.

Chapter 8 looks at the crux of the issue – implementation, or getting it done. Experience of major change projects, including the euro, integrating mergers and acquisitions, year 2000, process re-engineering, etc., all point at failure to implement as the most common and significant reason why organizations fail to embrace change successfully. This chapter looks at the main components of a successful implementation programme including sections on change management, the nature of projects and the critical success factors for your euro project: planning, resourcing, management, communication and control.

> I aim to give concise practical guidance to managers who are coping with the complexities and demands of the euro

Chapter 9 takes a brief look at integrating mergers and acquisitions – one of the strategic options which many companies have chosen as a response to the euro. Merger deals have become the primary instrument of corporate strategy, principally because strategic change in many of today's industries does not allow time for organic growth. If you want to compete, it seems, you have to grow, and to grow, you have to merge or acquire.

But research has shown that the long-term results of combinations are far from convincing. The main killer of value and post-merger results has been poor post-merger management. The impact of two major programmes, EMU and Year 2000, can only weaken organizations' ability to successfully integrate at this time. However, the business opportunities in some sectors are too strong to turn down. Consequently, managers will have to make some serious decisions when determining their integration strategy.

Finally, Chapter 10 concludes by drawing together the key message from the book to provide a salient reminder of the essential ingredients of a successful project.

I hope I can share some of the lessons from my line and project experiences as well as those of the book's review team. The last thing you have time for right now is to read an academic discussion – that's why I aim to give concise practical guidance to managers who are coping with the complexities and demands of the euro. Good luck.

Summaries from the book can be found at the author's website *www.namaste.com.*

# Impact of
# the euro

# CHAPTER 1

# A quick guide to the euro and its introduction

# ECONOMIC AND MONETARY UNION – WHAT DOES THAT MEAN?

Economic and Monetary Union (EMU), as conceived by the Maastricht Treaty, is a monetary union, an economic union to a limited extent, but not a political union. It is a monetary union because national monetary competencies are pooled within a European Central Bank (ECB) which defines and implements a single monetary policy, in a single currency – the euro – for the whole of the EMU area (*see* Table 1.1).

**TABLE 1.1**

**The EMU area**

| Eleven countries of the European Union will participate in EMU from 1 January 1999: | Four countries are in the EU but will not participate in the first wave (they are usually described as 'pre-ins'): |
|---|---|
| Austria | Denmark |
| Belgium | Greece |
| Finland | Sweden |
| France | United Kingdom |
| Germany | |
| Ireland | |
| Italy | |
| Luxembourg | |
| Netherlands | |
| Portugal | |
| Spain | |

With effect from 1 January 1999 the official national currency of the participating 11 countries is the euro. The rate of exchange between the euro and the old national currency will be irrevocably locked, each rate expressed to six significant figures, e.g., 1 euro = 6.54321 French francs.

Technically, it is not a genuine economic union since national authorities remain in charge of economic and budgetary policies. The transfer of competencies for national economic and budgetary policies to a Community body would actually have created a political union as decisions on these matters are, in all countries, an essential prerogative of government and parliament. This was not the intention of the Treaty. Nevertheless, these policies are directly affected by EMU, as governments and the ECB, as we have recently seen, continue to push for economic convergence.

# THE TIMETABLE

The transition to the single currency is a three phase process, for which definite dates have been set (*see* Figure 1.1).

## Phase A – Launch of the third stage of the Economic and Monetary Union (EMU):

Following the announcement of participating Member States in May 1998, the ECB was formally created. During the remainder of 1998 conditions for conducting the single monetary and exchange-rate policy have been finalized, and the production of euro banknotes began. The economies of participating countries, however, continue to function as before, in other words on the basis of the national currencies.

## Phase B – Effective start of economic and monetary union:

This phase begins on 1 January 1999 on which date the rates of conversion between the euro and the participating national currencies and irrevocably fixed and the euro becomes a currency in its own right. The currencies of the participating Member States are replaced by the euro which is denominated both in its own unit (1 euro) and sub-units (100 cents) and in national currency units (NCUs), i.e., the former national currencies of the participating Member States.

Organizations most heavily involved in international and European trade are the ones most likely to opt for early conversion to the euro unit of all or part of their operations. Public administrations will also continue to prepare actively for their own changeover where they have not already executed the changeover. This phase ends on 31 December 2001.

Note that there will be no physical euro notes and coins for three years, as they are not introduced until 1 January 2002.

**FIGURE 1.1**

**Planned timetable for the introduction of the euro**

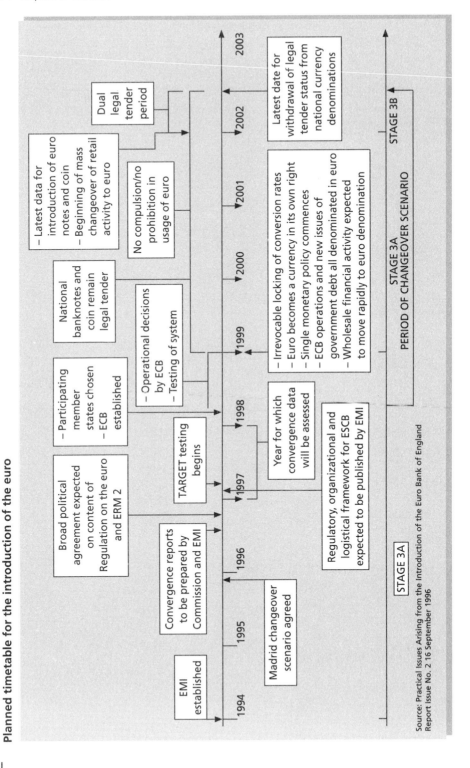

Source: Practical Issues Arising from the Introduction of the Euro Bank of England
Report Issue No. 2 16 September 1996

## Phase C – Definitive changeover to the euro:

After 31 December 2001, amounts which, on 31 December 2001, are still expressed in national currency units of the participating Member States will be deemed to be expressed in euro units, converted at the official rates.

On 1 January 2002, and over a short period (to be determined by each Member State but a maximum of six months), the new euro banknotes and coins will be put into circulation in substitution for banknotes and coins in the old national currency units. This phase should last no longer than is strictly necessary in order to minimize the complications for users that could be caused by national currency units remaining in circulation for an extended period alongside the single currency. The operation will end by 1 July 2002 (at the latest), when euro banknotes and coins will be the only banknotes and coins to have legal tender status in participating Member States.

# A SINGLE MONETARY POLICY

The Maastricht Treaty states that the primary objective of the ECB shall be to maintain price stability in the EMU area. The Treaty, however, does not stipulate how this should be achieved. It has been the job of the European Monetary Institute (EMI), the forerunner to the ECB, to propose the policies and instruments that can best achieve this objective. The actual choice, however, will be made by the ECB and implemented through the European System of Central Banks (ESCB) – which comprises the ECB and the national central banks of participating countries. Whilst maintaining the uniformity of monetary policy requires central decisions, the ECB will rely on the experience and operations of the national central banks. Table 1.2 outlines the structure of the ECB.

In practice, for the ECB to achieve its objective, it will need to monitor its progress through intermediate targets. It has principally two choices: firstly, direct targeting (i.e., forecast inflation targets); and secondly, some form of monetary aggregate. This intermediate target will act as a trigger to monetary policy instruments. Given the problems of time lag between effecting monetary policy and its consequent impact on inflation, the ECB is likely to go for a monetary aggregate approach. In addition the ECB would monitor a wide range of economic and financial variables rather than a single measure. Of central concern, however, has been the development of reliable euro-zone monetary statistics to work from (this is also a problem for econometric forecasting models used for inflation targeting).

> the primary objective of the ECB shall be to maintain price stability in the EMU area

As is the case for monetary policy strategies, differences in the design and use of monetary policy instruments exist across EU States.

However, there is broad consensus that the primary operational focus of the ECB should be the level of one or more short-term interest rates in the money market. In the majority of EU countries, open market operations play a pivotal role in the operation of monetary policy, being the primary instrument by which interest rates are steered.

As with national central banks at the moment, open market operations will feature heavily in the ECB's toolkit. The main instrument likely to be used for altering the balance of supply and demand for liquidity in the financial markets is through a system of weekly and monthly repo. A more controversial instrument is the use of minimum reserve requirements, whereby banks are required to maintain a fixed deposit at the central bank, as in Germany. There is general agreement that this kind of instrument should be available to the ECB, even if it is not actually employed. However, there has been much debate over this issue, in particular as to the level, if any, of remuneration. To the extent that reserve requirements are not fully remunerated, they may enhance the controllability of the monetary aggregate by the central bank. In July 1998, the ECB announced that it would impose minimum reserve requirements, remunerated at market rates, thus ending the debate.

Standby facilities differ from open market operations in that they are initiated at the discretion of individual banks rather than the central bank. As the Bundesbank does now, the ESCB is likely to provide a Lombard facility which gives participants access to overnight liquidity where there is an end-of-day deficit and acts as a sponge for soaking up surplus liquidity. By setting the deposit and marginal lending rates, the ECB would maintain a corridor for influencing market interest rates.

## THE LEGAL FRAMEWORK

The legal framework for the introduction of the euro comprises two EC Regulations:

- Council Regulation (EC) No. 1103/97 of 17 June 1997 (Official journal NO. L 162, 19/06/1997 P. 0001) on certain provisions relating to the introduction of the euro, which is based on Article 235 of the EC Treaty. This Regulation applies to all EU Member States, whether or not they participate in EMU, and concerns the one for one equivalence between the ECU basket and the euro, continuity of contracts, conversion and rounding rules; and

- Resolution of the European Council of 7 July 1997 on the legal framework for the introduction of the euro (Official journal NO. C 236, 02/08/1997 P. 0007–0012). This Regulation will be adopted on the basis of Article 109L(4)

**TABLE 1.2**

**Structure of the European Central Bank**

*The Executive Board*

| President | Wim Duisenberg | Netherlands |
|---|---|---|
| Vice-president | Christian Noyer | France |
| Chief economist | Otmar Issing | Germany |
| Payment systems, banking supervision | Tomasso Padoa-Schioppe | Italy |
| Statistics, banknotes and information systems | Eugenio Domingo Solans | Spain |
| Organization and control | Sirkka Hamalainen | Finland |

| Country | No. of ECB members | Population (m) | Population per ECB vote (m) |
|---|---|---|---|
| Austria | 1 | 8.5 | 8.5 |
| Belgium | 1 | 10.0 | 10.0 |
| Finland | 2 | 5.1 | 2.6 |
| France | 2 | 58.0 | 29.0 |
| Germany | 2 | 81.6 | 40.8 |
| Ireland | 1 | 3.6 | 3.6 |
| Italy | 2 | 57.2 | 28.6 |
| Luxembourg | 1 | 0.4 | 0.4 |
| Netherlands | 2 | 15.5 | 7.8 |
| Portugal | 1 | 9.9 | 9.9 |
| Spain | 2 | 39.2 | 19.6 |
| Total | 17 | 289.0 | 17.0 |

of the Treaty and will become legally binding in only Member States that participate in EMU, such as the substitution of national currencies for the euro.

This legal framework confirms that the euro will be the single currency of the participating Member States from 1 January 1999 and provides the necessary legal certainty for all economic agents. The legal framework for the euro includes several basic principles which are of importance for enterprises.

- The euro will be substituted for the currencies of the participating Member States at the fixed conversion rates applicable from 1 January 1999 (Articles 2 and 3 of the 109L(4) Regulation).

- As from 1 January 1999 every reference in a legal instrument to the ECU is replaced by a reference to the euro at a rate of one euro to one ECU (Article 2 of the 235 Regulation).

- Where in a legal instrument reference is made to a national currency unit, this reference shall be as valid as if reference were made to the euro unit (Article 6 of the 109L(4) Regulation).

- The introduction of the euro shall not have the effect of altering any term of a legal instrument or of discharging or excusing performance under any legal instrument, nor give a party the right unilaterally to alter or terminate a legal instrument. However, as the freedom of contract is respected, this provision remains subject to anything which parties may have agreed (Article 3 of the 235 Regulation).

- As from 1 January 1999 any amount denominated either in the euro unit or in the national currency unit of a given participating Member State and payable within that Member State by crediting an account of the creditor, can be paid by the debtor either in the euro unit or in that national currency unit (Article 8(3) of the 109L(4) Regulation).

## Definition of terms in the legal framework

The legal framework for the introduction of the euro defines the following terms:

- *Conversion rate:* The irrevocably fixed conversion rate from the euro unit to the national currency unit of a participating Member State. The conversion rates shall be adopted as one euro expressed in terms of each of the national currencies of the participating Member States;

- *Participating Member States:* The countries which, according to the legal framework for the use of the euro, adopt the single currency in accordance with the EC Treaty;

- *National currency units:* The units of the currencies of the participating Member States as those units are defined on the day before the start of the third stage of the Economic and Monetary Union;

- *Euro units:* Units of the single currency as defined in the Regulation on the introduction of the euro which will enter into force at the starting date of the third stage of the Economic and Monetary Union;

- *Transitional period:* The period beginning on 1 January 1999 and ending on 31 December 2001 (Phase B).

## No compulsion – no prohibition

In the legal framework, the fundamental principle applicable during the transitional period is that acts to be performed under legal instruments stipulating the use of one of the units – the national currency unit or the euro unit – shall be performed in the stipulated unit unless otherwise agreed by the parties (Article 8(1) of the 109L(4) Regulation). This rule ensures that economic agents will have to use only the unit to which they have agreed.

Article 8(4) of the 109L(4) Regulation contains provisions that allow for an early redenomination of debt and the changeover of organized markets. Apart from these specifically mentioned exceptions of Article 8(4), Member States may allow the use of the euro unit but can impose it only on the basis of further Community legislation (Article 8(5) of the 109L(4) Regulation).

The principles of 'no compulsion' and 'no prohibition' concerning the use of the euro were laid down during the Madrid summit. There is an inevitable trade-off between the freedom of the economic agents and that of the Member States. As a result of this trade-off enterprises may be faced with the following situations:

- It may not be possible to file tax returns for income taxes, value added taxes and customs and duties in euro from 1 January 1999;

- Other transactions with government bodies and agencies, such as payments of registration fees or sales and purchases, may only be possible in the national currency unit during the transitional period.

> few, if any, enterprises will be able to completely avoid using the euro before the end of the transitional period

The important conclusion is that economic agents will have to deal with amounts denominated in euro and national currency unit during the transitional period. Few, if any, enterprises will be able to completely avoid using the euro before the end of the transitional period.

## Payments in euro

Article 8(3) of the 109L(4) Regulation enables debtors to settle their debts in book money by making a payment in either the euro unit or in the national currency unit. Banks are under an obligation to convert such payments into the unit of account of the creditor. When an enterprise only maintains a bank account in the national currency unit, receipts in euro must be converted into the national currency unit. The euro Regulations do not expressly address the issue of charging for the conversion of amounts between the national currency unit and the euro unit.

## Conversion and rounding rules

Article 4 of the 235 Regulation lays down the conversion rules for the euro.

- The conversion rates shall be adopted as one euro expressed in terms of each of the national currencies of the participating Member States. They shall be adopted with six significant figures (counted from the left and starting with the first non-zero figure).

- The conversion rates shall not be rounded or truncated when making conversions.

- The conversion rates shall be used for conversions either way between the euro unit and the national currency units. Inverse rates derived from the conversion rates shall not be used.

- Monetary amounts to be converted from one national currency unit into another shall first be converted into a monetary amount expressed in the euro unit, which amount may be rounded to no fewer than three decimals and shall then be converted into the other national currency unit. This is known as triangulation. No alternative method of calculation may be used unless it produces the same results.

In addition, Article 5 of the 235 Regulation lays down the rounding rules for the euro. Monetary amounts to be paid or accounted for when a rounding takes place after a conversion into the euro unit pursuant to Article 4 shall be rounded up or down to the nearest cent. Monetary amounts to be paid or accounted for which are converted into a national currency unit shall be rounded up or down to the nearest sub-unit or in the absence of a sub-unit to the nearest unit, according to national law or practice to a multiple or fraction of the sub-unit or unit of the national currency unit. If the application of the conversion rate gives a result which is exactly half-way, the sum shall be rounded up.

The conversion and rounding rules do not specifically describe the conversion from a participating national currency unit to a third currency (a currency that is not taking part in EMU). Where a quotation between a third currency (for example USD) and a national currency unit (for example NLG) is no longer available the conversion should be performed as follows:

- *Conversion from USD to NLG:* The USD amount would first have to be converted into a euro amount by application of a USD/EUR exchange rate. The intermediate euro amount would then be converted into a NLG amount by using the conversion rate. It is only to this last calculation that the rounding rules of Article 5 of the 235 Regulation are applicable;

- *Conversion from NLG to USD:* The NLG amount would first have to be converted into the euro unit by applying the conversion rate. The intermediate euro amount resulting from this calculation would not have to be rounded to the nearest cent because this amount is not '... to be paid or accounted for ...' The intermediate euro amount would then be converted into a USD amount by using the EUR/USD exchange rate. This final step of calculating the USD amount is not covered by the Council regulation.

Article 5 of the 235 Regulation lays down the rounding rules for a 'Monetary amount to be paid or accounted for ...' These rules do not apply to converted monetary amounts such as price indications, which are not to be paid or accounted for. Therefore, it is not necessary to round prices, which are indicated with more than two decimals in the national currency unit, to the nearest cent after conversion into the euro unit.

# SO WHAT IS ALL THE FUSS ABOUT –
# POLITICS PERHAPS?

As you've no doubt noticed, there has been some debate around the pros and cons of EMU. In the UK, most of this has been in the media (even the *Sun* has taken up the debate) or behind closed doors. Since this is a practitioner's book, I do not wish to get drawn into a lengthy discussion of the macro-economic or political arguments surrounding the euro, since the majority of us have had little influence, other than our right to vote, over the politics. However, I thought it worthwhile to draw attention to some of the key elements of the debate – you can make up your own mind if you are for or against it. What is important for all of us, regardless of our opinions, is that it is happening. Such is the will of some highly influential politicians.

Personally, I am for it, but I have had serious concerns over the timing of the introduction of the euro and the risks that this represents. Some of the risks are not immediately apparent, especially to those who are far removed from the practicalities of introducing the euro. In many ways it is the risk of implementation, notably the state of preparations, that is the greatest concern. I shall look at this risk in more detail later, but for now, what has the debate been all about?

One of the most pressing and immediate questions for most commentators on Europe is whether the euro will be strong and stable. Many currency traders think that, because the euro embraces countries with a wobbly currency history and a pile of public debt, it will therefore be soft – certainly softer than the D-mark. The financial markets raise concerns, particularly at Italy and Belgium, and to a lesser extent Spain and Portugal. They have got into EMU, say the doubters, only by fudging of the Maastricht Treaty's qualifying criteria, especially the fiscal limits of 3% of GDP for budget deficits and 60% of GDP for public debt. France and Germany, too, have not escaped the fudging limelight.

But there has been a genuine convergence, both in inflation rates and in public finances. According to the European Commission's figures, only France among the euro-11 had a deficit that was even narrowly above 3% in 1997. However, only three of the 11 participating countries stand below the 60% ceiling. Both the European Monetary Institute, forerunner of the European Central Bank, and the German Bundesbank have criticized the high levels of public debt, notably in

Belgium (122.2% of GDP) and Italy (121.6%). Yet no country, not even the often strict Dutch, voted against letting in these two countries.

That is partly because debt is now falling, albeit slowly. But it may also reflect a belated appreciation that neither deficits nor debts will have much bearing on the euro's strength. Far more important will be the monetary policy pursued by the ECB. Expect it to be tough. Add to this a strengthening of economic recovery in Europe, a current-account surplus for the euro-11 of over 1% of GDP, the arrival of the euro after a long period of currency weakness and the likelihood of a portfolio shift of assets to the euro. The odds, then, seem good that, even with Italy and Belgium, the euro will be strong. However, how long can Europe remain immune from the economic conditions prevailing in the rest of the world, notably Asia?

The German-designed 'stability and growth pact', which seeks to limit budget deficits to 3% of GDP on pain of fines for miscreants. The big debtors can take some comfort from the declaration's lack of legal force. In any case, who really believes that those penalty fines, if levied, would actually be paid?

Debates about the euro's strength often follow this line. But why has everyone been so wound up about fixed targets that are questionable anyway? If you ever look at the compilation of national statistics there are quite a few assumptions, ambiguities and holes, so how can we have faith in the accuracy of the numbers to compare against the targets? And who is to say that the numbers are right anyway? This is the underlying reason why countries were able to 'fudge' in the first place.

Unfunded pension liabilities are conveniently left out of the calculations of public debt – that's certainly good news for France and Germany. A report from Britain's parliamentary social security committee in 1996 put the net present value of public pension schemes in the UK at 19% of GDP, France at 98%, Italy 113% and 139% for Germany. It said that 'the extent of unfunded pension liabilities in certain of our European partner countries casts serious doubt upon the long-term sustainability of their finances'.

More important, the convergence criteria were set in 1992 – would the econometric model produce the same targets today for an optimal single currency area? And what targets have been set for the other parameters in an economist's model of a single currency area? Unemployment, labour market flexibility, political control, fiscal transfers, etc. have all been left out. Is the ECB's primary goal of maintaining price stability not based upon the belief that such economic conditions are the basis for growth and employment? Then why have we not got such targets? Because we do not yet have political integration.

On paper, the ECB will be the most independent central bank in the world. Indeed, some reckon that the Maastricht treaty makes the ECB too powerful and by no means accountable enough. Even so, because of the farce over the choice of the bank's first president, Europe's governments have managed the unlikely feat of casting serious doubts over its independence. Nevertheless, who is the ECB accountable to? Whilst political control, the kind the French have shown that they desire, is undesirable, the ECB still has no direct counterpart in politics at present. Accountability lies at the heart of the success of both the Bundesbank and the Federal Reserve. Both these institutions operate in a clear political context in which they account for their actions, not just to politicians, but to a wider public.

And who, politically, is in charge of the euro? Who will speak for the euro at G7 summit meetings, or at the IMF and the World Bank? These questions have been largely ignored by European governments. Not surprising given the political 'hoo-hah' that resulted from the decision over the ECB president. In Britain's case, the policy of wait-and-see keeps the argument out of the public domain. Ultimately, the political ramifications of the arrival of the single currency, have barely been explored, but they are likely to be as, if not more, controversial as anything else about the euro project.

A further uncertainty concerns the relationship between the ECB and the national central banks. Power will be more dispersed between the centre and periphery than in other central banking systems and it is not clear who will prevail. While the ECB will be responsible for setting policy, the national central banks will conduct the bulk of money market operations and foreign exchange intervention. The ECB's policy-making council, which will decide interest rates, will consist of its executive board (based at its headquarters) and the heads of national central banks.

Whatever else the ECB does, it should make its operations as transparent as possible, something that goes against the grain of many central bankers. Both British and American experience has shown that immediate publication of the minutes of council meetings help to boost central banks' credibility. Unfortunately the early signs are that the ECB may not want to espouse too much openness – Wim Duisenberg, head of the ECB, suggested that no minutes should be published for 16 years! This may be somewhat unhelpful to its other role – looking after what will be one of the world's largest international currencies.

So, how much will the ECB be concerned with the euro exchange rate with the rest of the world? At present, foreign trade accounts for a third or more of most European countries' GDP, but in the euro-11 group the share of exports in GDP will fall to only just over 10% (because the bulk of their trade is with each other). That will make the euro economy as relatively closed as those of the US or Japan.

And what data will the ECB use to manage the EMU economy? Otmar Issing, formerly of the Bundesbank and now the ECB's chief economist, recently acknowledged that the quality of euro-wide statistics may not be as good as it should. Nobody is quite sure as to the reliability of available data, such as M3, a measure of broad money.

When the single currency is up and running, exchange rates will no longer be able to act as shock-absorbers; taxes and subsidies will surely be asked to do so instead. That demand will be hard to resist: it will be generations before Europeans are ready to move around their single market in pursuit of jobs as freely as, say, Americans move around theirs. And with such fiscal transfers will come equally irresistible calls for some kind of political supervision.

Whilst conventional wisdom has it that EMU will improve Europe's competitive position, mostly centring on scale arguments and consolidation and enhanced efficiencies in Europe's financial markets, there are a number of things that EMU will not do. For example, EMU will not reduce the continent's high labour costs in manufacturing. And it will not improve the efficiencies in Europe's bloated and highly regulated service sector – the sector that will have to pick up the slack as the continent restructures. In an era of privatization and corporate restructuring, the service sector is increasingly serving the role as a shock absorber to accommodate the job-shedding that occurs in competitive tradable goods industries. This surely gives added impetus to the deregulation of many European labour markets. However, this does not appear to be the case. The French have recently pushed through a 35-hour week and the works councils represented on many German boards are unlikely to be changed. What then is the net effect on unemployment?

> economists generally view rising unemployment and Europe-wide recession as the most plausible threat to EMU

Economists generally view rising unemployment and Europe-wide recession as the most plausible threat to EMU. Because the ECB wants to demonstrate its strength it is likely to go for a strong euro and high interest rates. There are concerns that this approach could exacerbate already high unemployment and kick the region back into recession. The best hope for EMU, says Franco Modigliani, is to make it reflationary, almost Keynesian, in approach. Certainly, lack of synchronicity between the economic cycles of European states will lead to severe economic and political strain in the first years, and that is the most likely reason for an early joint decision to end the experiment.

Analysts at Credit Suisse Private Banking foresee a severe test of political will ahead. 'Looking at the political landscape in Europe', they write, 'there is little to point towards speedy reforms of the labour market or towards the rapid development of a common legal and social security system. Probably the financial markets will first have to speculate on the collapse of the system to force politics to take action.'

## Is the euro-zone an 'optimal currency area'?

In 1961, Robert Mundell, an American academic, published a short article outlining a theory of 'optimal currency areas'. Refined versions state there are gains to be had from sharing a currency across borders – more transparent prices, lower transaction costs, greater certainty for investors, enhanced competition. For the EU the European Commission has put these gains at a substantial 0.5% of GDP.

One key strand to this theory is the area's response to asymmetric shocks. The factors include:

- free mobility of labour;
- flexibility of wages and prices;
- some automatic mechanism for transferring fiscal resources to the affected country.

Note that shocks should be rare, i.e., economies are on similar economic cycles and have similar structures.

Now, we know that the euro-zone scores more or less badly on the above counts, but does this matter? Let's face it, labour mobility is often poor within European countries, with little impact on the national currency. Shocks, such as German unification are reasonably rare in Europe *vis-à-vis* regionally specialized America.

However, the euro-economies' cycles are recognizably out of synch. In particular, Ireland, Spain, Finland and Portugal all seem to have pulled out of recession faster than France and Germany. That is why short-term interest rates in the peripheral countries have been higher than in the core. Now, when it comes to imposing a single interest rate on the entire euro area, the odds are that it will either be too low for the periphery or too high for the core – or both.

Under its statutes, the ECB must set interest rates without national prejudice. Privately, central bankers say that the core euro-zone states account for such a large proportion of GDP that their economic development will carry an overwhelming weight in the ECB's decisions, forcing most of the adjustment process on to divergent outsiders. The consensus among financial analysts is for short-term interest rates in the euro-zone to be around 4%.

The UK's cycle is even more out of synch. This is the central theme of the newly formed 'Business for Sterling' Group. This group, consisting of leaders of 100 blue-chip companies, was set up in June 1998 to co-ordinate a multimillion pound campaign to persuade British voters to block UK membership of EMU. In a letter to *The Times*, senior figures from the group stated:

'Whereas the Bank of England runs our monetary policy according to the UK's needs, the ECB would decide rates for the whole of the EMU area, of which the UK would merely be a region ... If the UK's economy mirrored that of the EMU area we would be less concerned. But it does not. The widespread use of variable rate mortgages makes Britons uniquely sensitive to interest rate policy. Moreover, the British and continental business cycles are out of step (as they have often been in recent years, notably at the time of the ERM crisis). Any convergence would probably be unsustainable, because of well-documented structural differences. Indeed there are inherent weaknesses in centralisation, with the threat of bureaucracy and over-regulation.' *The Times, 11 June 1998*

And what about fiscal transfers? Some commentators have pointed to the need for a significantly higher EU budget, even though some Member States continue to request a reduction to their contributions. Perhaps the most persuasive argument to counter such fears is the Maastricht Treaty's Article 103(a) provision which permits an aid package to a euro member that got into difficulties. I think that this provision is more likely to be utilized than those contained within the 'Stability and Growth Pact'. Do we really believe fines will be imposed?

The politics of EMU could not allow a country to fall into such difficulties as abandoning the euro would do enormous political damage to EMU-participants. In these circumstances, just keeping the single market together might become difficult. The lack of a viable alternative is itself a powerful, if negative, argument for going ahead with EMU to start with, and for providing an aid package to a suffering participant once EMU is up and running.

So is there any break-up risk? Monetary unions have been broken before. Some obvious examples are the republics which broke from the former Soviet Union, the Czech and Slovak republics, Rhodesia declaring unilateral independence in 1965, and Ireland de-linking itself from sterling to join the European Monetary System in 1979. But only in the Soviet case was there a complex network of cross-border assets and liabilities which had to be settled. And in the Soviet case the values, in transferable roubles and barter arrangements, weren't market sensitive.

A JP Morgan paper entitled 'Event risk under monetary union' says that to worry about such a risk, while others ignore it, would be to price oneself out of the market: 'The opportunity costs associated with managing denomination risk, combined with the low probability that such an event could happen, make it extremely likely that market participants will view the conversion rates as irrevocable.'

If doubts existed, market participants would be unwilling to net exposures in different denominations which would result in price differences between them – in swap markets, different denominations would not trade at zero yield differentials, while in bond markets investors would put a premium on issues with certain currency denominations. Perhaps credit risk models would be able to strip out from the premium the credit risk from denomination risk.

However, if the risk of this happening is not zero, then there is a price for it, which the riskier countries in EMU will have to pay – call it a credit spread, or a risk premium. It has been suggested that this premium should be quite high, given that, according to popular surveys, the perceived risk of an EMU break-up is quite high. An investor survey by Paribas in December 1997 had 39% of respondents seeing the risk of an EMU break-up ahead, 17% of them putting the date before 2002 and 22% after.

Break-up is not guarded against in any European Union literature. The subject is taboo, as if talking about it might encourage it to happen. As Neil Record, chairman of Record Treasury Management, warns in an article in his quarterly publication entitled 'The consequences of EMU's failure': 'Overt recognition of EMU's possible mortality may compromise its effectiveness and hasten its demise. Contingency planning may need to be conducted in private. Perhaps this is what the European Commission and member governments are doing. At the very least, organizations should consider the impact and investors in the euro area might like to do some contingency planning anyway.'

If doubts were to emerge about the durability of EMU, as there were about the ERM, what are the options? Leaving EMU is obviously far harder than leaving the ERM. A country wishing to get out might reintroduce its previous currency, but that would mean reneging on an international treaty and perhaps, say some Brussels lawyers, having to leave the European Union and losing access to the single market. The legal and economic, let alone psychological, problems of dis-entangling such a mess would be huge. Short of a political earthquake, such as the one that blew apart the Soviet Union's single currency, it seems unlikely that any euro member would ever want to go through all of this.

Ultimately, the role of the euro in the international monetary system will turn on the future stability and strength of the euro *vis-à-vis* the dollar and yen, and will be defined by the shares of the euro in official and private portfolios, international financial transactions and trade flows. Many Asian and US investors shifted out of the D-mark and into the dollar because of uncertainties surrounding EMU and the euro. However, as the euro and the ECB gain credibility and the euro markets acquire liquidity and depth, a significant rebalancing of portfolios can be expected.

# CHANGING FINANCIAL MARKETS

Hopes are high that the euro will provide the trigger for a revitalization of the continent's fragmented capital markets. At the very least, the single currency will lead to a profound shake-up in the operations of stock exchanges and financial institutions. In many ways, the international success of EMU will be influenced by the euro's ability to catalyze existing initiatives to enhance the efficiency of European capital markets (including early implementation of EU directives). The opportunities for beneficial structural changes are far reaching. They include the development of EMU-wide securities markets, the consolidation and restructuring of European banking systems, and the creation of a pan-European payments system.

As the deadline for EMU approaches, international investors have shifted their attention from the often debated questions of which countries will join EMU to more technical issues about the behaviour of European capital markets under EMU. In response, some investment banks have already launched euro indices. Merrill Lynch with a EMU Broad market bond index; Lehman Brothers with its Euro-Aggregate index, which tracks the performance of 6,882 investment grade bonds denominated in ECUs or EMU currencies. In addition, euro-zone equity indices have also been developed to respond to this demand from investors.

In May 1998, the *Financial Times* began publishing daily statistics on euro-zone equity, currency and fixed-income markets, including a 'synthetic' value for the euro itself. Euro-zone economic statistics are published every week. Until 1999, some of these statistics are purely hypothetical, however, as many are based on the ECU, which is not an exact representation of the currencies entering EMU. Nevertheless, it is a good proxy guide for investors looking at the euro-zone.

By removing the volatile currency risk component of intra-EMU cross-border financing costs, the introduction of the euro may eventually create the largest single-currency financial market in the world. Once the euro is introduced, borrowers and lenders will begin to seek lower costs and higher returns across national boundaries, European financial markets could become less segmented, and there could be more uniformity in market practices and more transparency in pricing. But there are still significant structural impediments to this process of transformation. The development of Europe-wide securities markets has thus far been impeded by a number of factors including:

- long-standing, inhibiting regulations for issuing, dealing and trading securities;
- elements of tax systems that encourage bank financing; and
- differences in market practices and in securities clearance and settlement systems.

There are currently significant differences in the practices and conventions that are used in the financial markets of the Member States. With the introduction of the euro these national markets will share a single currency and be subject to a single monetary policy, therefore, to create the most efficient and liquid euro-denominated markets it is clear that some degree of harmonized practices and conventions will be needed. Financial institutions operating either in a single domestic market or across borders will need to cope with the harmonizing of these conventions. Nonetheless progress is being made and probably the best indication of the future European markets is the current US market structure.

European finance has been dominated by bank intermediation, with EU bank loans accounting for 54% of outstanding financial instruments (bonds, equities and loans). US finance, by comparison, has been dominated by capital market intermediation, and bank loans account for only 22% of capital market activity.

Table 1.3 also shows the considerable size of the UK markets, notably the equity market, relative to the other large European countries.

The figures in Table 1.3 show how much has to happen before continental markets begin to look anything like the Anglo-Saxon model. Compared with the US and Britain, stockmarket capitalization is still low in relation to the size of the economy (24% of GDP in Germany, 95% in the US and 127% in the UK). The number of new issues on the stockmarket is also small on the continent, but hopes are high that restructuring and loosening ties to banks will stimulate considerable growth in new issues.

**TABLE 1.3**

**Size of selected capital markets, 1995, in US$ billions**

| | Population (in millions) | GDP | Stock market capitalization | Public debt securities | Private debt securities | Bank assets |
|---|---|---|---|---|---|---|
| EU-15 | 371.8 | 8,427.6 | 3,778.5 | 4,809.9 | 3,863.5 | 14,818.0 |
| EMU-11 | 289.0 | 6,804.9 | 2,119.4 | 3,903.8 | 3,088.6 | 11,971.6 |
| United States | 263.0 | 7,253.8 | 6,857.6 | 6,728.0 | 4,322.6 | 5,000.0 |
| Japan | 125.2 | 5,134.3 | 3667.3 | 3,447.7 | 1,877.1 | 7,382.2 |
| Germany | 81.6 | 2,412.5 | 577.4 | 893.6 | 1,284.5 | 3,752.4 |
| France | 58.0 | 1,538.8 | 522.1 | 681.7 | 801.2 | 2,923.0 |
| Italy | 57.2 | 1,087.2 | 209.5 | 1,222.0 | 396.8 | 1,513.5 |
| UK | 58.3 | 1,105.1 | 1,407.7 | 429.9 | 396.3 | 2,424.4 |

Source: International Monetary Fund

The globalization of finance has been transforming financial institutions, banking systems and securities markets worldwide for some time. Together with the ongoing changes related to EU banking and financial directives, the introduction of the euro is likely to accelerate the transformation of European financing. This will partly be the result of reducing, if not eliminating, the home currency advantages that EU banks currently have in their local retail deposit-taking and lend-

> **EMU will lead to stronger competition and integration of European financial markets**

ing activities, and by encouraging bank corporate customers to raise and lend funds directly in the EMU-wide markets, increasing the pace of disintermediation. So, what trends have we seen and what are we likely to see?

The existing trend of fast growth of OTC derivatives has been accelerated by EMU, notably non-USD swaps and the strong demand for stock index products as EMU triggers a pan-European equity approach. EMU has also led to a sharp rise in turnover of European futures exchanges and to the establishment of strategic links among and against each other. EMU-related innovations are mainly the launch of new products and the modernization of existing products.

EMU will lead to stronger competition and integration of European financial markets. In the money markets, the focus has been on the fixing of the reference rate and the ECB approach to monetary policy, notably minimum reserve requirements. In the bond markets, the focus has been on the benchmark issuer which will be determined by credit risks, liquidity and market efficiency as currency risks disappear.

EMU will lead to the contraction and concentration in the volumes of futures contracts with money market futures hit particularly hard. Among over 20 futures markets in Europe only Liffe, DTB and MATIF have a realistic chance to offer the benchmark contract. The major area of uncertainty is the structure of the euro bond future. The choice mainly lies between a single issuer basket contract, a multiple issuer basket contract and joint benchmark bonds (which differentiates Europe from the US in that US has a single issuer, the US government). The main problem remains that products that make up the basket need to be as homogeneous as possible, otherwise under current futures contracts, the bonds which become cheapest to deliver into the contract are automatically those implying the highest credit risk as they have higher yields.

Interest rate swaps could become the benchmark of fixed income markets in the euro-zone. Whilst European markets have benefited from the marked convergence of European yields and increased new issues, particularly in core countries, government bonds have not completely converged, particularly at the long end of the yield curve. This is due to the differences between national bond markets including:

- size of each market
- completeness of range of products
- modernity of market practices
- international acceptance of the market
- liquidity of instruments
- regularity of new issues, and of course
- credit.

Swap rates in the maturities beyond two years may become the natural extension of LIBOR, or EURIBOR, from the money market into the capital market segment. However, at the shorter end of the curve, spreads will probably not be large enough for the market to remain fragmented. Indeed, a euro yield curve has already developed *de facto*, at least for the issues of the core countries, since the yield spreads between government bonds from Germany, France, Austria, the Netherlands and Belgium have practically disappeared.

There is huge potential for equity-based derivatives with focus on a pan-European sectoral approach. Demand growth for these instruments has significantly outstripped growth in fixed-income products. Some products will disappear but markets should still expand. The euro swap market will play a significant role, pulling along with it a growing market for asset swaps and swaptions. Credit spread products will become more important with focus on hedging default risks and total return swaps, though price transparency due to unclear valuation methods, tax and regulatory treatment remains an obstacle to growth in these markets.

In the world of equities, there are two underlying drivers of change. Firstly, the relentless pressure for a single Europe-wide stockmarket and secondly, a dramatic switch in Europe's savings. EMU and the introduction of the euro act as a hugely accelerated further catalyst to this change. However, the synchronization of the national equity markets has been considerably slower than in the case of the fixed income markets. This is partly due to differing national accounting rules, corporate forms and investment mentalities.

Over time, however, the advent of the euro will have a profound effect on how European investors will approach sector and stock selection to come more in line with typical US investor view of Europe. An increase in cross-border investment seems inevitable.

All the talk is about pan-European sectors rather than individual markets. The FTSE committee has launched its own revamped set of Euro-indices, challenging the Stoxx indices, set up by Dow Jones and a string of continental partners. Several markets are already becoming redundant, with some individual stocks now looking too big for the domestic market. Nokia of Finland accounts for 44% of the local market by market capitalization. Novartis in Switzerland accounts for 20%.

As the euro-zone market develops critical mass, the US market will inevitably become the main competitor. Equally, it is the US houses that continue to set the pace in Europe, even in the domestic M&A market. For example, three US houses, JP Morgan, Morgan Stanley and Goldman Sachs topped the 1997 German M&A advisory league table. European institutions have some catching to do in order to match the continental presence of some of these players. In many ways, the Americans benefit from an even and balanced coverage throughout Europe, rather than being skewed towards any particular country like many Europeans.

The greatest benefits are likely to be realized by Europe's corporate giants, which have already seen their share prices multiply under the impact of global investment flows – much of it from the US. Consider the example of Daimler-Benz. Until only a few years ago, it was a confusing conglomeration. But now it has adopted a shareholder-friendly approach with sufficient self-confidence to launch, as the dominant partner, a merger with America's Chrysler. The strategic alliance between the London Stock Exchange and the Deutsche Borse further enhances these scale benefits, perhaps to the detriment of shares of smaller and medium-sized enterprises. Just as there is a premier league for football, so there will be a premier league for European stocks.

Much depends on the acceptance by European politicians and company executives of concepts such as 'shareholder value'. US and UK investors are inclined to insist that companies are run to benefit shareholders – which is still a controversial subject in several European countries where banks and trade unions have been much more important stakeholders. The wave of corporate activity in the past few years has shown that this process is well under way, producing lucrative business for investment banks.

Meanwhile, continental Europe is in the grip of a step-change in savings and portfolio flows: money is pouring out of low-yielding government bonds and money market accounts into equities. At present equities account for 38% of mutual fund money in Europe. Salomon reckons this could climb to 50% by 2008 (see Table 1.4). Flows into equity funds totalled close to $24 billion in the first quarter of 1998, the highest level to date in a significantly rising trend.

### TABLE 1.4
**Mutual funds allocation**

|  | Europe today | Europe 2008 |
| --- | --- | --- |
| Equity | 38% | 50% |
| Bond | 38% | 30% |
| Money market | 15% | 15% |
| Other | 9% | 5% |

Source: National associations of mutual funds, central banks and Smith Barney Inc./Salomon Brothers Inc estimates

Pensions have so far looked like being one of the last areas for harmonization because of the potential confusion caused by the different tax and social security systems in individual countries. However, a ruling by the European Court of Justice in May 1998 could help pave the way for Europe-wide pension funds, and may mean that companies could set up one pension fund in Europe and have all their employees in the same fund and everyone gets tax relief.

According to Lehman Brothers research domestic institutions in the UK own £866 billion of British stock and £224 billion of other European shares. The next most equity-orientated market is the Netherlands, where Dutch institutions own just £143 billion of domestic stock, with £152 billion invested in other European equities. Austrian institutions, meanwhile, have only £5.5 billion invested in Austrian stocks and £4.2 billion across the rest of Europe. The picture for private investors is much the same. Only about 6% of Germans own shares, compared with 21% in the US, 17% in Britain and 35% in Sweden. The implication is that if pan-European portfolios is the endgame, and sterling joins the euro, there is likely to be a massive outflow of funds from the UK market. Lehman estimates this at around £500 billion of continental stocks.

The emergence of a single European bourse with its own index will unleash powerful centripetal forces for a common company accounting system, a common regulatory system and even a common euro-zone investment tax. Indeed this is already happening. For example, the French government is to allow banks freely to determine interest rates payable on a range of taxable savings accounts. It also cut the interest rates on a number of tax-free savings products, and established an advisory committee which will play an important role in determining the level of the rates paid to depositors in the future. It is arguable that the creation of the euro would otherwise have put an unbearable pressure on the system by allowing other Europeans to open tax-free accounts supported by the French state.

The outlook for equities trading is unambiguously bullish compared with the mixed picture for the government bond and foreign exchange markets. Job cuts are inevitable in the forex markets, especially in smaller European centres; there are sharp differences of opinion on whether the EMU will give birth to a euro bond market to rival US Treasuries, or just kill the volatility that now enlivens European government bond trading. Equities trading has a much better chance of retaining its volatility after EMU and may well attract investors away from bonds, because companies will retain their inherent diversity and economic growth data will still move share prices.

As the markets become increasingly virtual – even the London International Financial Futures and Options Exchange (Liffe) brought forward the planned introduction of electronic trading by six months but not before the start of EMU – it is hard to see how geographical location matters for several types of activity. The fact that the largest share of the world's foreign currency trading gets processed in London is already an example of this fact. However, the increasing emphasis on credit research and the need to sell ever more complex and tailored solutions to institutional clients with different needs may put a premium on local presence for certain activities. Pension fund reform alone provides substantial local opportunities in all European financial centres. Many financial centres have kicked-off their own lobby groups, including leading industrialists, bankers and media representatives, to promote each centre as EMU approaches.

Some concerns have been expressed about the future of London as a financial centre as the UK stays out of EMU; Liffe losing its pre-eminent position in German bund futures, Europe's primary benchmark contract; Britain losing most of its powerful investment banks following the recent sale of the equities businesses of both Barclays and Natwest; and the creation of European strategic alliances such as the Euro Alliance. The Alliance, which has been formed between the Swiss, German and French exchanges, could prove to be a substantial competitor. It will form a common base for trading first derivatives, and eventually shares. The aim is to build a one-stop pan-European securities market which could, in theory, more than match London for speed of execution and price.

The Euro Alliance has agreed to launch futures contracts based on the Dow Jones Stoxx family of indices, in the hope of building a pan-European benchmark. Liffe's (and the Amsterdam Exchange's) alternative will be based on the Eurotop indices, FTSE International's competing pan-European product.

Nevertheless, there is a multitude of reasons why it will take more than the euro to dislodge its premier status. Firstly, London has a considerable head start in many markets. Its strength in foreign exchange, fixed income and derivatives trading has little to do with the physical location of the currency of trading. In an electronic environment, people will be physically located wherever they want to be.

However, the strategic alliance between Frankfurt's Deutsche Borse and LSE announced in July 1998 demonstrates the realization that co-operating is a better strategy than competing. They plan to provide a 'common access package' and 'a single point of liquidity' for German and UK blue-chip shares which means linking Frankfurt's Xetra system and London's Sets. Up until that point, the LSE was looking isolated. Whilst this is a big step forward in thinking, there are many issues and hurdles that the two exchanges will need to overcome, such as benchmarks, settlement, location and management.

In any case, London's competitive advantage stems more from structural and regulatory factors. English is the primary language of finance; London has the largest pool of skilled labour in Europe; it also has a cost advantage, helped by lower taxes and more flexible labour laws. Skilled labour has been London's greatest asset in preparing for the euro. Despite the uncertainty of UK entry, even the ECB president, Wim Duisenberg, has suggested that the City of London may be better prepared for the euro than a number of continental financial centres.

These advantages have been reflected in the run-up to the euro as many US banks have tended to concentrate their operations in London rather than move to the continent. Deutsche Bank also relocated most of its investment banking business to London, but following some serious pressure from the German establishment, has recently announced a new trading floor in Frankfurt. Deutsche plans to run its euro-denominated debt business from here and volumes could exceed those in its London base.

London's threat thus comes more from structural and regulatory changes rather than market forces. Capital market reforms should both reduce the cost of capital and improve its allocation. However, a genuine single capital market may take some years to emerge as the tax, regulatory and cultural differences amongst euro countries will continue to prevent totally free investing and borrowing across borders.

The introduction of the euro will thus have profound repercussions for the financial sector. All financial institutions will have to meet the challenge, within and outside of the European Union. The consequences of EMU will be more directly and immediately felt by the financial sector than any other sector of the economy. Other sectors can decide to adjust their business to the euro during the transition period at their own chosen speed. In contrast, the financial sector must be fully prepared to operate in euro and meet the challenges from the very start of EMU on 1 January 1999. The principle of 'no compulsion, no prohibition' is non-applicable for virtually all institutional investors and professional intermediaries. Here is a list of the main reasons for this.

- The European System of Central Banks ('ESCB') will be operating the single monetary policy in euro. Thus to manage liquidity (especially for those institutions that rely on central bank liquidity provisions to manage their balance sheets) and to participate in the ESCB's open markets operations it will be necessary for financial institutions to operate in euro.

- Governments will issue all new debt after the start of stage three in euro. Moreover all governments intend to redenominate the majority of their debt over the conversion weekend. In addition, equities will be quoted, traded and settled exclusively in euro within the euro-zone. Income (dividends and coupons) will, in many cases, be expressed and paid in euro, and even when declared in legacy currency, most likely will be paid in euro.

- Interbank payment systems across the euro zone, including TARGET, the pan-European real time payment system, will operate exclusively in euro.

- Businesses and citizens may decide to use financial products denominated in euro at any time during the transition period, all the more as, according to the euro regulation, the financial markets and stock exchanges in most participating Member States will switch to euro on 1 January 1999. A financial institution that failed to provide such services would run the risk of losing business.

- EMU will create a euro area within which national financial markets will become integrated, deeper, wider and more resilient. Financial institutions and financial centres themselves will face new competitive conditions which they must prepare for.

Therefore, financial institutions, payment systems and clearing systems will have to be prepared to operate in euro from the start of EMU. There is no doubt professional players will quote, trade and settle transactions in euro from the beginning of EMU. The question remains of how rapidly the single currency will be adopted by all the players that comprise the investment chain and their dealings with each other, from the market, which converts to the euro 'Big Bang' style at the start of EMU, to the end-investor who is likely to continue to operate in legacy currencies (*see* Figure 1.2). It will be interesting to see how long it takes the investment chain to wholly convert.

**FIGURE 1.2**

**The investment chain and the euro**

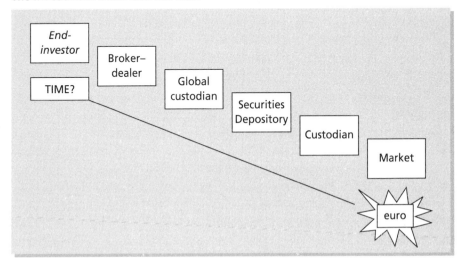

Whether professional intermediaries will continue to transact business with their clients in legacy currencies, or offer any sort of dual currency capability, is a business decision. The markets will work exclusively in euro. Institutions who see competitive advantage in offering flexibility will need to justify the overheads and implications of retaining business in the old legacy currencies for up to three years.

The elimination of costs to business resulting from the removal of exchange rate risk will translate into reduced profits for financial institutions, as the financial sector is the main intermediary for cross-border transactions. On the other hand, lower and more stable interest rates, flowing from the establishment of economic and monetary stability, should stimulate investment and growth. This will lead to increased demand from businesses and individuals for financial products and services.

Whilst EMU has the most immediate impact on the wholesale sector, the retail banking sector also has much preparation to do:

• how to prepare clients for the euro and retain their customers in the new environment;

- how to assess the likely timetable for the changeover of businesses and individuals to the euro;
- how to meet the possible needs of clients for dual displays of amounts in euros and old national currency units;
- how to define the business strategy in the new competitive environment;
- how to include the changes in time in the normal investment planning horizon.

National banking markets in Europe have undergone dramatic deregulation since the mid-1980s, partly under the influence of EU legislation such as the second banking directive of 1988 or the 1993 investment services directive. But despite these changes, Europe is still a long way from boasting a single market in banking services.

With the advent of the euro, companies will increasingly demand services such as the ability to pool euro cash balances held in several different countries. They are also unlikely to accept that charges for cross-border payments should remain at their current high levels, roughly 100 times higher than for domestic payments.

For personal customers, however, few bankers expect the euro will be enough to create a single market on its own, though most believe it will give a boost to cross-border sales of financial products and to multinational alliances between banks. Differences in mentality, savings regulations and fiscal laws will continue for several years to be very efficient barriers to multinational retail banking activity. Most banks remain nervous about their ability to march into new national markets and compete against strong local players with established customer bases.

EMU is, of course, only one of many events that are impacting the organization of financial markets. Others include technological change, consolidation in banking, the role of emerging markets, Japanese de-regulation. In the longer run, many believe the major shift in pension fund reform and general approach to public funding is likely to prove a much more powerful booster to the financial services industry than EMU itself. Nevertheless, it is unquestionable that EMU represents significant opportunities as a catalyst for the European equities and fixed income markets, which have a long way to go to match their US counterparts.

## Merger and acquisition (M&A) activity

1998 is set to be the largest year in M&A ever, with the value of deals possibly topping the $2,000 billion mark. Whilst the biggest deals have taken place between US companies, notably the $72.5 billion merger between Travelers

Group and Citicorp, activity has been dramatic in Europe, not just in terms of the number and value of deals, but also the nature of deals. The $39 billion all-share takeover of Chrysler by Daimler-Benz is notable as these types of deal involving Europeans are not common. European banks are also becoming more aggressive in their expansion activity overseas, notably South America, perhaps to compensate for loss of business in Europe.

However, a stream of deals directly related to the coming of the euro and the changes that EMU will bring to Europe, is the start of potentially years of activity. M&A specialists believe that 1998 will not be a peak year and deal flow is likely to be buoyant enough to maintain activity through any downturn.

One main reason for this is that the euro is accelerating and accentuating changes that would be inevitable over a longer period anyway. EMU is just speeding up trends such as globalization, a greater emphasis on shareholder value, and disintermediation – the greater use of securities at the expense of bank lending. The latter trend has knock-on impacts as the euro's most explicit effect will be to make companies within the euro-zone more transparently comparable to fund managers and to each other.

1997 and 1998 saw a spate of bank mergers in Europe, including:

- the takeover by the Dutch banking group ING of Belgium's Banque Bruxelles Lambert;

- Dresdner Kleinwort Benson's purchase of a two-thirds interest in Albertini, one of Italy's largest stockbrokers, previously owned by France's Société Générale, illustrating Dresdner's effort to broaden its presence in the euro-zone;

- a Bavarian marriage of Bayerische Vereinsbank with Bayerische Hypo-Bank;

- the merger of Bank Geschellschaft Berlin and Nord-LB, creating Germany's fourth largest bank;

- the acquisition of BZW, the Barclays investment banking arm by Credit Suisse First Boston;

- the acquisition of Natwest Market's equities business by Bankers Trust;

- the merger of Swiss Bank Corporation with Union Bank of Switzerland.

Continental Europe remains overbanked compared with the US and the UK: more mergers, branch closures and job losses are inevitable. Further cross-border deals and consolidation in Europe is likely, particularly banks with smaller home markets as they have the greatest need to reach critical mass.

We have also seen contested deals, hostile acquisitions, white knights – these are the characteristics of the US merger mania of the 1980s. But possibly the greatest barrier to the expansion-minded Europeans remains politics. This was amply demonstrated in two notable cases. Firstly, the French government insisting on 'reciprocity' following the takeover of AGF by Allianz: the takeover of

France's AGF by the German insurer Allianz, in a complex deal involving Generali of Italy, was allowed; however, the French authorities signalled that the next such deal would have to be French-led in the interest of reciprocity. So too in the case of CIC, France's fifth largest banking network. The government opted for Credit Mutuel over offers from Société Générale and ABN Amro.

Secondly, during the battle for Belgium's Generale de Banque, whereby the decision between rival bids from Fortis and ABN Amro was more to do with 'keeping it at home' than returns to shareholders, ABN Amro lost its (higher) bid for its Belgium neighbour in favour of an alternative domestic Belgian player, Fortis.

A similar picture is emerging in the insurance industry. Zurich (including Eagle Star, Allied Dunbar and Threadneedle asset management) merged with the financial services arm of BAT industries British American Financial Services (BAFS), which shed 1600 jobs when it demerged from the tobacco business. The cuts represent 10% of the combined British workforce, though most of the job losses will come from Eagle Star, Zurich's general insurance and pensions business. The newly merged entity hopes to grow its share of the savings market from 4.2% to 10%. The merger will cost Zurich $1.4 billion. BAT's shareholders will own 43% of the new company which will be listed in London and Zurich.

Merger mania is beginning to spread to the non-financial sector. In the new euro-zone price differentiation will give way to price transparency. Industries selling into most European markets – such as car and drugs makers – are all cutting costs and seeking partners in preparation for the pressure the euro may put on their margins.

Stora, the Swedish pulp and paper manufacturer, and Enso Oy, the Finnish forestry group, announced plans in June 1998 to proceed with one of the largest European industrial mergers, creating the world's biggest pulp and paper group. Officials said Stora's willingness to merge with Enso was due in part to the introduction of the euro, whereby Stora would gain access to reduced euro transaction and invoicing costs through Finland's Enso.

Much of this restructuring in Europe that the euro will promote, however, will only deliver benefits if companies can shed labour. Yet this could, in the short-run, increase Europe's already high level of unemployment. Perhaps this is why European countries are reluctant to change labour-market regulations that make it hard to fire (and costly to hire) workers. Comparisons between US and European bank mergers suggest that cost savings are twice as high in the US because jobs can be cut more easily.

Merger deals have become the primary instrument of corporate strategy, principally because strategic change in many of today's industries does not allow time for organic growth. If you want to compete, it seems you have to grow, and to grow, you have to merge or acquire. There is also significant opportunity to merge or acquire in some sectors of the economy, but at a time when organizations are facing, in some sectors, almost crisis levels of resource shortfalls. Companies must think carefully in deciding when and how to merge or acquire in the current climate.

Research has shown that the long-term results of combinations are far from convincing. The main killer of value and post-merger results has been poor post-merger management. The impact of two major programmes, EMU and Year 2000, can only weaken organizations' ability to successfully integrate at this time. However, the business opportunities in some sectors are too strong to turn down. Consequently, managers will have to make some serious decisions when determining their integration strategy. Chapter 9 looks in detail at the key success factors for companies wishing to integrate.

# WHAT DOES THE EUROPEAN COMMISSION THINK?

'The preparations for the introduction of the euro on 1 January 1999 are well under way. The Single Currency will contribute significantly to further market integration. It will not only increase market transparency by making prices more easily comparable. Cross-border transactions will also become more attractive as market operators will no longer be exposed to exchange rate risks and costs associated with currency conversion will be eliminated.

The Single Market is in turn one of the main pillars of Economic and Monetary Union. EMU is only possible thanks to the powerful impetus to economic integration which the Single Market gives. That is why the Single Market Action Plan adopted in the summer of 1997 sets a target date of 1 January 1999 for completing some important steps which will help to ensure that the Single Market delivers its full economic potential.

The introduction of the euro as the single currency will have a profound impact on the way enterprises operate. It will be one of the most important changes in the economic landscape of Europe in the next few years.

In order to take full advantage of the introduction of the Single Currency, businesses need to prepare themselves thoroughly for the changeover to the euro. The changeover will in particular have a number of practical consequences for the day-to-day operations of enterprises. One of those practical consequences is that information systems need to be ready for the use of the euro. Many people would agree that it is important to be well prepared for the euro and that careful planning is essential. However, recent surveys have shown that few enterprises, except perhaps for large banks and insurance companies, are actually preparing themselves for the introduction of the euro.'

*Mario Monti, Commissioner for the Single Market and financial services, Preparing Financial Information Systems for the euro, DG XV, European Commission, 15 December 1997.*

# A PRACTITIONER'S FINAL WORD

Everyone has their own views as to whether EMU is a good thing or a bad thing or whether it will last or not. The evidence seems to suggest that it is a good thing, certainly in the long-term, and that it will stay – that's not bad since the US took 100 years to create a currency union: Europe has managed it in 40. Suffice it to say that EMU is happening, whether you like it or not, with 11 participating European countries, from 1 January 1999. More countries will inevitably follow.

The integration of European capital markets and the added competitive pressure this brings to financial institutions will improve the cost and accessibility of the capital markets to issuers and the knock-on margin squeeze to traditional bank lending. This is good news for all, except of course to financial institutions. Strategy and preparation has become critical to survival for all of these firms, in many ways the 'guinea-pigs' for the introduction of the euro. In particular, financial institutions first have to cross the major hurdle of 'Big Bang Conversion Weekend' before they can aspire to longer-term strategic success. This is the subject of Chapter 4.

The best we, as managers of organizations of all shapes and sizes, can do is be professional and prepare for the short- and long-term consequences of this historic event in the best way possible. That means we should be thorough in our strategic analysis, meticulous in our planning and realistic in our implementation. This is the only way to respond to a fundamentally changing business environment which we must factor into our long-term strategic objectives. And perhaps this way we can ensure that the euro has the best chance of long-term success which is good for everyone. That's what the rest of this book is all about – getting it done.

# CHAPTER 2

# Business issues

# INTRODUCTION

In facing up to the challenge of the euro, many companies have begun with a decision to assess the impact of the euro on all their activities. Usually under the supervision of a senior executive, frequently the finance or IT director, the group making the assessment prepares a changeover scenario for approval by a strategic committee, whose members often comprise key functions such as accounting, legal, treasury, marketing, IT and human resources. Detailed plans would be developed by special groups drawn from each of these functions. Many companies which operate in more than one country then appoint a co-ordinator in each country, who is responsible for supervising the implementation of the changeover plan in that particular country.

This is the basic approach, but many have not even got this far yet. Those that have frequently realize that the implications of the changeover are broader and deeper than they thought. In particular, very few companies have yet to understand the strategic opportunities and threats, primarily because they have either been too preoccupied by the day-to-day practical issues of changing over, or political uncertainty has prevented practical action. Those companies which have taken strategic decisions have often decided to postpone strategic issues until 1999, 2000 or later, in order to focus on the practical essentials.

Whilst this strategy has the merits of pragmatism, particularly in the light of significant shortages of skilled resources as we shall see later, it also has the risk of closing off opportunities and wasted expenditure. Consequently, this survival strategy is unlikely to yield the greatest return on investment. Investing in the costs of changeover in a marginal business line or product may damage more profitable lines or products. This means that you must carefully weigh the strategic benefits of your changeover strategy against the costs of changeover in each line of business. Even though most of your time may be taken up with operational duties, strategic thinking in all areas of the company is an absolute must for a successful start to EMU. It will help to keep a lid on your operating costs and allow you to spend money where it is most needed.

EMU represents a unique opportunity to build competitive advantage – it involves the removal of a significant barrier between countries, the currency. As the advantages of national champions diminish, companies will have the opportunity to become pan-European. However, this will take time and the earlier an organization takes action, the better placed they will be to maximize the opportunity, benefiting not just in the short-term but also in using EMU for long-term strategic advantage. Consequences include:

- deepening of domestic markets

- price transparency
- opportunities for new products and services
- increased competition.

Today, there is a wide disparity of pricing throughout Europe for a multitude of reasons including historical, fiscal and cultural factors as well as cost. Pricing products and services in euros all over Europe will naturally increase the transparency of prices. Everyone knows, for example, that prices of the same model of car vary from country to country. A study by the European Commission in 1995 found that for 93% of models, pre-tax price differentials were above 20%. The single currency could wipe out these differences. Traders can be more confident that they can profit by buying goods in cheap countries and selling them in dearer ones; until now, the ability to do this has been curtailed by the fear that exchange rate changes might wipe out such profits. One known strategic response to this issue has been to harmonize prices but reflect the differing costs of production in models across countries by varying the standard set of features available for that model in each country. Call it feature-, as opposed to price-discrimination.

However, factors other than cost also contribute to market segmentation such as tastes, legal regulations, distribution, culture and language. The euro is just one element in the integration process. Nevertheless, it is likely that companies will move from national management to cross-border management, further enhancing their ability to reap other benefits such as economies of scale in logistics, products and distribution. Ultimately it is the consumer that should benefit from lower costs.

The dilemma facing organizations is whether to become pro-active or re-active to the introduction of the single currency. This will in part depend on an understanding and assessment of the risks and opportunities that organizations will face before 1999, during the transition period until 2002 and beyond. Many companies have already started to assess the impact of the advent of EMU on their business.

Organizations will need to assess the impacts of the euro both internally and externally to understand the implications for systems and processes. The policies and strategies that organizations develop towards EMU will have an impact on the relationships the organization has with its external customers, suppliers and stakeholders. These external drivers may make it necessary for an organization to become euro-compatible earlier rather than later.

> the dilemma facing organizations is whether to become pro-active or re-active to the introduction of the single currency

As a growing number of businesses recognize, the best way to view EMU is as a catalyst that forces change – and change for the better. If they are going to the trouble of preparing for the euro, why not look at ways to make the business operate more effectively, taking into account the advantages presented by price transparency and lower risks?

The large strategic issues must not divert an organization's attention from the impact that EMU will have on the day-to-day operations of the company. The number of systems and processes that will have to be amended will run into tens of thousands. They will take time, careful planning and co-ordination.

It is clear that EMU will have wide-ranging and significant effects on the operations of businesses. From major strategic opportunities and threats arising from changing markets and products to detailed operational aspects of adapting information systems to the euro, it is imperative to plan. Key questions you should ask include the following.

- What exactly do we need to do?
- Who will be responsible for each phase of the process?
- When will the process happen and how long will it take?

The timetable for the changeover will vary for companies. The date from which business is first carried out in euros by a company may be any time from 1 January 1999, and the particular date on which a company changes over will be determined by a number of strategic and operational considerations which are outlined in this chapter. For your own company, you must make sure you take all these considerations into account. Also bear in mind that you cannot manage the changeover in isolation – your timetable may well be driven by the approach adopted by your key customers, suppliers and competitors. Whatever you do, do not underestimate the time and effort involved. There are clear competitive, efficiency and cost advantages in getting your strategy for the euro right first time.

This chapter has been organized to revolve around the key factors influencing the strategy of your business, with summaries and questions provided throughout. You should be able to use this chapter to assess the impact of EMU on your business and check that you are examining the key issues. It is not intended to be fully comprehensive as this would be impossible, because of the volume of information, and because the issues for each sector can be quite different. The focus of this chapter is on the common issues affecting all organizations. Whilst this book can provide a summary you must also consider from where you can source more detailed information that you require. Further, you have to design a process to capture and manage all this information to support your ongoing euro preparations. Some guidance on knowledge management is given in Chapter 6.

## INFORMATION AND AWARENESS

According to IT services group CMG, in November 1997, 54% of Dutch companies started preparing for EMU, compared with 45% of their German counterparts and 31% of UK firms. Two-thirds of companies in the UK had not reviewed the changes required to their IT systems for dealing with EMU. In Germany, the level of awareness and preparation is far higher. CMG found that only 7% of UK financial directors thought that EMU would have an impact on their IT systems – compared to 58% for Germany.

Indeed, these figures probably mask a much greater lack of awareness among small and medium-sized organizations. Whilst governments, the banks and big business in almost all the main countries are driving the project forward, it is very uncertain as to whether the majority of industry in those countries, made up of small to medium-sized businesses, will meet the deadline.

A survey of 2100 European business conducted by the Federation of European Accountants at the end of 1997 found that, of the companies that had done no preparation for the euro so far, 58% stated that this was because of a lack of information. In other words, the more they are aware of the issues involved, the more they are mobilized. In many cases, however, the lack of mobilization has more to do with the type of information – the majority has been more to do with the political uncertainty of EMU than practical preparation for it.

A survey by MORI at the end of 1996 indicated that the majority of companies obtain their information from newspapers while 53% look to their banks to be educated (see Table 2.1). Being at the forefront of the changeover, banks will have to be prepared for the introduction of the euro before other businesses. Therefore, they should build on the technical expertise acquired from their internal adjustments to assist their customers.

Whilst the adjustment of companies will be less complex than for banks since money is not their primary product, they will still have significant difficulties. Various polls have shown that up to three-quarters of businesses would turn to their banker and/or accountant for advice. At the time of decimalization in the UK, banks organized some 18 500 meetings to inform their corporate customers. Meeting this expectation will certainly be a matter of intense competition between banks.

But what sort of information? Since 1996, most businesses have been inundated with information on EMU and banks are partially the cause of this, so they don't really need any more. Companies now need practical advice, but rarely have banks offered this advice.

A large company is likely to have specific departments for each function. But in a small company many functions may be carried out by the same people, so tackling all the issues may be a big problem. Either way you have to ensure that your approach to collecting and analyzing information from the many alternative sources needs to be carefully considered. Many organizations and bodies are looking at the issues of the euro changeover, and you could consult them. Alternatively, if you don't have the resources within your company you can plan to use the services of other companies and professionals to do the work, including:

**TABLE 2.1**

**Sources of information used by companies (%)**

|  | Total | France | Germany | Italy | Spain | UK |
|---|---|---|---|---|---|---|
| Newspapers | 60 | 57 | 74 | 66 | 55 | 48 |
| Banks | 53 | 48 | 87 | 34 | 35 | 63 |
| Specialist publications | 9 | 2 | 10 | 5 | 15 | 13 |
| Seminars | 9 | 24 | 13 | 2 | 5 | 3 |
| Television | 7 | – | 10 | 17 | – | 8 |
| Various associations | 5 | 5 | 8 | – | – | 13 |
| Internal sources | 5 | 2 | 5 | 5 | 10 | 5 |
| Association of treasurers | 5 | 21 | – | – | 5 | – |
| Financial institutions | 4 | 2 | – | 2 | 3 | 13 |
| Working group | 4 | 2 | 13 | 2 | 3 | – |

Source: MORI survey, 1996

- *Business organizations* – your relevant trade association may have prepared briefing notes or leaflets on EMU, or they may be able to give you such information prepared by other bodies and organizations.

- *Accountants* – your accountant should be a member of a professional body that is analyzing the changeover requirements, and should be able to give you advice on how to tackle the issues of the changeover.

- *Banks* – banks are also preparing for the new environment which will impact them more dramatically than any other sector. They should be more advanced in their preparations and should be able to offer advice. Talk to your bank and see what information they can give you. By so doing, and expressing your own interests and concerns, you will help them develop the kinds of services you might need.

- *Computer systems companies* – you are probably already dealing with computer system companies, software suppliers, etc. You should talk to the computer system companies and examine how they view the changeover and what solutions they are offering.

- *Other companies* – you may want to get together with other companies similar to yours, so that you might jointly develop solutions for the changeover. These might include sharing the costs of new systems developments or training courses.

- *The Internet* – there is a mass of information available on the web. The big problem here, though, is avoiding the danger of reading the same material and issues again and again. Nevertheless, www.euro-emu.co.uk is a good place to start as it provides a wealth of useful information as well as links to other sites.

- *Consultants* – many consulting companies have been assisting companies preparing for the euro. As a result they have acquired considerable knowledge of the changeover process and strategies to deal with it. However, they are not within all companies' budgets, but you should weigh this against the time savings and experience you will receive.

It is of paramount importance that rather than defining your approach to the euro in isolation, you exchange your views with your peers and service providers, bearing in mind there are essentially three types of EMU requirement:

- *mandatory requirements*, such as redenomination and triangulation;
- *discretionary requirements*, where some degree of flexibility is allowed, such as dual pricing regulations. This allows for some decision-making, but be aware of the time it takes to do this; and
- *strategic requirements*, which are changes that you wish to pursue as a result of the euro. These are unique to each company.

The European Commission has only agreed rules for currency conversion and they have said that all other accounting and reporting regulations must be set by the national governments. This means individual project managers, programme managers and indeed companies in general, have to seek information from each country, all of whom are working to different rules and timescales. Until recently, and in some countries this is still the case, markets have had to make some assumptions and work around the lack of details to compensate. Consequently, no-one has been able to obtain a single set of standard requirements.

Even where requirements are known, they can still be complex. For example, to handle 'triangulation' in currency conversions is not so straightforward as you might think. All currencies must first convert first to the euro and then convert again to the national currency using the published cross-currency rate to the euro. This means that nearly every accounting software package will have to be rewritten in order to handle the intermediate euro stage, even existing multi-currency systems.

The information needs of individual firms will vary depending on size, sector, internal structure, location of activities and so on. Ultimately, each company is responsible for its own decisions in preparing for EMU and for establishing its specific information requirements for this purpose. The first step to take is to designate responsibility for the collection and analysis of information. Alternative approaches are outlined in Chapter 6.

# CUSTOMERS

## Customer base

EMU may significantly affect your customer base and how you conduct business with them, both during and after the changeover process. Issues include:

- managing your customer relationships;
- discussing relevant issues before the changeover;
- defining your marketing strategy including pricing strategies;
- managing supporting technology; and
- assessing new products, services and markets.

Your approach to these issues depends upon the nature of your customer base. Since EMU is a complex issue, companies who sell primarily to the general public will face significant challenges. Issues will include pricing, invoicing, explaining the transition process, converting balances to euros and helping to minimize disruption to customer relations. You will need to design a comprehensive process of communication, particularly to train staff to deal with customer issues.

For enterprises with a small number of major customers there is a particular risk that those customers will be in a position to dictate the timing of changeover to euro pricing and transaction processing. The changeover may be sooner or later than otherwise planned and bear in mind that larger companies are likely to convert earlier (particularly those that operate in a number of countries likely to participate in EMU). It is therefore essential to discuss this issue with your major customers as soon as possible, to understand clearly their likely conversion date to euro.

Given that each of your customers has a choice of dates, within the three-year period from 1 January 1999, to convert their operations to dual currency or to euro only, the most difficult issue to deal with may be the variety of customer conversion dates, causing an extended period of dual currency operations for your business.

For companies that do not export to EMU countries, opportunities may arise to compete in these markets once the foreign currency barrier is removed. Although this is just one barrier to trade, it may be a significant barrier in your, or your competitors', case. If you export outside the EU, you are less likely to have to change your customer management process. However, you may choose to invoice in euros as a more internationally acceptable currency than your home currency. This is particularly plausible for companies exporting to the US.

Enterprises dealing in large volumes of cash will have particular conversion difficulties during the dual currency period following the introduction of notes and coins. Remember that your customers will be free to pay cash in either euros or national currencies within the euro-zone for a period up to six months. However, these dual currency issues may well be mitigated by the increasing use of electronic payment methods, such as debit cards, smart cards and Internet-based banking.

## Market share

As the barriers for entry into markets are removed, it is inevitable that some national organizations will seize the opportunity to become more international and access more profitable markets within EMU countries. Multinational companies will also become more attracted to the enlarged market and may increase their efforts and presence to gain market share. This increased competition will present both opportunities and risks to companies.

If your customers are likely to remain loyal throughout the changeover process, and you have clear lines of communication to discuss and deal with particular issues as they arise, the potential impact of the euro is likely to be low. However, if customers are not particularly loyal, they may well be more inclined to buy from your overseas competitors once exchange risks and transaction costs are eliminated, and the prices being offered in different countries become more comparable. The transparency of prices for products sold across Europe will increase greatly with customers querying euro-based price differentials that cannot be explained purely by transportation costs.

## Pan-European marketing and branding

Rethinking of company strategy in the light of EMU and the changeover to the euro may identify new opportunities and challenges, requiring long-term planning and strategy development. But even with no changes in market strategy there are many issues:

- pricing policy
- price lists, catalogues
- display of prices
- review of distribution channels in EMU participating countries
- payment handling
- EMU positioning.

The dynamics of the market environment will begin to affect the way in which organizations communicate with consumers/customers across the euro marketplace. The introduction of the euro may increase the trend to Pan-European products and marketing. Indeed, if the strategy is to treat 'euroLand' as one market then the customer will expect a common look and feel across the zone.

The adoption of the single currency will increase the transparency of prices for similar products across member countries. Hence, customers will be more inclined to shop around. You may need to adjust your branding strategy if you are not confident that your existing brands provide sufficient protection against market shifts caused by EMU. Few companies are in the happy position of being able to rely extensively on this factor for protection.

From 1 January 1999 to 1 July 2002 at the latest, the euro and EMU-participating currencies will both be used in transactions. Only in the final six months will companies be legally obliged to accept both currencies. Until then it will be competitive pressures under the rule of 'no prohibition, no compulsion'.

It is important that you discuss the preferences and intentions of your key customers and suppliers in relation to the dual pricing period, as this is likely to be a major influencing factor for deciding on the timing of your transition. Consider the lead time and IT implications of preparing and producing new price lists, bar coding and catalogues and ensure that you incorporate regulations for price displays and price rounding.

> the adoption of the single currency will increase the transparency of prices for similar products across member countries

One of the greatest challenges is explaining EMU to the man in the street. Dual pricing can facilitate the acceptance process, but for how long do you provide dual prices? Consumer groups favour the longest possible period, but what is the cost? Some logistical and technical questions also need answering.

- Overloading the quantity of information provided to consumers: up to eight different prices could be shown – price/item, price/unit and promotional price equivalents all need converting to euros;
- *Timing:* when do companies start displaying dual prices?
- Will cash registers and displays both need to show dual prices?
- Pricing printed on items, or mail-order catalogues;
- Avoid consumer belief that rounding up of prices is hiding unfair inflation;
- Queuing times at cash registers as consumers line up for explanations.

Whilst, at the time of writing, the EC has yet to legislate on this issue, agreements have been reached between industry associations and consumer groups. The EC has decided to provide a label to companies who comply with six principles:

- applying EU rules for conversion and rounding of prices;
- abstaining from charging higher prices to consumers paying in euros;
- providing practical information on the use of the euro;

- pricing receipts and products on display or subject to special offers in euros as well as the national currency;

- ensuring that staff are capable of providing information on the euro; and

- signalling whether they accept payments in euros (but not necessarily accepting card or cheque payments in euros).

Channels of distribution may be affected by changes in direct selling, such as Internet or mail-order, as price transparency and increased cross-border trade increases. A company exporting may be currently using different distributors in different countries. There may be scope for rationalization if the countries are all members of EMU. Alternatively, if a company identifies new sales export opportunities in countries where it previously had no dealings, new distribution channels may be required. Possible options include using local agents, direct selling, licensing arrangements or electronic media such as the Internet.

Businesses may have to deal with euro electronic payments during the three-year transition period. All companies in participating Member States will have to accept both electronic and paper euro from 1 January 2002. Can your payment-handling systems, such as cash registers, storage facilities and vending machines, cope with the new specifications for euro notes and coins, and particularly, can they handle two sets of notes and coins? Companies must also ensure that their bank accounts, credit cards and electronic facilities are able to deal with the euro from the moment they invoice and accept payments in euros. Obviously staff will need training on dealing/transacting in the euro in a way that minimizes disruption to the business.

Your customers may be confused by the changeover and suspicious of price increases during the changeover period. These customers will need assistance in understanding how the euro will affect business with your company. You need to develop a clear communication strategy which may include factsheets, letters, shop notices or conversion charts.

You may also want to use your changeover strategy as a selling point. What is your EMU positioning? Do you want to be, and be seen to be, an early user of the euro? Consider the benefits of this approach, including the IT implications and impact on your customers and suppliers. You will however lose the chance to learn from the mistakes of other early converters.

## Products/services

EMU may affect the design and positioning of your products/services. Think beyond the monetary issues and don't miss out on new product opportunities that might arise from closer economic union as well as the changeover process itself.

If your products rely on particular price points (e.g., under £10), once the euro becomes the accepted medium of exchange, the price points are likely to shift. This may need a re-evaluation of the target pricing for your products and even result in a need to reposition or redesign products. You will need to consider changes to production line, service process, IT, training needs and storage. Is your production labelling equipment flexible enough to incorporate dual prices and the new euro symbol?

If you apply the conversion rates strictly, it is unlikely to result in an ideal new psychological price point such as €9.99. In order to maintain profit margins while adjusting to new price points it may be necessary to redesign your product, in terms of size and/or quality. For example, a confectionery manufacturer may alter the number of sweets in a packet, or a shoe manufacturer may change the quality of leather. For companies currently selling products to meet a range of different price points in different European markets, the euro provides an opportunity to standardize products for all EMU markets.

Fixing new threshold prices by adjusting product or packaging sizes presupposes that variation is an option. However, EU regulations stipulate that prices must also be stated per kilo or litre, thus limiting this option to a certain extent. If sizes cannot be varied it may be necessary to reposition the brand over the longer term, or analyze the entire value chain with the aim of tapping improvement potential and thus arriving at new threshold prices.

The deepening of the single market associated with EMU is expected to favour companies whose production processes and costs compare favourably with their international competitors. Less efficient producers are expected to come under increased pressure. This is extremely important to producers of internationally traded products who may not have the necessary cost and efficiency structures to benefit from increased cross-border trade.

A clear benefit expected from EMU is the elimination or reduction of foreign exchange handling and transaction costs. If these costs are significant for you, make sure that the benefits materialize as soon as possible.

## Legal issues

You will need to ensure that you comply with any existing or new regulations concerning the euro. For example, EU directives already refer to pricing display. In addition, you may need to review your contracts. Legal agreements most affected are likely to be in multi-currency areas, where contract terms extend beyond the conversion dates. Where simply substituting a national currency amount for a euro amount is not a comprehensive solution, difficulties may arise. In particular, complex legal agreements drafted without any consideration of the EMU process will need to be reviewed. Also of concern is the impact of EMU on contracts drawn up under the jurisdiction of non-EU countries.

Some changes will have more far-reaching implications. One example could be long-term contracts set in an old currency. This example might cover the payment and management of pension funds, staff contracts, long-term purchasing and supply contracts, as well as loans, stocks, bonds and debentures. Hence, there may be a need for the corporate legal department to review and re-negotiate each contract with each client in each subsidiary.

## Market research

If you plan to use EMU as an opportunity to expand into new markets, it will be necessary to obtain information on local customer preferences, buying patterns, distribution channels, etc. You may need to build new customer profiles to assess if their needs are significantly different from those of existing customers, with possible implications for product design. There may also be opportunities to exploit niche market opportunities which were not viable pre-EMU due to the limited size of the customer base. You will also need to re-organize your sales department to enable it to maximize the potential of new opportunities, including new language skills. You should also review the prices of your products and services against those of potential EMU competitors to assess whether price transparency is likely to be an issue for your business.

### *Customers*

Are you affected by your customers?
Do you sell to the euro zone, or to customers that will want to use the euro?
From what date will your customers require bids to be submitted in euro?
Will existing long-term contracts have to be re-costed?
Can you quote in euro and handle the exchange rate risk?
Will the currency conversion endanger your signal prices?
Will you need to standardize prices across the euro zone?
Will you need to establish new price points in euro?
When will you change the prices on product labels?
What rules need to be complied with, such as conversion of currencies to and from euro?
When will you reprint advertising material?
Should you change and streamline your product range?
Should you change your product design for a larger market?
Should you rethink your distribution strategy and network?
Can you print invoices in euro?
Do you have the production capacity to expand your market?
Will you need a multi-currency accountancy package?

▶

> Will you use the euro as an opportunity to redesign old structures in the marketing department, distribution and logistics?
>
> How will you analyze your customer structure and demand patterns?
>
> Have you talked to your customers about their needs?
>
> What are you doing to ensure that your customers notice that you are gearing up for the future Europe?

## SUPPLY CHAIN

The challenge is that, when exchange risks and costs are eliminated by EMU, European players will be much more inclined to compete, both as buyers and sellers, on a pan-European basis. The issue here is that the supply chain is about far more than just logistics and distribution. It is now the most important process for any organization, whatever products or services it is delivering to customers.

For manufacturers, the supply chain is the set of processes that starts with taking customer orders, and ends with delivering products or services and customer satisfaction. It involves sourcing, buying and delivering raw materials and components, as well as managing the labour needed to produce finished goods.

At the moment, the costs of raw materials and labour across European countries are not transparent. Although it is possible to know in theory what costs in individual countries are, changing exchange rates mean that it is not always possible to know what costs will be at a certain point.

After EMU, that uncertainty will be removed. Organizations will be able to source components or promise to sell goods in certain countries at a set (albeit market-set) price. This so-called price transparency will have far-reaching effects, not only on the cost of living, but on the ability, willingness and desire of organizations to introduce truly pan-European processes.

One way to do this is by reducing the number of distribution and storage facilities across Europe, or even changing their operating bases. Another is to be more reactive when it comes to sourcing raw materials and components. Without the added risk of buying materials or selling products and services at unpredictable prices, it will be easier to base buying decisions on other factors – such as quality or quick availability – all within a smaller timeframe.

The source and cost of supplies of goods and services will be significantly affected by EMU – particularly by the timing of changeover to the euro by your major suppliers. New purchasing opportunities will arise with alternative European sources, but you may have your conversion timetable influenced by the behaviour of important suppliers. There is also an increased opportunity to buy directly from producers in EMU participating countries and to bypass, to some extent, wholesale distributors.

Although suppliers' margins will come under pressure as customers re-assess contracts and prices due to the single currency, the transition to EMU will not cause everyone to flock to the lowest-priced supplier as buyers do not look at price alone. However, it will lower the barrier to intelligent sourcing and may well cause significant shifts of business. If there are significant non-foreign-exchange issues involved in buying overseas, such as high transportation costs, the opportunities for diversifying overseas suppliers and generating cost savings are reduced.

As a pre-requisite for 'winning' business, suppliers may be required by their customers to become euro-compatible throughout the supply chain. A cascade effect will occur as governments and large industry sectors adopt and seek euro compliance from their suppliers for purchasing and invoicing throughout the various economies involved. British Telecom (BT) has already insisted that all its suppliers demonstrate Year 2000 compliance to continue doing business with BT. Equally, several companies have already indicated their intention to start invoicing in euro at the beginning of the changeover process.

## Suppliers

Are you affected by your suppliers?
Do you buy from the euro zone?
Do you buy from multinationals outside the euro zone?
Will your suppliers insist on using the euro?
Can you handle the exchange rate risk?
Will you need a multi-currency accounting package?
Could you pay your suppliers in euro?
Could you purchase from new sources once price transparencies are clearer?
Have you talked to your bank about the euro services they offer?
Will long-term procurement projects have to be rethought?
How will you rethink your supplier relations?

# COMPETITORS

As a major step in the process of deepening the single European market, the most significant economic impact is expected to be an increase in competition across European borders. This is an opportunity for you to increase your penetration of European markets, but it also gives your competitors the same opportunity.

For companies that compete primarily on price, the risks of EMU are clearly greatest. Overseas competitors may well have the financial resources to attack new markets with aggressive pricing. Opportunities to price discriminate between EU markets will diminish and direct comparisons across markets will be far easier than at present.

Organizations whose competitors, domestic and foreign, currently see intra-European foreign exchange risk and transaction costs as substantial barriers to cross-border trade, are likely to review their plans for European market penetration post-EMU. Once the pricing of your product is in euros, potential competitors will have a far clearer idea of how profitable it might be for them to attack your markets. However, non-price barriers to competition such as customer loyalty, exclusive distribution channels, transportation costs, delivery times and quality issues may cushion the immediate impact of the euro. Can you build barriers to entry on the basis of such factors rather than price?

Competitive strategy involves positioning a business to maximize the value of the capabilities that distinguish it from its competitors. A central aspect to this process is competitor analysis. The objective of competitor analysis is to develop a profile of the nature and success of the likely strategy changes each competitor might make, each competitor's probable response to the range of feasible moves other firms could initiate, and each competitor's probable reaction to industry and market changes brought about by the euro.

> for companies that compete primarily on price, the risks of EMU are clearly greatest

This is generally harder in practice than in theory. Many companies do not collect information about competitors, both existing and potential, in a systematic fashion, but act on the basis of informal impressions, conjectures and intuition gained through the titbits of information about competitors every manager continually receives. Key information that you should consider about your competitors includes the following.

- What is the current strategy and future goals of your competitors?
- What assumptions do you make about the industry in which you compete?
- What are your competitors' strengths and weaknesses?
- How will they respond to the euro?
- Is each competitor satisfied with its current position?
- What likely moves or strategy shifts will your competitor make?
- Where are your competitors vulnerable?
- What will provoke retaliation by your competitors?

You should ensure that you have a clear picture of what your current and potential new competitors are up to. If you have so far had different prices in the national markets, can this price differentiation be maintained within the EMU countries?

Whilst the complexity of the euro project is exacerbated by the uncertainty of competitor reactions, customer requirements and the speed of any changes, you should try to get a feel for the state of preparations of your competitors. Have they developed an EMU strategy? Have they commenced both business and systems changes? Have they initiated customer and staff communications programmes? The relative positioning of your company should, at the very least raise concern, and give you added impetus to your own sensible and planned response.

### Competitors

Are you affected by your competitors?
Do you face competition from companies from the euro zone, in the euro zone, or internationally?
How will lower transaction costs affect your competitors?
When will you review your costs and prices?
Do you know how your competitors' behaviour will change?
Could you afford to match price reductions?
Could you purchase from new sources?
Are you affected by virtue of your organization?
Do you have factories, shops or offices in the euro zone?
Should you rationalize your operations?
When will you review your distribution channels?
When will you review your cash handling operations?
When will you review your sourcing arrangements?
Should you consider a merger or partnership arrangement?

## FINANCIAL MANAGEMENT

### Financial planning and capital procurement

What changes are expected with respect to the funds your company will need as a result of EMU and preparations for it? You should consider the amount of funds, when they are needed, the impact on your current investment strategy, and factor in changes to investment planning and budgeting. In particular you should set aside resources for conversion.

To date most of the work in quantifying costs has been carried out in the financial services industry. However, the Gartner Group estimated that the overall cost of preparing European companies' IT systems to deal with EMU has risen to between $15 billion and $40 billion. And IT represents, on average, only around 50% of the total cost of changeover. The other main drivers of cost include business process change, project management, marketing, staff training, and consolidating operations.

Gartner analysts estimate that, over a seven-year period to 2003, the cost of adapting IT systems to cope with EMU could exceed some estimates of the cost of dealing with the Year 2000 problem. Due to the overlapping of EMU and Year 2000, companies are left with little spare or discretionary spending to invest in new IT systems or develop new applications. More worrying is the potential shortfall in skilled resources required to tackle EMU and Year 2000.

Research carried out by BZW suggested the cost to companies of implementing EMU strategies will far exceed the cost of addressing the Year 2000 issue. Estimates for Year 2000 compliance are $15 billion across Europe, where EMU totals a staggering $24.4 billion (*see* Table 2.2 for estimated costs of EMU by country). The cost of EMU compliance is, however, far from clear largely because there is no such thing as a set standard of compliance. This is demonstrated by the wide variations in cost estimates that have been made.

EMU-compliance for one organization is not necessarily compliance for another organization with a different strategy. Whilst IT represents a fair proportion of the changes and hence budget required, the size of budgets allocated to marketing and internal training have varied enormously. Deutsche Bank estimated that an average of 15 minutes will be needed to train each customer, in addition to the time spent training the staff first.

Few IT systems are already fully equipped to deal with the changeover and conversion issues of EMU. The conversion costs may be significant and must be included in future IT strategies and budgets. If you are reliant on IT for your key business processes, you will need to focus significant effort on your IT.

**TABLE 2.2**

**Estimated cost of EMU by country**

| Country | Est. cost ($m) | Estimated by |
| --- | --- | --- |
| Belgium | 400 | Belgian Banking Association |
| France | 4000 | Association of Credit Institutions |
| Ireland | 125–160 | Irish Banking Federation |
| Italy | 900 | Italian Banking Association |
| Luxembourg | 250 | Luxembourg Banking Association |
| Netherlands | 600 | Dutch Central Bank |
| Netherlands | 600–900 | Rabobank |
| Portugal | 650 | Portuguese Banking Association |
| Spain | 2000 | Spanish Banking Association |
| UK | 2300–3200 | British Banking Association/APACS |

Source: Sema Group

Given the scale of cost, it is unlikely that you can squeeze the cost of changeover into your existing budget. Further, you will have to justify the investment in changes made to your business and supporting IT environment.

You should also clarify to what extent the fixing of exchange rates could have ramifications for profitability. Prepare yourself for the fact that from 1999 the costing basis in many markets will change (e.g., through the disappearance of hedging costs and transaction costs, but also as a result of changes in procurement and sales potential as well as the price structure).

Do you expect changes to balance sheet ratios and earnings statements? What about the consequent impact on existing loan agreements? Take a look at the agreements reached in loan contracts or in other agreements, e.g., with respect to maintaining certain ratios in the balance sheet or earnings statement (minimum equity capital, interest cover ratios, etc.). You should discuss any changes in projections with your lender. In addition, the changed market environment could offer you new opportunities such as changing the terms of your loan.

How do you plan to benefit from new opportunities to raise capital in the financial markets? As the interface between the company and the financial system, the treasury department is in the unique position of being impacted by the 'Big Bang' conversion in the financial markets. The future bond market will be substantially larger and more liquid than today's national bond markets. Yield spreads between the member countries will narrow. Interest rate differentials will in future depend on the credit rating of the borrower, market liquidity, the availability of derivative hedging instruments and differences in taxation. Today's fragmented equity markets in Europe will become one European equity market in which the cross-border valuation of certain industrial sectors will have much greater significance.

You will have access to this market and you should develop financing strategies in line with future market structures and investors as well as identifying the ramifications on your existing borrowed capital. If you are planning to issue securities over the medium-term, which currency, maturity and market should you be looking at?

On the other hand, lending and borrowing operations, as well as asset and liability management, will be much easier conducted in one currency only instead of in the euro-11 currencies. Apart from this more technical advantage, you should consider how you can benefit from the emergence of the huge euro-capital market. It will be a more competitive market and, therefore, credit quality will be even more critical for borrowing. A better credit standing gives you a better position to benefit from the greater depth and liquidity of the euro-market in terms of improving your borrowing costs. Lower borrowing costs, in turn, will alleviate some of the margin pressure from price transparencies.

Those companies that have traditionally turned to the banks for straight lending should be looking to drive the rates down. Alternatively, maybe now is the time to consider floating and raising funds directly from the capital markets. The search for credit and the expansion of equity markets will be providing attractive flotation conditions; and intense competition between banks will keep costs down.

---

**Business finance**

Will there be new opportunities to raise finance?
Will you be exposed to exchange rate risk?
Can you deal with the exchange rate risk?
Do you have any outstanding shares or bonds that you wish to convert?
What euro services do you require from your bank relationships?
How will your current investments be affected and should you consider taking professional advice?
Are you affected by your investment strategy?
Are your investments in the euro zone or in national currency units?
When will you review your investment strategy?
How will your budget planning be affected?

---

As well as the impact on cash management and foreign exchange operations, you should also analyze the impact of the euro on strategic investments. Differentiate initially between these investments, such as equity holdings which secure sales markets or increase market presence, and operational investments, such as positions which you have to hold to maintain your current liquidity.

## Exchange Rate Risk

A manufacturer can see the profitability of his exports vanish overnight as a result of exchange rate fluctuations. He therefore has two alternatives: either he shoulders the risk, and accepts that he might have to export at a loss if his currency revalues too much, or he seeks to insure himself on the financial markets. The cost of hedging against the exchange rate risk can be ascertained in advance. But it comes on top of the traditional transaction costs and other costs of multi-currency management.

Thus, the elimination of exchange rate instability and the associated costs will encourage greater cross-border trade and investment and enable companies to better exploit the opportunities of the single market. Further, the introduction of the euro will lead to a more unified, deeper and more liquid market in public and private debt. Firms can expect to see this translated into reduced financing costs as banks and other financial institutions seek to increase their lending opportunities.

From 1 January 1999, the conversion rate of the participating national currencies to the euro is fixed by the ECOFIN Council through a unanimous resolution. The procedure for fixing the conversion rate was not defined exactly in the Maastricht Treaty – but there has been no doubt that market rates would be used.

With foreign exchange transactions including currency swaps, the euro will replace the national currency of a member country. You should analyze how this impacts different types of transaction that you may have, including traditional forward currency transactions (including currency swaps which provide for both parties to make a one-off final payment in each case on the basis of a different spot and forward rate), fixed-rate currency swaps (i.e., which provide for only fixed, same-day periodic payments by both parties on the basis of identical spot and forward rates), and combined interest rate and currency swaps.

Have you identified your short- and medium-term currency risks? Differentiate foreign currency positions by maturity, check the structure of short-term financial funds and ensure the validity of hedging transactions beyond the start of EMU. In addition, you should ensure you can benefit from the cost savings arising from eliminating conversion costs, reducing price of cross-border payments, increased netting opportunities and reduced discrepancies between value dates, and streamlined cash management processes including the number of bank accounts.

The management of the exchange rate risk puts SMEs at an unjustified disadvantage compared with large companies, which are better equipped to manage exchange rate variations. Structurally, SMEs do not have the critical size which gives them access to the most modern (and least expensive) hedging instruments such as futures and options. Nor do they employ the qualified staff who would enable them to discern exchange rate risks accurately. Lastly they are obliged to use the services of intermediaries, which increases the final cost of the insurance. EMU effectively removes this disadvantage.

## Interest rate management

From 1 January 1999, money market rates in the euro-zone will be uniform. The interest rate level on the money market will be steered by the ECB. The volatility of interest rates on the euro money market will depend above all on the monetary policy instruments of the ECB and the frequency of its market interventions. Within the euro-currency zone, currency-induced yield spreads on the bond market will disappear; yield differentials will, therefore, be determined primarily by credit rating and liquidity differences between issues. The euro interest rate level will, as before, reflect the economic situation, the development of inflation, current monetary policy, etc.

You need to identify which exposures in your interest rate agreements are expiring. Remember that rates on fixed-rate loans extending into EMU remain in force. Variable-rate loans and loans with rate adjustment clauses will be adjusted to the new level at the time pursuant to the conditions of the contract. Draw up interest rate scenarios for financial and liquidity planning and check possibilities to lock in long-term financing.

During the transition period, treasurers will have to deal with the change in liquidity risks and funding possibilities available in euro and national currency. You will need to ensure you identify changes to price and reference rates and understand the use of new financial products available in euro.

Finally, it is worth remembering that where exchange rates are held constant, stresses are likely to manifest themselves in interest rates. Witness the UK's exit from the ERM or unemployment in Spain, France and Germany today. Once exchange rates cannot be moved, the risk measure may migrate to interest rates. Governments of countries with high social security costs may be forced to borrow at ever higher rates. The volatility of foreign exchange markets may re-emerge in national debt rates.

## Treasury operations

As corporates review their Europe-wide banking arrangements, and decide which accounts they no longer need, the advantages of concentrating common financial control activities in one centre will become evident. When expanding into new countries, European companies often simply recreate the majority of their domestic functions within each country or adapt those of an acquisition.

It may well be possible for you to streamline company treasury operations as a result of the harmonization of money and capital markets. For example, you may be able to centralize the decentralized financial activities of subsidiaries by reducing the number of treasury departments. The number of banking connections can be reduced where bank accounts of subsidiaries can be replaced with internal settlement accounts.

## Accounting and fiscal issues

During the transition period companies must select the desired reporting currency, be it euros or existing national currencies, in which their financial statements will be presented. After this period, all financial statements will have to be presented in euro. Even large multinationals outside the euro-zone have been considering this issue. The key determinant will be the requirements of users of financial statements such as shareholders, stock exchanges, bankers, public administrations, customers and suppliers. Several options are available including:

- continuing publishing accounts in national currency and converting to euro some time during the transition period;

- publishing two sets of accounts, one in national currency and one in euro; and
- publishing a single set of financial statements with amounts shown in national currency and the euro.

If you expect your account users to be pan-European investors, you are more likely to want to publish accounts in euro, which coincides with the conversion of euro-zone stock exchanges. One important factor to consider is the treatment of prior year comparatives in financial statements. It is important that users are aware of the conversion method used to translate prior year national currency figures into euro. There is a range of alternative converison rates to use, though the most common is likely to be the simplest – the official conversion rates as at 1 January 1999. There is a legal requirement that foreign exchanges gains/losses will not be generated by this conversion process.

As far as filing annual returns, such as accounts or tax returns, is concerned, public administrations in each EMU country are still in the process of determining whether or not they can accept euro. Many still have a long way to go in their preparations. Nevertheless, you should keep a watchful eye on the preparations of national fiscal and public administrations.

The changeover to the single currency will give rise to a number of accounting issues that need to be addressed. More detailed guidance on these issues should emerge from national accounting associations which are liaising closely with the FEE (European Federation of Accountants). The principal issues include:

- recognition of changeover costs;
- accounting for foreign subsidiaries;
- accounting for foreign currency transactions;
- share capital denomination;
- changes in asset values;
- taxation, including expenses of conversion to the euro, revenue administration issues, realisation of gains and losses, and derivatives contracts;
- fiscal treatment of gains and losses arising from conversion;
- choice of exchange rate for translating historical data;
- depreciation of investments related to the preparations for the introduction of the euro;
- rounding of amounts which will become cumbersome in euro and subsequent discrepancies resulting from successive conversions of a given amount.

You should seek guidance on these issues from your accountants. You will also have to ensure that accounting systems can cope with euro transactions, including the potential to process transactions in national currency and euro.

Given that the costs of conversion to the euro are significant, including the costs of altering IT systems and documentation, staff training and communication and maintaining customer service, it is important that you incorporate these costs into your budgeting process.

One key element of costs relates to the provision of functionality to cope with dual currency accounting and reporting. You will need to consider carefully whether you want to allow this flexibility in accounting systems, e.g., adding the euro as an extra currency, and permitting a switch from the euro to national currency and back.

## OTHER STAKEHOLDERS

Other than customers, suppliers and competitors, there are three other key groups of stakeholders that you will need to consider during your preparations for the euro: investors, bankers and employees. The euro and your specific preparations for it will stimulate a great deal of interest and uncertainty from these groups and you should ensure that you can meet their requirements. This will allow you to secure both long-term and working capital at competitive rates from investors and bankers. Meeting the needs of your staff is crucial as you are fundamentally dependent upon them to prepare for the euro.

Significant benefits from EMU are expected for companies who will be in a position to access pan-European capital markets. Primarily, this is due to new opportunities to obtain funding outside domestic banking arrangements and the expectation that EMU will significantly increase competition between European banks. But this in turn requires you to respond to the requirements of the financial markets. For example, the importance of internationally accepted credit ratings will increase as financiers seek to rely on such independent measures of credit risk in competing for business in new areas of the euro zone.

One of the key goals of EMU is exchange rate stability which will allow more predictability for investments and markets. This will make it easier for companies to plan their investment strategies and reduce the risks of cross-border investments. Shareholders will expect organizations to be ready. European firms will naturally become more exposed to the rigours of shareholder value as global fund managers and other investors focus their attention on the euro-zone's single equity market. In particular, company restructuring to gain European scale and the resulting need to raise capital for takeovers will force companies to take greater account of shareholders' needs.

Joint ventures and large co-operation agreements such as in aerospace, defence and large scale capital projects will require euro reporting to EMU partners. Subsidies and investments may be dependent on organizations being euro-compatible during the transition period and subsequently post 2002.

Some organizations will come to be viewed as large euro earners in the same way as multinationals now are viewed as large dollar earners which have a dependence not only on how their operations are performing but their exposure to variations in exchange rates.

With exchange rate risk largely eliminated by the single currency, investment decisions by pan-European companies, not least the investment in your euro strategy, will involve a closer scrutiny of operating costs and, inevitably, a greater emphasis on regulatory and tax issues. The investment decisions of large companies have already driven certain European countries to adopt similar regulatory regimes to their neighbours. This trend is likely to accelerate as the euro exposes structural differentials across European countries.

Banks face the toughest issues. Some commentators have suggested that banks simply face a lose–lose scenario due to the combined effect of increased competition, loss of foreign exchange revenue and profit, consolidation of inter-bank accounts, substantial conversion costs, a complex impact in all business areas, as well as coping with a period of dual-currency accounting. For banks across Europe, EMU means intense competitive pressure. Corporates, particularly multinational companies, are expected to rationalize not only their treasury operations but existing banking relationships in the euro-zone as well as their correspondent banking ties.

Organizations perceiving potential advantage, whether from the point of view of operating efficiency (single accounting system), elimination of currency risk within a major market, or simply conforming to head office requirements (offshoots of euro-zone organizations) will all demand euro banking at an early stage. Banks without such services risk customers migrating to those that do. This is a chance to capitalize on a period of intense banking competition.

A study by MORI at the end of 1996, commissioned by IBM, looked at how European corporations saw their banks responding to EMU and the services they expect from them. According to the survey, over 50% of companies were expecting help in preparations from their banks, from seminars and literature, to expertise and consulting; 35% said they had been approached by banks other than their current relationship, the Germans being the most active in this activity. The majority of companies deal with several banks in Europe. Almost three-quarters work with over nine banks, while 3% use only one bank.

And what about your employees? A survey by Deutsche Bank and Towers Perrin published in June 1998 indicated that of 200 multinationals surveyed, over half expected EMU will lead to pan-European pay agreements and levels of remuneration, principally as a result of increased pay transparency. Equally you will need to assess potential changes to staff pension arrangements and other benefits.

One of the most important and potentially time-consuming issues to be addressed is the training of staff, including cash handling and conversion rates, invoicing procedures, dealing with customer enquiries, inputting transactions into accounting systems as well as understanding the basics of EMU and the implementation of the companies' euro strategy.

> **one of the most important and potentially time-consuming issues to be addressed is the training of staff**

The staff of the company will need to be able to implement the company strategy for the changeover and to carry out the operational changes needed to achieve it. Issues include:

- drawing up the main lines of the training programme;
- detailed training requirements specification as the date for the changeover approaches;
- planning for outsourcing of additional training resources if required.

Finally you must consider the type and number of resources required to deal with the euro. For example, how and who will assess the impact of the euro on your business? How many skilled professionals will you require to implement planned IT changes? Do you hire permanent staff, contractors, consultants, or do you outsource or upgrade? These questions must all be answered at an early stage in your euro preparations.

## RESOURCING

Within the financial services industry, dealing with the euro is the first project to simultaneously involve more than one financial market in all its aspects, and virtually every financial institution globally. It has required a significant effort and co-operation from all the parties involved. The all-encompassing nature of the euro project in financial institutions has exposed some of the more difficult managerial issues, in particular coping with the lack of experience in managing a major conversion project. There are some key lessons to be learned from their experiences.

The key message for managers is to focus on staff retention whilst stressing the importance of all functions. This is particularly the case when operations, technology or back office staff require the engagement of the front office as is the case on all euro projects. Who has the tougher job – the operations manager and technologist trying to create an environment that supports the euro, or the trader that tries to make money from speculating on future euro volatility?

The answers to the specification questions are more pressing for the IT specialist who's got to get the corporate system or the national settlement system singing and dancing rather than for the trader. Traders trade, if it's cucumbers or gold bars, they'll quote you a price, and they're pretty agile at it.

Often the best sales staff and traders are those that understand what goes on around them that allows them to do the job they do. It's not difficult to get on the phone and buy and sell some stocks, particularly when it is a customer order anyway. Without funding, operations and accounting, these trades would not be possible. Processing the transaction from conception to completion necessarily requires the involvement of all functions and management structures should recognize this. How many accountants do you know that do not at least feel a little intimidated when they deliver their first P&L to a trading desk? Who do you think will be responsible for converting the billions of dollars' worth of positions on the books of investment banks?

The cross-functional nature of a euro project necessitates a team drawn from all functions, but who has responsibility? Is the project manager the man or woman with the greatest project management skills (in particular, man-management skills) or is it the manager who has risen through the ranks on the back of technical success? The euro requires a strong team who can work together to achieve a common objective. There is little room for front-office/back-office politics with such a tough fixed deadline. The ability of the manager to build an effective team is often related to that manager's ability to break down some of the traditional human barriers between different functions of the organization.

Personality management is one of the more complex issues that managers within financial institutions have to face. Front office managers are faced with huge salaries and even bigger bonuses coupled with an exceptionally high staff turnover rate. Such statistics certainly give credence to the view that the financial institutions compete for resources in a largely individual, ego-driven marketplace. Who you know means everything – let's face it, the largest intangible asset any investment bank has is its people and their contacts.

The job of rewarding and retaining staff is becoming more difficult, particularly as the marketing machine increases its focus and attention on individuals. Whilst protecting talent (and market share) is a critical issue for organizations preparing for the euro, managers are increasingly being faced with how to grow and integrate with new mergers and acquisitions.

The easiest way to grow the most important asset (i.e., gain market share) is to gain the people, particularly those with the right contacts. At an individual level, recruitment consultants earn huge fees for successfully moving people from one firm to another. At an organizational level, the dynamics of an acquisition demonstrates the problems of retention most acutely. Prior to the announcement, senior managers effectively cherry-pick the best staff, give them huge financial incentives to stay, and leave the rest to fend for themselves.

Perhaps the premium paid by most acquirers is cheaper than the aggregated fees that would have to be paid to recruitment agencies in order to grow organically. More importantly, an acquisition is certainly a much faster process of getting new people in the door, but often the return from this investment is less than expected.

This is largely due to the inability of firms to retain key staff. Most noticeably, those people who are mostly ignored during an acquisition – the operations, technology and back office staff – are the ones who move on. It is these people that often give rise to the greatest integration success and failure, but they haven't been retained in the same way as 'front office' staff. Most of the research on M&A activity points to poor post-acquisition integration management as the principal cause of lower than expected returns and most of this work is carried out by non-front office staff. If the staff in the know are no longer on site, it is very difficult for the remaining staff to do as well.

The application of organizational behaviour and the process of management take place not in a vacuum but within the context of an organization setting. Organizations come in all forms, shapes and sizes. However, despite the differences among various organizations, there are at least three common factors in any organization: people, objectives and structure, to which can be added a fourth factor – management. The qualities of these factors determine organizational effectiveness.

The formal organization can be distinguished from the informal organization and from the social organization. The formal organization is deliberately planned and created, and is concerned with co-ordination of activities. The informal organization arises from the interaction of people. It serves a number of important functions and has an influence on the morale, motivation, job satisfaction and performance of staff.

It is important to maintain the balance of the socio-technical system. This calls for effective management of human resources and a style of managerial behaviour which helps to minimize problems of business and technical change.

It is important that priorities are spelled out correctly and resources allocated effectively. Ready or not, most London-based banks were at least starting to expand their in-house staff by late 1996. Many organizations took the view that they had to be prepared come what may. In particular, the investment decisions had to be taken before the political decision to proceed with EMU.

Computer experts will be well-placed to bid for big bonuses for solving EMU problems. Banks will be recruiting them to bring the euro on line at precisely the time when companies in all sectors are seeking urgent help in reprogramming older 'legacy systems' to recognize the Year 2000. The British government-sponsored group taskforce 2000 has estimated that up to 80% of computers will be affected, and that there may not be enough experts to tackle both EMU and Year 2000 at the same time.

Even those businesses which have advanced plans to achieve euro-compliant systems (whatever that is) acknowledge that the collision of the euro and Year 2000 redoubles the complexities and risks of IT management. Many are discovering that human and systems resources are going to be seriously over-stretched for that whole period.

The skills and technology gap that has already developed can only get worse. It was estimated in some quarters that every skilled person in the European IT industry as a whole could theoretically be fully occupied by EMU-related software conversion activities in the next two years!

But time is still desperately short – so you will need to allocate resources carefully and prioritize strictly. Delay is likely to result in a competitive disadvantage compared to organizations that are prepared. The smaller the window for preparation, the more resources will need to be concentrated to focus on the euro rather than other business issues.

The question of availability of IT resources (hardware, software but perhaps above all human) requires close attention. EMU impact assessments have revealed that there is a substantial technology development and implementation man-day requirement. You should understand the conflicting demands for resources of both technology and operational staff as a consequence of other initiatives such as Year 2000 and major systems implementations.

You should identify any skills shortages as there may be insufficient skilled and knowledgeable staff within the company and the marketplace generally, to cope with the complexity and issues surrounding EMU. Whilst staff may need to be transferred from areas of surplus to areas in deficit, they are unlikely to have the exact skill set required. Manpower planning has become a key attribute to successful euro implementation strategies.

# CHAPTER 3

# Information technology issues

# MANAGEMENT

IT systems represent a large share of the global euro changeover project; however the switch to the euro cannot be reduced to mere IT problems as it involves major strategic and organizational issues. Therefore, information system experts in all departments should be closely involved in conducting the project, but they should not head the project.

In many cases, companies have focused on the IT issues to the detriment of both the business and IT. This has created significant problems, uncertainty and delay to IT as responding to the euro has to be business-led. Frequently the IT department comes under pressure from the business to prepare for EMU but does not specify its requirements.

Consequently, for many IT departments, the battle may well be an uphill one as IT staff often have to assume the mantle of prophets, of organizers and awareness-raisers. Raising EMU awareness may be a difficult task especially as EMU has occurred at the same time as business managers are becoming more aware of the implications of the Year 2000 issue. The two have become inextricably tangled in the corporate consciousness, which can make the IT manager's task that much more difficult. Raising awareness, getting a business project team moving, mobilizing the business and finding (willing and committed) sponsors are tasks that should not be underestimated.

> frequently the IT department comes under pressure from the business to prepare for EMU but does not specify its requirements.

Effective prioritization across major programmes, including EMU, Year 2000, integration and other major projects such as a system replacement or implementation, has become critical. Without the right information or a lack of leadership from the business, IT is perpetually struggling to meet continually increasing, and in some cases unrealistic, demands.

## Competing priorities

Given the uncertainty that has surrounded the start of EMU, there is a question over how ready even the best institutions can be. The financial sector is probably further ahead than most others in its awareness of the Year 2000 and euro issues, though even here there are still lots of open issues and questions.

Vendors of complex financial software are having to delay the announcement of 'EMU compliant' products because they are still waiting for guidance on the detailed implementation of the euro. But guidance should come from the users, and this has not been very forthcoming as strategies have varied significantly.

German banks have pretty much agreed to co-operate rather than compete in preparing for the euro. The German Banking Association produced the *EMU Bible* as well as running seminars and offering advice to customers at every level. In Europe as a whole though, preparations are generally less well developed than in Germany.

In the UK, for example, general scepticism towards EMU is reflected in the greater priority attached to Year 2000 projects. Continental Europe is far more concerned about the euro demonstrated by the fact that continental European companies are far less advanced in their Year 2000 preparations. Softlab recently surveyed nearly 1000 major European organizations to find 54% thought Year 2000 was more important than the euro problem, while just 12% said the opposite.

The combination of Year 2000 and EMU is stretching IT resources to the limit. For Year 2000 alone there is a considerable shortfall in available resources. The UK Department of Trade and Industry estimates that the UK alone requires 30–50 000 more IT professionals. The shortfalls in other EU states are understood to be similar. The US has some 190 000 IT vacancies and is actively recruiting overseas, as well as subcontracting work to Europe, India, South Africa and the Far East.

A recent survey of *Fortune 500* IT officers conducted by Cap Gemini America found that four out of five large American organizations are finding a 'tight labour market' for skilled personnel is hampering their ability to achieve Year 2000 compliance. The skills shortage is aggravated by the concurrent timetable for EMU which will require IT systems to be modified in order to process the euro.

Whilst IT resourcing is a major issue for both EMU and Year 2000 projects, there are differences in skill sets required. The skills required to implement EMU must come from both the user and IT departments, since EMU requires in-depth analyses as well as programming skills. Year 2000, on the other hand, is a relatively simple task compared to EMU: fix the dates so that they properly reflect the correct century. This requires little involvement from the users (other than for end-user computing) and, with respect to the code changes themselves, little in-depth analysis. In the words of Peter de Jager, Year 2000 requires 'a squadron of competent programmers, operating under a fully funded, comprehensive, closely monitored and well-managed project plan, can complete the task.'

But whilst the Year 2000 is largely a technical problem, EMU is a much greater challenge as it touches all areas of a business. The main challenge of EMU and Year 2000 lies not in the monetary cost but rather finding enough people with the right technical skills. Before worrying about how to fix their code, companies need to first spend time and money conducting a detailed business analysis and producing a master plan.

This can act as a guide to ensure that good project management is put in place to ensure deadlines can be met, even if the workload grows beyond budget. There is a difference between increasing the level of awareness and doing something about the problem. There is a lot of inertia, particularly in large organizations, to get a big project up and running.

The most important driver for the adoption of the euro is the activities of large organizations. Some large European corporates, such as Philips, already publish annual reports denominated in ECUs. As soon as the ECU converts to euro on 1 January 1999, they automatically operate on a euro base.

## THE YEAR 2000 PROBLEM

There is worldwide concern that many systems and services will fail at the start of Year 2000 (Y2k). The process of identifying where there is a problem and making the necessary changes commonly demands more resource than is available. There is growing concern that staff shortages and turnover will lead to increases in serious systems failures, exemplified by the difficulties in obtaining insurance cover for Year 2000 problems or liabilities. Year 2000 problems are now commonly uninsurable as cover is removed from standard product and service liability renewals because even those who have taken reasonable measures to be compliant cannot be sure of the behaviour of components, sub-systems and interfaces. In response, many software companies have dedicated a substantial amount of resource to avoiding liability.

Commenting on the proposed $32 billion merger between Wells Fargo and Norwest, both North American banks, the *Economist* noted in an article on 13 June 1998 that 'because of the millennium computer-bug problem, banks that strike merger agreements any later than now [June 1998] will be faced with an awkward choice: postpone linking computer systems for over a year, or rush the job and hope for the best. Other prospective brides and bridegrooms might prefer to put off the big day – at least until 2000.' And these banks, being fundamentally dollar-based, don't even have to worry about the euro! Unless of course, they are planning to use their combined size to make new moves in Europe's direction.

The source of the Year 2000 problem lies in the six-digit date field used in the majority of business programs. To save valuable storage space, programmers regularly indicate the year by using just the last two digits of any given date, so that 1998 is seen as 98. But when the date rolls around to 2000, any program that is date or time sensitive will assume the date is 00 and that we have gone back in time by 99 years to 1900.

There is a multiplicity of examples of what might go wrong as a result. The main challenge does not lie within the technicalities of the conversion itself, but the sheer scale of the problem. Using a traditional, manual approach, it takes an average of three days to locate, test and implement each program. So, for the typical company with an average of 10 000 programs, it will require 30 000 man-days or over 150 man-years to solve the Year 2000 problem.

Compounding the requirements of rectifying computer systems and desktop computers is the problem of embedded microchips. Because these are so common, the number of devices that have the potential to cause problems is very large. By some, this issue and its knock-on effects is being taken seriously. An economist from Deutsche Morgan Grenfell predicted that the Dow Jones will break 10 000. But now he warns that:

> 'the "Year 2000" problem is a serious threat to the US economy: a recession, collapsing to deflation, and a sharp drop in the Dow. Investors could lose $1 trillion if prices drop as they did in 1973–74 (42%). He has raised the odds of a severe global recession to 60%. His worry is that the world's leading (and computer driven) economy will succumb to a systemic failure to handle the switch to 2000.' *The Sunday Telegraph, 10 May 1998.*

As with euro conversion, the most time-efficient solution is to use highly automated conversion routines. For Year 2000 solutions, Cap Gemini has found that using an automated toolset, rather than in-house manual resources, can reduce Year 2000 project workloads by more than 40%.

During the testing phase of Year 2000 projects, the error rate for automated code renovation is very low, but where, through necessity, manual changes have been made, the error rate is much higher. Euro conversion is the same in this respect. Companies taking the manual approach to Year 2000 preparation or euro conversion should be aware that they must assign a substantial proportion of the project timetable to testing systems and implementing corrective measures.

## Managing EMU and Year 2000 simultaneously?

The changeover to the euro is often compared to the Year 2000 problem, probably because both are related to information systems and occur at roughly the same time. The basic rule is that those systems that use dates, directly or indirectly, can be affected by the Year 2000 problem. This means that hardware and software that is not used to process financial information can still be affected by the Year 2000 problem. Since most financial information systems also use dates, they must be reviewed for problems associated with both the changeover to the euro and Year 2000.

The preparations for the introduction of the euro, on 1 January 1999, and the Year 2000 will necessarily need to be made at the same time. Therefore some enterprises have decided to combine preparation for both issues in order to avoid modifying the same information systems twice.

The economic, administrative and managerial benefits of concurrent change management have strong appeal. However, whilst there are significant similarities, there are good reasons for managing the subsequent phases of the projects separately. The IT director should examine this ideal with respect to criteria such as those shown in Table 3.1, and in particular should be aware that the combined project could be of unprecedented size and complexity, and may become too difficult to manage.

**TABLE 3.1**

**Comparing EMU and Year 2000 projects**

| Similarities | Differences |
|---|---|
| 1. For both projects an information systems inventory must be made. | 1. The Year 2000 problem is largely a technical problem in information systems, whereas the euro changeover requires additional functionality in information systems, and also affects an enterprise in other areas. |
| 2. Savings can be gained by combining the testing infrastructure for EMU and Year 2000, particularly since both projects relate in part to the same information systems. | |
| 3. Decisions to fix or to replace information systems in view of the euro changeover and Year 2000 problem cannot be taken independently. | 2. EMU-compliance for one organization is not necessarily compliance for another organization with a different strategy, whilst Year 2000 compliance is more easily defined and agreed. |
| 4. Both projects have externally-imposed deadlines that IT managers cannot miss. This means that sound project management and contingency planning techniques are of significant importance. | 3. Deadlines for the euro and Year 2000 projects are different (a delay in the euro IT project should not lead to a delay in the Year 2000 fix). |
| 5. Organizations are no longer isolated from their environment. The entire supply chain in many industries now relies on the transfer of electronic data. Managers must liaise with every member of the supply chain to ensure that all interfaces are fully prepared for EMU and Year 2000. These interfaces include suppliers, customers, payments and the Internet as well as the more obvious information vendors. Systems that are not ready for either the euro or Year 2000 may infect those that are. The fulcrum of EMU will be the interface between retail, manufacturing and commercial organizations and the banks. | 4. Year 2000 has a single date, EMU is a continuum with fixed deadlines contained within a period of transition. Different types of organization will have to meet different deadlines.<br><br>5. EMU starts earlier, and may go on for much beyond 2002, dependent on successive 'waves' of entrant currencies.<br><br>6. Much of the detail in EMU is continually changing. Thus an earlier start might require revisit(s) to some programs or suites as the rules and practices unfold. |

Unfortunately, it is difficult to achieve significant savings in cost and time by handling EMU and Year 2000 changes together. While the projects may be run in parallel, there are fundamental differences between them which mean that systems changes should be undertaken separately. There are apparent similarities, not least because they coincide chronologically. However, EMU must be handled as a single project spanning the whole of the enterprise, both business and IT, whereas Year 2000 is by and large, an IT issue. Thus, the business process changes and re-engineering will to some extent drive the pace, sequence and shape of IT change.

Development complexity rises non-linearly as more functions and/or lines of code are changed. The risks arising from complexity should not be underestimated. Either EMU or Year 2000 'failure' is sufficient to risk the business. To 'fail' on both by trying to manage an unwieldy project coupled with the added complexities of converting systems simultaneously is recipe for disaster. No CEO is seeking the lowest cost way of going out of business! In addition, resources for parallel coding and especially parallel testing may be limited, to the detriment of both Year 2000 and EMU projects.

The IT director must assess the factors and risks very carefully before essaying the obvious optimum of concurrent change. Concurrent change must be the first option in planning, but note some current predictions, that 30% of combined projects will incur increased costs rather than the intended economies. New systems and processes may be planned in support of an entrepreneurial business plan designed to optimize opportunities opened by EMU. In this case, it is particularly advisable to segregate the two campaigns.

> unfortunately, it is difficult to achieve significant savings in cost and time by handling EMU and Year 2000 changes together

# CHARACTERISTICS OF THE EURO PROJECT

Whilst advising caution on merged Year 2000 and EMU projects, an invaluable starter on EMU will be the inventory created during the Year 200 impact assessment. However, it is not just a case of specifying or identifying, developing, testing and implementing changes. There are a number of factors that complicate the IT planning and development process for the euro including:

- compliance
- depending on third party software
- scope and nature
- scale and volume
- uncertainty and indecision

- new business processes
- testing
- training and awareness
- resources
- internal controls
- opportunity cost.

## Compliance?

From 1 January 1999 participating countries enter into a three-year period of 'no compulsion, no prohibition' during which the euro will be available for transactions that do not involve the exchange of physical cash (as notes and coins will not be around until 1 January 2002) in parallel with transactions in the national currency. No organization has to do anything in the new currency, but it can also do anything it wants. Various European companies are announcing what they intend to do and it is this freedom of choice that underlies the danger of statements about 'euro-compliance'.

As with Year 2000, it is likely that a company's partners may soon be demanding 'euro-compliance' in some form or other, but certainly with an IT emphasis. But compliance is undefined. It is almost impossible to find two sets of 'compliance' requirements that are the same, either for the same system for different companies, or for the same company for different systems. And how can you judge awareness and preparedness?

Even so, 'compliance' may be requested or even demanded from a company's bankers, investors, auditors, insurers and trading partners, and it may be requested sooner rather than later. But who is to judge and what are the criteria?

It is impossible to compose an objective definition of 'euro-compliance' as it is a subjective decision. You must refuse to make any statement whatsoever about 'euro-compliance' unless you have agreed a clear definition of what is meant in that specific instance with the supplier or user community.

Terms such as 'EMU-compliance' or 'euro-compliance' have become common expressions amongst the EMU 'marketplace'. This has occurred because the terminology for the Year 2000 issue, where the issues are fairly well-defined and understood, has been transposed onto the EMU topic.

Even at this late stage there are still very few externally imposed mandatory EMU requirements with which any organization has to comply. 'EMU compliance' is a subjective matter for each and every company and not objectively determined. This is destined to continue as it is unlikely that there will be an abundance of regulations on what is, in essence, a commercial decision for each company.

The following statement from the *Report from the Business Advisory Group* of Her Majesty's Treasury, published in January 1998 suggests:

> 'The Advisory Group concluded that it is difficult to have an all-encompassing warranty for euro-compliance, since requirements will vary from system to system. Rather it is a matter of specifying the functions required and ensuring the IT supplier will deliver them. The Fédération des Experts Encomptables (representing the European accountancy profession – the FEE), the Business and Accountancy Software Development Association (BASDA) and others are currently working on a specification and means of accreditation.'

All companies, whether in an 'in' country or a 'pre-in' country such as the UK, will need to determine their 'euro-vision', i.e., their strategic vision of where they wish to be in post-EMU Europe.

## Depending on third party software

Most enterprises use third party software to some extent. Despite the fact that some software vendors have announced that their software will be made 'euro-compliant', very few have been able to show working products.

Defining 'euro-compliant' is difficult because it requires an evaluation as to whether a particular financial information system meets the particular functional requirements of an enterprise changing over to the euro. These functional requirements depend both on the business of the enterprise and the changeover strategy it has adopted. Therefore, no standard definition of 'euro-compliant' exists. Hence, enterprises should always verify for themselves whether 'euro-compliant' software actually meets their needs.

Five aspects of the dependency on third party software warrant special attention.

- Enterprises usually have little influence on the type of changeover solution that the software vendor will choose in dealing with the euro, and little influence on the euro functionality that is added or not.
- The lack of influence over the software vendor can impact the choice of the timing of the euro changeover. If the software vendor has not completed software modifications then the enterprise cannot change over to the euro.
- Software vendors may not have the financial and human resources necessary to successfully complete a euro changeover project.
- The 'euro-compliant' software may turn out to be less reliable than the previous release of the same software. The enterprise should allow itself sufficient time to evaluate the new version of the software and time to develop alternative possibilities in case serious problems do surface.
- The price of the 'euro-compliant' upgrade of the existing software is uncer-

tain. The price of an upgrade can be excessive when the original software was poorly designed, a substantial amount of unnecessary functionality was added, or when the software vendor takes advantage of the situation.

Enterprises that depend on third party software should not wait until the very last moment to plan their changeover to the euro, nor should they unconditionally rely on the good intentions of their vendors. At the very least you should discuss the following issues with your software vendors.

- Satisfy yourself through enquiry that the product is compliant with known external requirements and with the euro positioning of your business.

- Include in the contract between yourself and the third party supplier a 'euro warranty'. This clause will warrant that the product is 'euro-compliant' (depending on the exact circumstances) and requires the third party to compensate you for any loss you may suffer or any liability you may incur if their product turns out to be non-compliant. But specify what you mean by 'compliance'.

## Scope and nature

Several difficulties will probably arise during the impact assessment phase.

- Key vital systems are very old, and possibly written in outdated programming languages.
- Documentation is no longer available.
- Specifications are unknown.
- Currency references and/or thresholds are hardcoded in the programs.

Before starting the actual work on planning the changeover to the euro, an enterprise must have a good overview of its information systems. This step is rather technical because it requires the enterprise to do the following.

- Make a list of information systems that deal with financial information. Increasingly enterprises are discovering that they use more information systems than they previously realized. Often branches of larger enterprises have implemented information systems that provide functionality beyond that of the standard software used by other parts of the organization. Many systems, ranging from cash registers to spreadsheets, are often conveniently forgotten when discussing information systems. Underestimating the number of systems that need to be changed can cause enormous problems once the changeover strategy has been determined.

- Conduct a systems inventory: this has clear common features with the approach taken in dealing with the Year 2000 problem and if tackled in this light the synergies can be exploited to help reduce overall costs and efforts.

- Document technical details as to the way information systems are implemented.

- Ask whether the software was purchased from a third party, or if it was custom designed for the enterprise.

- Ask what programming language or technique was used to implement the systems. Well-documented systems that are programmed in a modern programming language using an underlying (relational) database management system are easiest to modify. However, systems that (i) are programmed using utilities no longer used by the enterprise, (ii) are programmed in a spreadsheet, (iii) that use a unique data format, (iv) that are poorly documented or (v) that are programmed by an employee who has left the company, may be particularly difficult to modify.

- Ask whether the hardware is affected by the changeover to the euro. Some software problems are also hardware problems because the software has been embedded into systems as firmware (software that is encoded in hardware, ROM). Such software can be upgraded only by replacing the hardware (for example, cash registers).

- Determine dependencies between systems. Dependencies through links or interfaces determine to a large extent whether a gradual approach towards the changeover is feasible. It is important to realize that not all dependencies are internal (within the enterprise), but that external dependencies (for example with customers or suppliers) might exist as well. Additionally, dependencies between systems greatly increase the complexity of the changeover problems.

Describing the existing systems and determining the quality of those systems is extremely important. Attempts to modify poor quality software are seldom successful. However, there is a risk that enterprises may embark upon such an attempt anyway.

- It is not uncommon for enthusiasm or the wish to make difficulties go away to lead to overly optimistic assessments of IT projects.

- Organizations may have a subconscious tendency to favour incremental changes over fundamental changes that are perceived as being riskier.

Enterprises may want to take the opportunity to replace existing information systems, although there is always a trade-off to be made between the costs of doing this and the risks which will be run by not doing it. It is important that enterprises do not overlook the option of completely replacing existing information systems; though be realistic when determining an implementation programme in conjunction with your current workload.

## Scale and volume

According to the Association for Monetary Union in Europe (AMUE), estimates for a middle-sized company with one single location, the analysis of applications could require around three months, and the implementation phase six to nine months. These figures should probably be doubled for a company with multiple sites located in different countries. Costs are divided between:

- evaluation of changes required
- actual changing of programme lines
- development and running of tests
- management of the IT project.

Direct costs can be attributed as follows: programming and testing both new and upgraded systems; package upgrades; data conversion; training for existing systems; training for new systems; roll-out; hardware; management of change; synchronization/concurrence with Year 2000.

The two most difficult direct costs to compute (unless based, fortuitously, on Y2K impact analyses) are the world of the PCs in all their guises, and most difficult of all, the cost of uncertainty. Uncertainty derives not just from Brussels, nor simply from domestic/national politicians, but possibly from uncertainties of direction within the IT department over corporate strategies.

More indirect costs might also arise as a knock-on effect of changes made for the euro including: database 'overflow'/growth; new generations/releases of packages; over-consumption of development/testing resources; the imposition of 'duality'; traffic growth from new ventures; new demands at the interface to external agencies; diminished batch windows due to longer processing; extra hours working to synchronize with European partners/branches on different time zones and with differing public holidays; extra demands from the public, on call centres, help desks, etc., over longer days and out of hours.

In terms of size, the adjustment of systems for the introduction of the euro is a large project in itself and requires appropriate project management. Companies should:

- organize the project into manageable domains/systems/processes; and
- assess the sequence of conversion by order of priority including temporary solutions as required during the transition period.

Whilst using converters would provide a technical facility which would simplify the management of two currencies, it would not solve all of the problems. The transfer and exchange of information from one system to another needs to be read and understood and this allows for a great possibility of errors. However, converters inside the company could reduce the shortage of data processing capacity.

The problem of duality – be it dual pricing or dual reporting – is a significant factor in scale and volume. Couple this with potential database revisions, redesign and re-sizing, a conversion workload and a programming plus testing workload exacerbated by Year 2000 and other changes. IT directors may be faced with a 'last straw' that breaks the carefully tuned architecture and computer services regime (will that age-old system just not hang on any more, where EMU forces an unplanned system replacement?) Databases, servers and networks may not cope. Certainly, problems will occur in staffing, resourcing and outsourcing with so much change and so much activity in such a short period.

## Uncertainty and indecision

What is known is dwarfed by what is unknown. The momentum of legislation, practices and interpretations was slow to start but has now accelerated beyond easy control. For IT departments, the problem is when to change, what subsystem to change, and which rule to code. You cannot code uncertainty, but you cannot afford to revisit code on multiple occasions as decisions unfold. Equally, an IT director cannot wait until the last 'i' is dotted and 't' is crossed, because by then it will be too late!

With two, three or even more 'waves' of entrant currencies, IT departments may be faced with dealing with this re-actively, or perhaps pro-actively by scrapping old systems in many countries and going for a universal, multi-currency, new package solution.

## New business processes

Some organizations are taking a defensive stance and minimizing the short-term costs by focusing on requirements to simply stay in business. A significant number of businesses, however, will be aggressively building EMU as an opportunity, perhaps in new channels, with possibly new products or services, certainly new customers and markets. And other businesses will have to adapt their structures to benefit from new opportunities or fend off competition.

To support these entrepreneurial ventures and competitive responses, it is likely that new business processes will be needed, others dramatically re-engineered. To support these new developments in turn, technology will be central and IT in all its facets, vital.

More fundamentally, the currency changeover will inevitably entail organizational changes. These restructurings will naturally impact IT systems. These impacts are likely to be more complex and costly to implement than mechanical impacts. Some issues include:

- Are your IT suppliers of an adequate size to operate on a European scale?
- What is the reactivity of your IT system towards new activities?
- Does your system accept multi-language use?

How many organizations already have well-developed conversion routines across all their systems and processes? Developing and testing these routines is an enormous strain on resources, especially as many conversion routines will be manual in nature. So too is the decision about when to convert each application.

EMU will also accelerate many current trends and stimulate new ones. Active businesses will be investing in new ventures and backing them with appropriate business processes and demanding the IT to support these. Demands may range from the innovative and hitherto unattempted to the more mundane extensions/expansions of emerging technologies like electronic commerce in all its guises, smart cards, electronic purses, etc. A completely re-vamped help desk and call centre strategy may be needed during the vital, customer-oriented transition period.

The IT department may well be faced with a raft of new build projects, probably with challenging new technologies, under the banner of EMU. Who said it was 'just another currency'?

## Testing

Given the scope of the project it will not be possible to arrange a multilateral street test of conversion functionalities and communication links. It is unlikely that all market participants will be ready to test at the same time; the logistics and complexity to perform a street test with potential implications of Year 2000 is unmanageable. Differences in the approach taken by various countries will serve only to exacerbate these difficulties.

Nonetheless, all conversion procedures will need to be carefully prepared and tested, many of which will be required sooner rather than later. It is recommended that all institutions, prior to arranging any bilateral testing (such as between service providers and clients), test their developments possibly using a standard set of test data and expected results. Naturally, time constraints will limit the number of tests that each institution will be able to carry out.

## Training and awareness

Above all EMU is a business issue. The IT implications will affect every area of the business including its developers, testers, end-users, customers and even the general public, certainly for bankers and retailers. The load on training all the users, in the widest sense, will place enormous burdens on traditional IT staff, whilst the implications for call centres, help desks and intranet and Internet sites is likely to be enormous.

EMU will bring IT to the forefront of staff retraining, across the whole spectrum of users. Further, the use of new forms, the exploitation of new channels, the output of new forms, bills, printed media in the new currency and/or both, will bring IT even closer to the end customer, his very retention by and loyalty to the business. The commitment of IT to the design and roll-out of new awareness and training programmes is perhaps even more crucial than involvement on mass roll-outs.

## Resources

The need for careful planning, for long-term commitment to staff and contractors, the proper provision of development and testing environments, reviews with outsourcing partners are paramount. The costs, particularly of last-minute corrective actions can be considerable. The coincidence of Y2K and EMU is less than helpful in the current systems development marketplace.

It must be recognized, also, that electronic point of sale (EPOS) vendors of both hardware and software will be at full stretch, such that only 'life support' may be obtainable; further, that currencies joining in the second and succeeding waves may benefit from the experiences of these vendors from the first wave, but may not be able to tear the resources away from fire-fights in first-wave countries. Further the relatively relaxed transition period may not be available as generously to later entrants. Indeed, it is expected that transition periods for second-wave entrants, such as the UK, will have a shorter transition period.

> it is expected that transition periods for second-wave entrants, such as the UK, will have a shorter transition period

## Internal controls

Introducing new information systems or modifying existing ones is not a routine process in many organizations. This in combination with the euro changeover, which by definition is not routine, leads to certain risks for which enterprises need to be prepared.

- *Testing new systems* – changes in the information systems should be adequately tested before these systems are put into operation.
- *Data conversion* – Sufficient controls should be in place to avoid fraudulent insertion, modification or deletion of financial information during the conversion of data files to the euro. Substantial risks exist, especially, where users need to revise and correct the data files manually.

- *Suspense or clearing accounts* – a well-known procedure for dealing with exceptional or unsettled transactions and differences is to put them in a suspense or clearing account by giving them a special code. The risk exists that the conversion to the euro will give rise to a substantial number of these 'suspense' or 'clearing' items. These items need to be analyzed and resolved in time to ensure that no irregularities have occurred, particularly where users tend for convenience to classify other differences as euro conversion differences.

- *Unusual transactions* – many users rely on their experience to recognize and investigate unusual amounts and transactions. After the conversion to euro it will take some time before they regain these skills.

- *Access privileges* – some users may need additional access rights to the information systems in order to resolve euro changeover differences. Granting too much access rights to a single user could expose the enterprise to risks.

## Opportunity costs

The IT department, faced with both Y2K and EMU (and possibly new business opportunities arising from EMU) will possibly be incapable of completing current business developments, or incapable and lacking resources to embark upon new ones. Budget may not be the answer, in that resources of the right calibre and skills may not be available and the development, testing and creative environments could be difficult to 'ramp up'. The management and control of exciting new projects on top of the (inevitable) Year 2000 and (imposed) EMU may also present new challenges.

# WHAT SYSTEMS ARE AFFECTED?

All processes and systems that handle currency transactions will need evaluation and upgrading. Anywhere that hardware or software handles or interfaces with a participating currency, real or plastic, smart or virtual may require extensive software, and probably, hardware updates. This is true of individual domestic systems, such as purchasing, billing and payroll, as well as the more obvious corporate foreign exchange risk management and reporting systems. Some changes may be technical (e.g., changes in interest rate calculations and currency denomination). Dual reporting of both the existing and new currency may also be required during the transition period.

To prepare an enterprise's information systems for the introduction of the euro it is important to establish which information systems are affected by the euro. The basic rule is that only systems that are used to process financial information in one of the participating national currencies can be affected by the euro changeover. This means that many information systems, principally those dealing with non-financial information, will not be affected by the euro at all. However, strategic changes to systems may be required as the business responds to the competitive challenges of the euro. Nonetheless the most obvious and immediate systems that are affected are those that contain financial information. Here are some examples of financial information systems that are affected by the introduction of the euro.

- *Accounting software* (general ledger; accounts receivable and accounts payable subledgers; inventory subledgers, which record the value of inventory; fixed asset subledgers, which keep track of fixed assets, their value, and calculate the depreciation charge for the period). The government will also play a role here, probably late in the day, doubtless with much complexity, especially in the realms of excise duties, VAT, tax, vouchers and credits, rates and rents, levies, etc.
- *Electronic payment systems* including invoicing and billing systems.
- *Payroll systems* including wage rates, pensions, taxes, commissions, social security charges, and all the other minutiae of payroll administration will be profoundly affected. Even if you've 'outsourced' payroll processing, contracts of employment and pension agreements will need to be altered and maintained. The effects on database and HR records, including pension records will be significant and will persist well beyond the millennium.
- *Legal databases* containing financial contracts, agreements, leases and schedules will need to be altered, as will insurance policies, claims and risk management systems.
- *Other EDI systems*, notably interfaces throughout your supply chain and interface network including: extranet (a growing exchange with partners), contracts, concessions, insurers, bankers, shippers, transporters, franchisees, insurance/warranty/after-sales service providers and direct home deliverers.
- *Financial planning and budgeting software* including work-in-progress systems; costing systems; treasury management systems.
- *Enterprise resource planning (ERP) systems* which are used to plan and manage business functions or processes from order processing and procurement of supplies to manufacturing, accounting and personnel.
- *Cash registers and other types of point-of-sale terminals* which process financial information. These systems may store comparative historical information (such as the turnover on the same date last year), calculate cumulative turnover figures (which are used in cash reconciliations). These are often linked to other financial information systems, and in some cases are not able to deal with decimals.

- *Financial models.* Some enterprises use statistical models based on historical data expressed in the national currency unit. A credit card company may have software that reviews the incoming transactions for abnormalities. The system could for instance scan for withdrawals of rounded amounts (such as 100, 500 or 1000 D-marks) that are unusual for credit cards. It is of little use to convert those amounts to 51.60, 257.99 or 515.98 euros.

The above list of financial information systems is certainly not exhaustive. Many categories of information systems that will also be affected by the euro are sometimes easily overlooked. Organizations often have more financial information systems that process financial information than they themselves realize. This is especially true for large enterprises that have standardized on a certain software package. Many branches of such large enterprises use additional software packages that the parent company is not aware of. Often small spreadsheet applications and databases are developed locally that give the branch the additional information systems functionality that the standard software package does not offer.

Some financial information systems are not used by the accounting department, such as software for making cost calculations or databases used by the marketing department. It is easy to overlook these applications if the euro changeover is initiated from the accounting department.

Banks have a much more significant issue as the majority of the systems they use contain information concerning financial transactions. In the case of one large European global investment bank, the euro impacted over 600 individual IT-supported systems and over 50 000 business applications (mostly spreadsheets).

## Packages

The current IT portfolio may well comprise multiple packages, possibly some of them old, most tailored and a complex web of interfaces, supported by rafts of bespoke applications. Some of the applications may well be interfaced to packages used by business partners. IT departments may well have the luxury of one major enterprise-wide package, but this is relatively rare.

Rather like with Year 2000, the speed, competence, reliability of package vendors to support EMU, and the ability of the IT department to synchronize and co-ordinate all the upgrades is a potential nightmare.

It is likely that a mixed environment of packages and bespoke applications will be used to support the business. Interfaces between these will abound, whilst there may be interfaces to packages shared or exploited externally with business partners or outsourcing contracts.

In this situation, the various vendors will be taking different strategies and different timescales to deal with EMU. Some vendors may well be non-European, and thus may be taking a more relaxed attitude to the challenges. Some packages may require a new release, or for the IT department to accept and install a latest release. Also, not all package vendors have concurrently transformed for Y2K and EMU.

The IT department could be faced at best with a sequence of 'upgrades' to packages (and their interfaces), at worst with wholesale upgrades to new releases, with consequent rework of all modifications and enhancements, as well as interfaces.

The question of a complete change of package strategy must be considered, especially if the company has different packages in different countries within the EU, these countries 'joining' in successive waves. The case for commonality across the board may thus be strengthened by the imminence of EMU.

For those enterprises with a single enterprise-wide package philosophy, the IT director is in a stronger position, but should his sole vendor fail to support, then perhaps this is the weakest of all positions! Whilst vendors of such solutions may be well advanced in EMU readiness, it must be borne in mind that there is unlikely to be a straightforward implementation. As versions may vary across enterprises in different countries, support may also be variable in different countries. The key here is to begin immediate dialogue with the vendor. This dialogue must be two-way, both parties detailing all policies, rules and interpretations, both highlighting needs and expectations from the other. It should be recognized that upgrades of packages, especially when new releases are obligatory, are likely to engender physical resource demands, which could have a knock-on effect on infrastructure, particularly since EMU itself will inevitably demand more resource.

## Personal computers (PCs)

The number of PCs in European business probably number tens of millions, each with personalized and/or corporate applications, many networked, most using simple tools and certainly using currency fields. All of these may need changing or replacing.

These PCs come in all shapes and varieties, many configured on networks, most working or used semi-autonomously. The usual tools and facilities from Apple, Microsoft *et al.* abound. There are many, many personal applications, and currency will doubtless figure in many of these. The problem cannot be ignored, particularly where users access and even update common data sets, perhaps even corporate data files.

Fortuitously, the inventory taken during Y2K impact studies is a good starting base for EMU work. Have you documented the use of all personal applications?

## Spreadsheets

Financial models are often implemented as a spreadsheet model. The major advantage of spreadsheet models is that even people with a very modest background in information technology can build these models. These can play an important role in pre-processing input for other financial information systems and in processing output received from other systems. The link between spreadsheet models and the other financial information systems often consists of retyping financial information or downloading print files.

Modifying spreadsheet models so they will work with euro instead of the national currency unit is extremely complicated for several reasons.

- *Spreadsheet models can be very large.* A spreadsheet of one megabyte will contain 20 000 to 25 000 individual spreadsheet cells. Spreadsheets models of this size are not uncommon in many enterprises.
- *There are different types of spreadsheet cells.* They contain: (i) text; (ii) formulas; (iii) non-financial numerical information; (iv) financial numerical information; (v) dates and (vi) links to other spreadsheets or data sources.

In order to prepare spreadsheets for the use of the euro only the cells with financial numerical information and some cells containing formulae must be modified. Identifying only the right cells to modify, not forgetting any or selecting too many, is a lot of work.

Enterprises may be using certain valuation models, based on discounted cash flows, in making investment decisions. If the model's discount rate were to be multiplied by the fixed conversion rate (which is incorrect) or if some of the cashflows remained in the national currency unit (which is also incorrect), then the model could produce dangerously inaccurate results. Such an error can be hard to detect and may lead to incorrect investment decisions.

It is important for enterprises to get an overview of the different spreadsheet models that are used. Most enterprises will be unpleasantly surprised by the variety and quality of the models that are in use. The preferred option will often be to rebuild the spreadsheet model, rather than trying to convert an existing spreadsheet model. Unfortunately, it is impossible to design a utility that can automatically convert all spreadsheet models to euro.

## HOW ARE THESE SYSTEMS AFFECTED?

Within all programs and files, references to national currencies, interest rates and other financial information will have to be modified for the changeover to the euro. These operational impacts of the changeover are generally not complex to solve individually, but the sheer size of the operation and the interlinking of programs can cause many difficulties.

Whilst many euro requirements are unique to each company due to varying business responses there are a number of common issues to consider. Usefully, they can be grouped under three main headings: conversion, functionality and interfaces.

## Conversion

For most organizations, there is a choice of when to convert to the euro under the rule of 'no compulsion, no prohibition'. All organizations in participating countries will need to change over to the euro by 31 December 2001. A company can make its own decisions about how soon after 1 January 1999 it will make the changeover to the euro, but customers and suppliers may have a different timetable. Computer systems may therefore need to be flexible enough to deal with the old and new currencies and convert between the two. Among the issues confronting IT are:

- choice of changeover times for company systems;
- choice of strategy for changeover (e.g. parallel systems, replacement systems);
- relationship to the Year 2000 issue;
- resource implications in terms of equipment, software development and staff training; and
- interface with supplier and customer systems.

Conversion for financial institutions and users of financial instruments is looked at in detail in Chapter 4, as it is the most significant issue for these organizations. For banks, conversion comprises upwards of around 75% of the man-day effort required for EMU whilst representing the most significant operational risk. This is due to the 'Big Bang' nature of conversion in many of the capital markets, notably European equities and government bonds plus their associated derivatives.

For other organizations there is considerably more scope for strategic changeover to the euro at the management's discretion. Should you go big bang at the start of EMU, or delay a big bang for some other time, perhaps 2002? Should you stagger your changeover strategy and if so, what converts when and how? When in the year should you convert? There are several good reasons for avoiding a changeover to the euro at the end of the year.

It may not be attractive to change over at year-end when the previous financial periods must remain 'open' or 'active' for an extended period (more than a few weeks). An alternative would be a changeover during the financial year, when financial periods may not need to remain 'open' for so long.

Most organizations are subject to a seasonal business cycle. It might be attractive to change over during the seasonal low period (where it does not coincide with the financial year end), when the information systems contain relatively little current data and employees can be spared from the operational activities.

Organizations that have planned to introduce new information systems during a financial year may want to consider to start off in euro, rather than starting off in a national currency unit and having a separate euro conversion at a later date. The end of an enterprise's financial year appears to be a more or less natural moment for changing over from the national currency unit to the euro. Because the end of the financial year is an important measurement point, enterprises go to great length to ensure the correctness of their financial data. Changing the base currency of the information system in the middle of a financial year could pose problems with respect to the presentation of comparative figures, calculation of certain cumulative figures and the audit of the financial year.

And how do you convert? There are a number of options:

- manual conversion;
- conversion utility;
- modifying information systems; and
- encapsulation.

These options are explored in more detail in Chapter 7. Be warned – the devil lies in the detail and sheer volume – the conversion of balances, the calculation of depreciation, of interest, of timing, rounding and reconciliation.

### Converting historical data

Historical financial information denominated in the national currency unit will have to be converted to euro. Although not all historical financial information may be equally relevant, it is necessary to convert all data that has a future use to the euro.

Relational database theory requires normalization of databases to ensure that information systems do not store the same information more than once. This is a sound principle. However, for performance and other practical reasons, software developers often find themselves in a position where they have to depart from this principle. Therefore, many financial information systems store the same information more than once.

- Subledgers are used to store the details of transactions, while the general ledger stores part of that data in a summarized form.
- Identifying all the instances in which an information system duplicates data can be a daunting task in itself.

When converting historical data, it is important to ensure that data that is stored more than once remains consistent. If the underlying information is converted to euro, but the cumulative or summarized data is not converted to euro properly, financial information systems may produce either unreliable data or refuse to operate normally. Conversion of historical data requires that all instances of the same data are converted in exactly the same way, otherwise unpredictable results and errors may occur.

### Converting thresholds and ranges

Very often financial information systems use threshold values that define the actions of the system, for instance:

- *Generating reports* – applying the fixed conversion rate to calculate a new threshold of EUR 247.80 may not make sense if the previous threshold in a national currency unit was a 'user-friendly' round amount. It is probably more appropriate to use EUR 250 which implies a degree of arbitrary rounding up or down.

- *Calculations* – systems can have built-in rules for making certain calculations, such as, 'when the order is for less than 10 000 charge 200 for postage and packaging'.

- *Authorization level* – in many enterprises junior employees may authorize transactions up to a certain threshold value only.

- *Validity checks* – in order to improve the quality of data input, information systems perform validity checks on data and use data input masks. Validity checks (that, for instance, test whether an amount falls within a certain range that is considered reasonable) will work differently than expected when the data is input in a different currency unit. Checks on the reasonableness of amounts or prices per unit will no longer function as expected. Data input masks (that can filter out certain keystrokes such as the decimal point '.') may need to be modified to accept decimals.

- The issue of 'psychological' prices and amounts.

Changing threshold values is not something that can be done automatically because the thresholds must be set at rounded amounts that people can remember. Having thresholds converted automatically to awkward amounts such as EUR 247.80 will normally not be satisfactory. Moreover, changes of threshold values are often quite important management policy decisions and as such require management attention (for example in the case of discount levels and credit limits of customers).

## Functionality

### Decimals and rounding

Some national currencies are normally expressed without decimals (examples include the peseta and the lira). Financial information systems that were designed to work with amounts expressed in such currency units usually cannot handle decimals. As the euro is subdivided into 100 cents it is necessary to modify these systems so they can handle two decimals.

The rounding and conversion rules of the Article 235 Regulation prescribe in detail how amounts must be converted from a participating national currency unit to the euro and another participating currency unit. These rules reduce the number of rounding and conversion problems significantly, but problems still remain. Converting amounts between the euro and participating currency units will unavoidably cause rounding differences. The effects of these rounding differences vary from being merely a nuisance to being able to bring information processing to a halt.

The Article 235 Regulation requires that when converting amounts from one participating currency unit to another, the conversion is processed as follows.

- Translate the amount from participating national currency unit A to the euro using the fixed conversion rate quoted to six significant figures.

- Then translate the amount from the euro to participating national currency unit B using the fixed conversion rate quoted to six significant figures.

The intermediate product in this calculation, the euro amount, must be expressed to at least three decimals. This means that even when systems can handle amounts expressed in two decimals, it may be necessary to modify these systems so they can handle the three decimals necessary for the intermediate product in this calculation.

This process, known as triangulation, seems relatively simple, though for countries like Portugal, Italy and Spain that have never had decimal points in currency since computers first appeared, it is sometimes a tricky problem. Common to all countries, however, is the fact that most systems currently do not process such a two-step conversion, requiring additional functionality.

### Input problem

In most cases the financial information systems of an enterprise are built with the implicit assumption in mind that all transactions take place in the same currency unit. That is, the financial information system expects the user to input all financial data in the same currency unit. What happens when such an enterprise is suddenly faced with a situation in which it has to deal with two different currency units at the same time? Depending on the situation, the organization has the following options: a manual solution, using standard software, modifying information systems, using parallel systems or sequential changeover.

### Base currency

The base currency is the currency unit in which a financial information system processes and stores financial information. Normally it suffices to use the national currency unit as the base currency for a financial information system, but there may be advantages to using multiple base currencies.

## Output problem

Problems may occur where important customers or tax authorities insist on receiving financial information in the national currency unit while the enterprise has already changed over to euro or where customers would like to receive financial information both in euro and in the national currency unit. Financial information systems rarely have the built-in capability to print the same information in two currencies on one schedule.

Alternatively, the enterprise has switched over to the euro, but needs to keep its historical data available in the national currency unit in order to maintain the existing audit trail. It will often not be acceptable that the transaction amounts recorded in the information system suddenly no longer match the amounts on the underlying physical documents (such as invoices and contracts) that are still denominated in the national currency unit.

Furthermore, in most countries national law requires enterprises to keep their accounting records in their original form for at least five to ten years. Here an enterprise must always be able to reproduce the accounting records in their original form.

## Forms

Wherever 'forms' are used, either as output such as bills and receipts, or inputs, by the public or the in-house user, there will be a considerable IT impact, with associated changes to business processes and training requirements.

## Reports and screens

Any layout with currency may need to be changed, even if field length is not affected. The problem of decimal points, of segregating millions, thousands, hundreds by point or comma is important. In many countries the decimal point is in fact a comma.

## Programs

In many cases, EMU is considerably more 'invasive' than Year 2000 in terms of complexity. There are significant logic changes, new rounding rules, changed field sizes and/or characteristics internally as well as on input and output fields. For financial systems, interest calculation periods, public holidays and accrual methods are likely to figure in changed calculation criteria.

Very often financial information systems use threshold values that define the actions of the system. These thresholds must be converted to euro to avoid unexpected actions by the information system.

## Databases

Major changes may be required to schema and design, simply to accommodate new flags and switches, conversions and tables. Consolidation may add a whole new dimension to these changes. Some financial information may be stored in the description fields of a database and converting such information to euro may often not be possible.

## Duality

There may be a legislative requirement, and almost certainly a business requirement to adopt multi-currency systems, if only for the transition period. For a large multinational, there may be a series of such transitions, with several waves of entrant currencies. Duality of reporting, and in retail especially, duality of pricing are major issues for the IT department. To print and/or display two currencies even for a limited time will require major surgery by IT. Functionality must be added to the information system to enable it to show the information in two currency units.

During the transition period, and possibly some time thereafter, it would be convenient to display the same amount both in the national currency unit and the euro. From a technical point of view, presenting amounts in two currencies may pose certain problems.

● The amount of space (number of columns) available on computer displays and printed reports is limited.

● Adding a column to an existing screen layout or report may not be possible without some serious redesigning.

Including totals and subtotals when presenting two columns of figures (one in the national currency unit and the other in euro) will certainly give rise to the rounding problem associated with cumulative amounts.

However, in many cases it is sufficient if comparative figures in a second currency unit are presented at the subtotal level only, without really providing details in two currencies for all individual items.

> to print and/or display two currencies even for a limited time will require major surgery by IT

For retailers, dual pricing, in store, at checkout, on shelf-edge, in advertising, the Internet, catalogues, all media, perhaps in EDI exchange, anywhere the retailer makes an offer presents a unique set of IT problems as well as commercial and legal ones. The ground rules are not yet established and intensive dialogues are taking place continuously in Brussels. Whatever the outcome, the costs will be steep for both the business and IT. Brands and suppliers will also have an influence and an effect on this most contentious of subjects.

In many instances financial information systems display amounts under the implicit assumption that all amounts are denominated in the same currency unit (for instance all amounts are D-marks). Where information systems are capable of displaying amounts in one of two currency units, or in environments where not all information systems use the same currency unit, it is important that all amounts displayed or printed are properly labelled. If this is not done the resulting confusion will surely lead to a higher number of clerical errors.

Ticketing and labelling, including in-house, by third parties, or by suppliers sounds simple, but it is a likely area for legislation, oversight and control whereby companies are obliged to offer dual prices for a considerable period (not yet defined). These apparently simple IT tasks may need many extra checks and controls to be built-in. Table 3.2 shows some of the myriad of formats and media that price displays may appear in.

**TABLE 3.2**
**Price displays**

Point of sale
Shelf edge (might be electronic)
(Electronic) kiosk (in store, in mall, in third party)
Pumps/dispenser
Weigh scale, or volume or length measuring device
Packs and outers
Internet
Intranet
Extranet
TV
Media
Catalogues
Teletext
Advertising in general
Ticket and label printers
LEDs/LCDs

## Interfaces

Many enterprises have linked their own information systems to those of other organizations and they must decide together how and when these systems are changed over to the euro (examples include: electronic banking systems, links to external databases, and the use of EDI messages). Enterprises that have linked their information systems must decide together how and when these systems are changed over to the euro. Where it is not possible to reach agreement on changeover issues, some of the organizations may need to modify their interfaces to the external information systems. Developing interfaces between systems that use different currency units is often more complicated than expected because of rounding differences.

When one system still uses the national currency unit while the other systems use the euro, it is necessary for the interface between the two systems to be modified in such a way that it will be able to translate the amounts from one currency unit to the other.

Given the fact that some rounding problems are unavoidable, it may be difficult to develop a straightforward currency converter that can take care of everything. This means that the costs of temporarily modifying the interface between two information systems can be excessive.

When different financial information systems are changed over to the euro at different points in time, a problem arises with respect to the communication between those systems. Several approaches exist with respect to the interface problem:

- *Building converters* – It is possible to build interfaces that not only link two systems, but also convert the amounts from one currency unit to the other. However, technical problems (such as rounding) can make this approach very unattractive.

- *Simultaneous changeover* – Change all information systems to the euro at the same time. This eliminates the need for interfaces between information systems that convert amounts to and from euro.

- *Autonomous groups* – Identify groups of information systems that are relatively autonomous, that is, groups of information systems that have no or only a few links to other information systems. These groups of information systems could be changed over to the euro at different points in time, while requiring few interfaces that can convert between currency units. This approach, which combines the advantages and disadvantages of the other approaches, can be a practical solution in some situations.

For organizational or practical reasons it may not be desirable to change over all financial information systems at the same time. A good example of a system that most enterprises will want to change over to euro at a very late stage is the payroll system. Generally, employees are not interested in receiving their payroll slip in euro when they do not yet have a bank account in euro.

Special care needs to be taken to avoid information systems accidentally combining amounts expressed in euro with amounts expressed in the national currency unit (data pollution). Mathematically there is no problem with adding up these amounts, but the result of the calculations will be complete nonsense. Enterprises should therefore take special precautions in order to be able to restore the original data in case of such accidents, such as making frequent backups.

Because some data is used only periodically, data pollution could go unnoticed for quite some time. It is no use having backups that go back one month when all of these backups contain polluted data. As a precaution it may be necessary to review data files specifically for possible errors as a result of using different currency units. Manually restoring lost or polluted data can be extremely expensive and time-consuming.

# CHAPTER 4

# Conversion in financial markets

# 'BIG BANG' CONVERSION WEEKEND

The introduction of the euro is the single most complex change to be undertaken in global financial markets. With only several months left, some markets had failed to formalize their basic conversion criteria. The delay in some countries in ratifying and publishing market processes to ensure an orderly introduction of the euro has significantly exacerbated the problem. The obvious impact of delay is that firms have had less time to prepare properly, hence the likelihood that some organizations will not be ready, and others will not be able to meet preferred market practices.

The smooth establishment of the euro financial markets at the start of EMU fundamentally depends on the successful implementation of the conversion weekend. The following main tasks will have to be performed by each financial institution.

- Processing of the end of day 31 December 1998 including the receipt and reconciliation of legacy currency positions from custodians;
- Converting or redenominating securities positions (including all 'in' currency equities, government bonds and associated derivatives);
- Converting cash balances from legacy to euro;
- Converting pending trades (redenominate security and convert cash countervalue);
- Converting all impacted static and reference data;
- Converting all account data such as nostros;
- Converting all historical data where appropriate;
- Revising communication links to reflect the introduction of the euro;
- Receipt and reconciliation of post-conversion euro positions and transactions with custodians and clients.

Sounds simple? There is no conversion in history of this scale and complexity, either in terms of the volume of data to be converted, the type of data to be simultaneously converted, the number and variation of conversion routines to be processed or the number of institutions simultaneously processing both autonomous and inter-linked conversions. Simply identifying all instances of data to be converted across multiple databases and systems is hard enough. Designing, testing and conducting the conversion will fundamentally test the skills and resources of financial institutions.

> the smooth establishment of the euro financial markets at the start of EMU fundamentally depends on the successful implementation of the conversion weekend

For each institution, public and private, the euro conversion weekend at the end of 1998 represents an unprecedented additional workload on their year-end processing. Critically, this additional workload has to be scheduled coherently across many complex interacting systems, both in-house and third party systems, and the interfaces between them. And all this has to take place in the space of, at most, 80 hours. How many financial institutions can honestly say that they had completed the necessary tasks? Ask yourself the following questions.

- Have all business lines completed their conversion plans?
- Have we accurately mapped and tested the critical path of conversion across all of our processes, systems, and interfaces, including communication links to counterparties, clients, custodians and depositories?
- Have we built a tried and tested global command and control structure to manage the conversion weekend?
- Do we have all the resources in place to conduct the conversion, much of which will be manual?
- Do we have a contingency plan in case systems fail or conversion routines collapse or are delayed?

When you add to this scenario the management issues for conversion weekend, summarized below, from Chapters 2 and 3, the situation is far from ideal. The risk of systems and counterparties being unable to operate on the morning following 'Big Bang' conversion is considerable. There is a strong possibility of gridlock and bottlenecks over the weekend, slowing down the conversion process and increasing the risk. Some entities will be slower in responding to queries, reports, reconciliations and/or system failures. It is not impossible that the volume of enquiries over the transition weekend and in the days following 'Big Bang', may cause severe delays even with round the clock coverage. There is consequently a huge risk of widespread failure occurring following the conversion weekend.

## Key management issues for conversion weekend:

- A large number of organizations have significantly underestimated the effort required to successfully convert to the euro. This has created a serious resourcing bottleneck as banks look externally for skilled resources to do the work required, even in London which has the largest pool of skilled resources of any European city.

▶

- The business (or front office) in many institutions is not sufficiently engaged or aware of the issues, especially in supporting the work of operations and technology, often due to a sufficient lack of priority attached to the euro project (such as in a merger scenario). Over conversion weekend, the most significant workload savings can be achieved by the business as conversion activity is primarily volume-related, therefore the operations workload remains very high.

- Poor risk management and reporting leaves senior managers without information about implementation risk – the risk that all required activities/conversion tasks cannot be done in the time available. Consequently public statements about euro-readiness rarely reflect the true state of preparations internally. Even if senior managers are aware of this, they are unlikely to share this information with external parties, notably regulators, auditors, counterparties or clients. Therefore it is very difficult to get a true picture of the state of readiness of an organization, let alone a financial centre.

- Institutions rarely have a sufficient command and control management structure in place to plan, test and manage the conversion weekend which requires the entire organization to act in concert. Politics and functional separation of activities have made it extremely hard to organize in a way that transcends traditional front-office/back-office as well as business line barriers.

## Inconsistency and its consequences

The Bank of England stated in one of its *Practical Issues* that 'reliable information about exchanges' and issuers' plans is needed by the market as soon as possible. This includes methods of redenomination of bonds, equities, preference shares, convertibles and other specialized securities.'

According to Paribas, in a paper issued on the conversion weekend, international financial intermediaries who have to contend with all 11 markets have two urgent requirements.

- It has become extremely critical that the regulatory authorities in each of the 11 countries finalize, ratify and publish their detail plans for transition to the euro.

- A consistent approach as far as practically possible across the 11 markets to issues relating to redenomination, reconventioning, outstanding trades and how potential failures caused by redenomination are managed.

The Securities Conversion Workshop in October 1997, hosted by IBM, and attended by eight of the main US investment banks, recommended that:

'Full detailed information regarding the conversion weekend and beyond for each market must be finalized by 31 December 1997. Without this information there is an increased likelihood of severe market disruption as participants will not have sufficient time to prepare. In particular, detailed ratified information is required from governments, stock exchanges, derivatives exchanges, central securities depositories and clearing agencies on methods of conversion, quotations of securities, securities settlement practices, plans for delivery, plans for testing, legislation, tax, etc.'

> **detailed and reliable information about which, when and how individual securities will be redenominated is essential for the timely reconciliation of market firms' positions after redenomination**

These are just three examples of the cries for consistent and timely information. But much of this information was not made available until the second quarter of 1998, and some is still outstanding, notably the plans and procedures from some derivatives exchanges. In part this has been due to the delays in publishing national changeover plans for the cash markets.

So timeliness has been poor, but inconsistency will cause a great deal of confusion and incorrectly converted positions and incorrect accrual calculations. Some of the inconsistencies include:

- methods of redenomination
- reconventioning of existing issues
- price sources and feeds
- pending trades
- operating days
- derivatives exchanges
- start of conversion weekend
- testing.

## Methods of redenomination

Participating governments decided to redenominate into euro some or all of their national currency debt over the conversion weekend, but they have not been consistent in the methods of redenomination that they proposed to adopt. Whilst there are some similarities, Table 4.1 highlights divergent approaches. Redenomination by other issuers, whether of debt or of equity, over the conversion weekend should be kept to the minimum, and should preferably not take place until some time after the conversion weekend. However, some corporate issuers had announced their intentions to redenominate over the weekend.

**TABLE 4.1**

**Inconsistent redenomination methods**

| Majority of countries will: | But: |
| --- | --- |
| Redenominate at investor holding level | Austria is redenominating the face value of each individual bond; and Italy will redenominate minimum nominal denominations. |
| Round nominals to nearest euro cent | France will round down to nearest euro; and the Netherlands will also round to the nearest euro, either up or down. |
| Apply a new minimum nominal amount of one euro cent | The Netherlands will apply a new amount of one euro; and Italy and Spain will apply further new amounts during 1999. |
| Not change ISINs | France and the Netherlands will change ISINs |

Detailed and reliable information about which, when and how individual securities will be redenominated is essential for the timely reconciliation of market firms' positions after redenomination. Euroclear is providing a detailed list containing Euroclear-eligible debt securities to be redenominated and this list is updated on a regular basis.

## Reconventioning of existing issues

If governments intend to change market conventions on existing issues, market practitioners have recommended that they should not do so over the conversion weekend. In the case of Treasury bills, where existing issues will quickly run off, changes should apply only to new issues. In the case of bonds, issuers should only change day-count conventions on an interest payment date or give sufficient notice of a 'Big Bang' change so that investors can plan for the consequent changes to accrued interest. However, these market recommendations are not being adhered to in some cases.

For example, the Belgian authorities are moving to an actual/actual day-count convention and TARGET business days for the calculation of accrued interest on secondary market trades in Belgian government bonds from 1 January 1999. The accrued interest on all trades that settle after that date will be calculated on the basis of the new convention for the entire period from the previous coupon date to the settlement date. Likewise Belgian Treasury certificates will be discounted using the actual/360 rather than actual/365 day-count from 1 January 1999. The Spanish authorities are also taking a 'Big Bang' approach to change to actual/actual. At the time of writing, the date of the switch is yet to be fixed, but it is likely to be after the conversion weekend. The Italian Treasury Ministry is recommending a change in the day-count convention on each of its government bond issues to actual/actual from the first coupon date in 1999.

Market associations have recommended harmonized market conventions for new issues of securities in the euro money and bond markets, and for the foreign exchange market. These proposals have been welcomed and supported by the Council of the EMI and endorsed by the European Commission. They need now to be adopted by the governments of individual Member States, which will also help to give a lead to the private sector.

## Price sources and feeds

Price sponsors which have not so far stated how they propose to replace disappearing price sources should do so as soon as possible. All price sponsors should inform the market and the screen services as to the display of successor rates. Should national reference rates be replaced with EURIBOR or the BBA's EUROLIBOR?

There has been a lack of information on what price feeds will be available from exchanges and data vendors over the conversion weekend. They quote prices in national currency until the close of trading in 1998, and then in euro from 4 January 1999. Some market practitioners would find it helpful if exchanges also requoted the closing prices for 1998 in euro to give a seamless series of external prices. Price providers should clarify their intentions as soon as possible as a lack of adequate price information will cause significant delays and problems for financial institutions.

LIBA hosted a workshop in May 1998 for the main information providers, including Bloomberg, Datastream, Dow Jones/Telerate, Financial Times/Extel, Reuters and telekurs. A number of issues came out of the workshop including the significant difference in their state of preparations, as well as inconsistencies in approach. The vendors were taking individual approaches to testing, releases of new information and treatment of historical data.

The problem has been circular as banks have asked the vendors to lead on this issues, but the vendors have asked for input from the banks. Historical data is not an easy issue as there is no one answer. The best solution is often dependent upon the use as this determines the level of accuracy required. For example, do analysts and traders require exactly the same history for the euro? Unlikely.

## Pending trades

The market needed more information about how CSDs would treat pending trades over the conversion weekend: in particular, whether they will handle discrepancies between the buy and sell sides of transactions following redenomination and rounding using the preferred 'auto-give-take' approach.

## Operating days

The market needed to know whether national RTGS systems plan to close on some TARGET operating days, if so on which dates, and whether RTGS opening days have implications for national and bank holidays.

## Derivatives exchanges

Some of the derivatives exchanges in the prospective euro area were noticeably late in disclosing their approach to the conversion weekend. Those that had were often not prescriptive with different conversion methods and mechanisms being proposed. This is important as the impact on hedging ratios and risk management cannot be determined until the conversion method is finalized.

Proposals have differed between exchanges. Here are some of the different methods proposed for different products within exchanges.

- *'One for one'* ECU to euro. ECU contracts convert to euro at the rate of 1:1. This is the simplest conversion method.

- *'One for one'* NCU to euro. Contract parameters (i.e., strike price, tick value, nominal, etc.) are converted to euro at the conversion rate, producing non-round amounts. These are quoted to zero, one or two decimal places. The remainder is ignored.

- *'One for one'* NCU to euro, *plus cash*. Contract parameters are converted at the conversion rate to rounded amounts, with cash settlement of the residual. *'One for two'* (i.e., one contract is replaced by two new contracts, 'A' and 'B'). Contract 'A' has a large rounded nominal and rounded tick value. Contract 'B' has a small nominal and tick value, possibly up to six decimal places. Once the conversion rate has been published, exchanges can finalize the new 'A' and 'B' contract specifications on the principle that the value of 'A' plus 'B' is equivalent to the value of the NCU contract. The 'A' contract is actively traded. The 'B' contract is expected to trade out within a short time, and is marked daily with the price of 'A'.

- *'One/many to one/many'* (i.e., not a linear conversion). Positions are converted at a flexible ratio. For example, an exchange may convert a one lot position in the NCU contract to one lot in the euro contract, but a 2000 lot position in the NCU contract might be converted into 1520 lots of the euro contract.

- *Parallel listing*. Exchanges list a new ECU product during 1998. The equivalent NCU contract is listed in parallel until expiry. Settlement of, or delivery into, NCU contracts remaining after 31 December 1998 may be in euro.

The various mechanisms for converting from the old product to the new include the following.

- *'Big Bang'*. Positions are converted over the conversion weekend at a contract, trade or position level.

- *Exchange conversion facility*. A mechanism to facilitate conversion before the conversion weekend from ECU to euro, and after the conversion weekend from NCU to euro. The administration of the facility varies from mainly manual to largely automated. At least six different variations of this mechanism have been under consideration.

- *Spread trading facility*. A spread trading facility will be made available by some exchanges to facilitate conversion from NCU contracts into their ECU equivalents before the conversion weekend.

This summary demonstrates the complexity that market firms have faced in converting listed derivatives. In order to allow firms adequately to prepare for EMU, the Futures Industry Association (FIA) urges exchanges to standardize approaches both within and between them, and to publish detailed plans as soon as possible. Exchanges should confirm that the information that firms will require over the conversion weekend will be made available, and when.

> the Futures Industry Assocaition (FIA) urges exchanges to standardize approaches both within and between them, and to publish detailed plans as soon as possible.

The situation with OTC derivatives is further complicated as contract conversion has to take place on a client-by-client basis rather than being market-wide as with exchange-traded instruments.

## Start of the conversion weekend

The market needed to know which exchanges and settlement systems would be open on 31 December 1998 and which would be closed. Market practitioners would prefer new trading on that day to be kept to a minimum, while settlement systems should as far as possible be open. This should serve to reduce the volume of trades to be converted over the conversion weekend by allowing market firms to complete the maximum volume of settlements before it starts.

In particular, firms operating in global markets on a single IT platform have had to consider how to handle conversion in one location whilst maintaining a presence in markets that are open during the European conversion weekend, notably Asian markets.

The rates for the conversion into euro of the national currencies of participating Member States should be set as early as possible in the conversion weekend, and the procedure for setting them and timing of the announcement should be made public as soon as possible. At the time of writing, no decision had been finalised, though there appears strong market support for the proposition that the relevant event should be the last official ECU fixing. Since New Year's Eve is not a public holiday throughout the EU, but market trading usually winds down early, the last official ECU fixing is expected to be at 11.30am Central European Time on 31 December 1998. (The normal afternoon official ECU fixing at 2.15pm does not take place on New Year's Eve.)

However, the actual conversion rates announced by the EU Council of Ministers at some time on 1 January 1999, cannot be guaranteed to correspond exactly to the ECU fixing rates despite the 1:1 conversion between the ECU and the euro. Market pressure for certainty has forced the EU to provide guarantees that rates would be legally ratified on 31 December 1998 in order to give maximum time to carry out processing of conversions.

## *Testing*

The main technical risks over the conversion weekend appear to be: the risk of failed trades; the risk of inability to handle the volume of client enquiries; the risk that operations and support staff will be swamped; the risk of loss of integrity and accuracy of books and records; and the risk of loss of upfront trade matching controls. To keep these risks to the minimum, it is essential that market firms conduct dress rehearsals for the conversion weekend, but this is very difficult to do well in practice.

If an in-house dress rehearsal is this difficult, it is no surprise that a synchronized 'street test' is not feasible, in particular because:

- all market participants will not be ready for testing at the same time;

- the logistics and complexity of performing a test across thousands of participants is unmanageable; and

- the complexities and vagaries of the different countries cause too many problems.

The reality of testing has demonstrated that a much more pragmatic method of ensuring firms are ready has had to be used. For example, the creation of a set of test cases that any market participants will be able to use as references to check the logic and mathematics of their internal conversion and redenomination processes are working correctly and can be reconciled before they test with each other. But is this enough?

> the reality of testing has demonstrated that a much more pragmatic method of ensuring firms are ready has had to be used

Given the scale of the work to be undertaken, it is important that market firms should review their contingency arrangements in advance, and consider what steps they may need to take to ensure that they can conduct their operations effectively over the conversion weekend.

Firms should already have in place arrangements to carry on their business in the event of disruption caused by loss of electrical power or computer failure. These plans should be reassessed in the light of the additional demands of the conversion weekend, and adjusted as necessary.

## Payments and settlements

To achieve an integrated euro zone, the central banks have developed TARGET to link national RTGS systems. TARGET will allow correspondent banks in each EU member country to transfer euros to correspondent banks in other member countries. In addition, the Euro Banking Association (EBA) is developing a private sector net settlement system for the settlement of euros. The TARGET and EBA systems, along with the opening of existing RTGS systems for cross-border access by correspondents, will enable correspondents to offer euro-clearing services across the EU.

The existence of a large number of euro payment and settlement systems throughout Europe will mean that large institutions in particular will have a number of separate pots of liquidity and collateral. Most large institutions will seek to manage those separate pots collectively, typically from centralized treasury operations, in order to minimize the cost and inconvenience caused by imbalances between them. Some institutions may pool their liquidity and use TARGET, provided it operates efficiently, to move the liquidity to where it is needed. Ultimately, competition between the different payment systems, in terms of capacity, efficiency and cost will determine the most popular payment system.

> the existence of a large number of euro payment and settlement systems throughout Europe will mean that large institutions in particular will have a number of separate pots of liquidity and collateral

This infrastructure will, in theory, allow correspondents to move NCUs to euro accounts and, euro to NCU accounts, both within national borders and across borders. Funds moving across borders will be converted to EUR, and then converted to NCUs by a domestic correspondent bank. For example, a correspondent in Germany will be able to deliver euro to a correspondent in France from either a DEM or EUR account that can be credited to either an FRF or a euro account.

Banks in participating Member States are required (by virtue of EU Regulation 1103/97 under Article 235 of the European Treaty) to provide a conversion service between their local NCU and the euro which allows a payer to send either NCU or euro and the payee to receive the payments in the denomination of their account, either NCU or euro. This facility is the practical implementation of the principle of 'no compulsion, no prohibition', allowing one party to a contract to use euro (or NCU) without compelling the counterparty to do the same.

However, as services provided by euro correspondents vary, institutions and their correspondents should agree on services that can be expected when converting NCU amounts to euro, and *vice versa*. For example, will correspondents be able to provide conversion between NCUs and EUR? How will correspondents handle local holidays that are not TARGET holidays? How much will they charge for their services?

Further, participants should recognize that the validations currently in their system to prevent cross-border payments will need to be relaxed to support the euro-settlement environment. In addition, banks should be aware that not all counterparties will have removed the system validations that prevent payments to a destination bank in a country different from that of the paying agent.

At present, banks generally maintain at least one nostro in each country in order to make payments in that country's currency via the local payment system. The euro is different because it will be possible to make euro payments to any participating Member State from one account held in any Member State (and also via CHAPS euro from or to a euro account held in the UK, despite the UK being 'out'). Thus it will be possible to hold only one nostro account for making and receiving euro payments relating to euro transactions throughout the EU.

> banks should be aware that not all counterparties will have removed the system validations that prevent payments to a destination bank in a country different from that of the paying agent

However, it is recommended that national currency nostros should be retained in each country to receive incoming payments relating to outstanding NCU deals which may still be directed throughout the banking centre of the currency of the underlying contract. The nostro agent can be requested to remit funds received each day to the main euro nostro, and this one nostro used to make all payments.

Correspondent banks should make available accounts in euro as well as NCUs. Banks need to decide what nostros they need from 1 January 1999 and their long-term nostro account plans so that they can advise appropriate standard settlement instructions (SSIs) in good time to all their dealing partners. If a high volume of SSI changes take effect on the same value date, settlement problems could be significant. Any problems would then need to be investigated, leading to possible liquidity constraints for market participants and/or correspondent banks.

The implementation of SSIs advised for the euro will be a major task for many banks. If, in addition, banks are requested to change settlement instructions on existing deals, there is a risk that some changes will not be made correctly and that, through weight of numbers, some requested changes will not get processed. The result of this might then be a significant increase in payments going astray at a time when banks are adjusting to new dealing and nostro patterns, potentially leading to substantial delays while the errors are sorted out. The BBA recommended that particular attention is paid to the resources available to implement settlement change requests and to manage misdeliveries or failures to settle in the first weeks of 1999.

In the absence of SSIs, euro deals will require specific instructions, reducing 'straight-through' processing volumes and increasing operational risk. It will certainly not be feasible, and would be operationally risky, to wait to make substantial numbers of SSI changes over the conversion weekend. However, the relevant accounts and use of SSIs may need to be 'switched on' and tested at that point.

The rounding rules specified in Council Regulation 1103/97 can lead to small differences in the end results when payments involve conversion from euro to NCUs, or *vice versa*. Parties to transactions need to recognize this potential error, and to decide how their institution will handle small rounding errors. A best practice would be to determine a threshold; rounding amounts under the threshold would be written off. With this method rounding errors will, for the most part, net out for most institutions.

> a best practice would be to determine a threshold; rounding amounts under the threshold would be written off

For the purposes of payment netting, it is recommended that amounts in underlying transactions that are in different denominations of the euro should not be netted, even if both parties use euro nostros. This is because most market participants do not have the systems capability to perform netting across the different denominations of the euro. If participants wish to net, it is probably better to convert NCU transactions to euro and to then net in euro.

If an institution chooses to maintain both a euro account and an NCU account with the same correspondent in the same location, it is suggested that the operating procedures be reviewed to minimize postings to a wrong euro account. Institutions should seek to institute a pooling agreement for debit and credit interest with their correspondent. These actions may help reduce operational settlement problems and will ensure that, when problems arise, costs are kept to a minimum.

Processing of euro deals will be different from other currencies because there are a number of payment systems available for executing payments and because the number of participants in these systems will be much larger than in the existing national payment systems. This means there is a greater likelihood of a bank finding itself paying away more than it is receiving in a particular system, despite having matched inflows and outflows overall, and that it will be more difficult to find out where the surpluses corresponding to a bank's deficit are held.

In the case of RTGS systems, banks may not be able to make payments pending receipts and there is a potential for gridlock. Particularly during the first few days of the euro, major settlement banks will need to maintain higher levels of liquidity and monitor which system payments are being made through as well as the nostro accounts involved.

There is the possibility of a hiccup in one payment system, leading to hiccups in the others. There is a danger of liquidity problems for individual banks in a real-time gross settlement system such as Chaps euro which is outside the euro zone. Such a system has no end provider of liquidity. In a crisis, banks may not be able to complete payments. Real-time gross settlement means that the TARGET system will be safe, but a liquidity crisis outside it could hit the banks as they fail to find collateral to complete trades.

> a service level document for TARGET provides a summary description of the service it will provide for cross-border payments only (national RTGS systems may provide different or additional local services)

A service level document for TARGET provides a summary description of the service it will provide for cross-border payments only (national RTGS systems may provide different or additional local services). The document summarizes the service that will be available in normal circumstances, and also how abnormal circumstances will be addressed. However, the document is not very detailed on this latter issue, making clear that the participants themselves must meet their responsibilities to ensure that the system as a whole can operate efficiently.

# WHAT ARE THE RISKS?

## Conversion failure

Given that the financial markets generate millions of prices and other data each day at tremendous speed, errors are inevitable. All financial activity generates data: market makers put out bids and offers; deals give transaction prices. Volatility and correlation data follow, as do futures and options prices. All sorts of other information feeds this process and flows from it – data on economic fundamentals, trade statistics, company accounts, market analysis and so on.

> human error is one cause of bad data and, unfortunately, a substantial proportion of conversion processes will be manual

Many of those involved in collecting and supplying data are taking steps to improve the quality of their output. But the data vendors cannot solve the problem alone. In many cases, the same data is replicated across systems, institutions and markets meaning that simultaneous conversions of the same data will have to take place. This significantly increases the risk of data pollution and reconciliation breakdown. The issues of who owns market data and who is responsible for its quality are unclear and sensitive. Consequently, a comprehensive solution will be achieved only by a concerted effort across the industry.

Human error is one cause of bad data and, unfortunately, a substantial proportion of conversion processes will be manual. Some problems arise through software bugs, or hardware or communications equipment breakdowns. Transmission systems fail from time to time and errors can result if the service is resumed and data is missing or the user misinterprets the relationship between the last data received and the new data.

For example, a source might generally give only the third and fourth decimal places of a price except where there is a change in the second decimal place. The user could miss a change in the second decimal place if it occurs while the system is down. If we assume that rounding occurs randomly, then the average fractional amount on a €100 bond will be 0.5%. On total outstanding bonds of say €5 trillion, this equates to €25 billion. This calculation illustrates the non-trivial nature of this issue and the urgency of coming to a practical decision. In many cases, banks will have to significantly adjust existing matching and reconciliation tolerances.

There is little correlation between the volume and the quality of data. For example, much of the foreign exchange market is automated so the data quality is relatively good, principally because it is captured at source, in real time. In some less automated markets, notably the OTC markets, there is a slow process of contribution – data is put on paper, passed about, then keyed in. This process naturally allows more errors to creep in.

Traders' systems will need to be converted over the conversion weekend, so that the euro is included as a currency and NCUs are linked to it via the conversion rates. All spreadsheets, composite screen pages or other front-office applications used for trading, ticket-writing and position-keeping purposes will need to be amended to reflect the new currency and the new market conventions. These changes should all be checked and reconciled internally to settlement and other back-office systems as the data will in many cases be converted independently in these systems and reconciliation is critical. They will also have to be reconciled to the conversions of clients, counterparties, exchanges, custodians and depositories.

> traders' systems will need to be converted over the conversion weekend, so that the euro is included as a currency and NCUs are linked to it via the conversion rates

Automated price feeds (such as for money market rates and foreign exchange rates) will need to be updated to refer to their euro equivalents. Many of these changes can be prepared well in advance, and automated price feeds can be tested if 'dummy' feeds are available. Screen providers have amended formats to display euro data to assist in the amendment of data feeds. Nevertheless, the feeds and other applications may still need to be finally tested for accuracy during the conversion weekend once price feeds are 'live'.

The more instruments that are being updated in a volatile market, the faster the flow of data and the greater the danger of losing price transparency. The market will become inefficient if clogged with data.

'The ultimate danger is that traders will not be able to get prices and transact deals and so the market crashes. Although such catastrophes are rare, the system is frequently under strain. Even relatively small events, like a change in interest rate by a central bank, can have huge repercussions on the flow of data through the linked markets. So maintaining transparency and the efficiency of markets is becoming a key issue.' *Risk Magazine, July 1996.*

If this is true under normal market conditions, consider the impact of the massive conversion of all participating interest rates, equity prices, government bond nominals, etc. at the end of 1998. Equity markets are significantly at risk from such a large-scale big bang conversion due to the sheer volume of positions and open trades that will need converting over a single weekend. The bond markets are even more at risk as they have, in addition to volume, the added complexities of redenomination and reconventioning to deal with.

> the risks to the organization of not completing conversion in the time available are significant

The risks to the organization of not completing conversion in the time available are significant. For an investment bank, examples include the following.

- **Operational risk.** The inability to track and reconcile payments or the inability to settle outstanding transactions or the inability to process transactions.
- **Market risk.** Both volatility in the market and the inability to understand and manage market and credit risk post 4 January 1999 as exposures have not converted correctly or completely.
- **Credit risk.** The inability to track companies experiencing operational difficulties, liquidity difficulties or becoming over-exposed to various forms of market risk.
- **Liquidity risk.** The inability to fund due to lack of the right information or operational failures that may leave a bank exposed to a lack of funds coupled with the potential for gridlock within payment systems.
- **Legal risk.** The loss of client positions and accounts or the loss of audit trails required for accounting data.
- **Business risk.** The inability to trade on and after 4 January 1999 may result in a loss of business as clients trade with organizations that can.

The total risk exposure to an organization rises exponentially the longer it takes to complete conversion successfully beyond 4 January 1999. ISMA concluded in its report, *The Repo Market in Euro: Making it Work*, that 'the chances of total chaos on 4 January 1999 are low: perhaps 1%. The chances of a relatively high incidence of settlement failures are much higher: perhaps 20%. The chances of at least one major firm having a software problem which may ripple over to other firms are higher still. The systems complexities are in danger of being seriously underestimated and this is becoming increasingly urgent as each day passes, with final decisions being postponed.' I think this is still quite an optimistic picture, though they are right in suggesting that if there are problems they are likely to show up early in the repo market.

This is because of the relative short-maturity and settlement-intensive nature of the repo. The scope for confusion as one segment of the market is redenominated and/or reconventioned in one way and others in another will be immense. The fact that the repo market is closely linked to government bond trading activity, the futures market for government bond options (being used for hedging activity by these markets), and other short-term money markets, means problems with redenomination will cause major issues for repo trades. Problems could be further exacerbated due to weak cross-border linkages between domestic depositories and the implicit risk of 'ripple' settlement failure across the euro area arising from failure of these linkages.

This is a key concern for the ECB as repo is critically important to the operation of monetary policy being the primary mechanism for conducting open market operations. Liquidity could be severely squeezed if firms lose access to secured funding via repo.

Risk management has always been a key area of regulatory supervision as well as a tool for deriving competitive advantage. But techniques for managing risk have so far focused on quantifiable risks, such as market, credit and liquidity risks. Conversion is, let's face it, a huge, unprecedented event, and banks have no in-built, tried and tested methods of managing this risk, much of which will result from operational failure during data conversions. But implied failures would need to be treated as potential credit problems, as it could be hard to immediately differentiate a simple operations failure from a default.

Even with sophisticated market risk management techniques, examples of risk management failure are well-known. For example, an article in *Risk Magazine* comments:

> '"How could one man, just 13 years out of puberty, bring down a 200-year old bank?" asked one banker at a recent London conference. A good question, which has since been joined in the annals of risk management by such conundrums as "how could one man hide a billion dollars of loss-making bond deals?" and "how could one man have lost billions in copper over 10 years?" Attempts to answer them often reveal a common theme. In each case, senior management, regulators and investors seem to have been left in the dark because of their physical or organizational separation from the trader, highlighting the need to eliminate such failures of communication.'

The scenario under which a single operation runs amok is not as pressing for non-financials, whose risk management and trading are most likely to be auxiliary to the core business. But, haunted by the ghost of Metallgesellschaft, whose New York arm implemented an apparently carefully planned hedging policy which still went dramatically awry, many companies have responded by centralizing risk management at their global headquarters. Nevertheless, hedging strategies will have to be carefully reviewed to ensure that converted cash or derivative positions do not give rise to any unexpected exposures.

Continuity of contract provisions generally provides that all contracts entered into in an NCU will be available after 1 January 1999. To date, legislation or regulations that assure the continuity of contracts exist in all EU jurisdictions (including those that are not 'in' countries) as well as New York and Illinois. If an institution has contracts governed within a jurisdiction that has not adopted laws or regulations to assure continuity of contracts, legal counsel should be sought.

ISDA has created a protocol to provide for continuity of contracts, price source fallbacks, payment netting, and basic definitions for the euro and euro business days as well as other 'housekeeping' matters. This protocol serves to amend existing ISDA master agreements on a bilateral basis between parties who have subscribed to the annex.

Banks active in the swaps market have been queuing to adopt the EMU protocol. It addresses issues such as how to amend a French franc swaps contract based on Pibor, the Paris interbank offered rate, when that ceases to exist. In May 1998, ISDA said that they had 35 to 40 firms adopting the documentation, with some commentators hailing it as 'a major step towards legal and contractual security' and 'an effective tool for every market participant trying to master ambiguous questions' posed by EMU.

From January 1999, dealers will have to be able to look at their positions in the participating currencies as positions in euro. If a bank chooses to convert all deals to euro, no additional position-keeping functionality will be needed. If, on the other hand, the euro is treated as 'just another currency', capacity to create combined positions will be necessary. Other risk management functions will similarly need to be able to combine national currency and euro-denominated assets, liabilities and off-balance sheet positions.

VAR models and other risk analysis tools use historical data series to provide statistical information as a basis for risk assessment. Specific requirements for these data series are laid down by regulators if models are to be used as a basis for capital adequacy calculations.

There is no data for the euro prior to 1 January 1999 and therefore no data series. Banks using models for capital adequacy purposes should decide how they will construct proxy data series for the euro and agree with their regulator that the methodology proposed is appropriate. Regulators will not agree or publish a particular data series – it is part of the management responsibility surrounding model usage.

Thus for an interim period, proxy data series will be needed for many credit and market risk algorithms using historical volatilities and correlations until sufficient data has been generated to calculate true euro volatilities and correlations. Many market participants are expected to use DEM or a basket of NCUs as a proxy for euro. Other possibilities are the use of ECU and a derived/synthetic euro. Each institution must decide for itself what is best.

A report published by the Bank of England on 11 June 1998 warns that unit-trust (mutual-fund) managers might use the euro conversion as a chance to 'modify' track record. Equally, companies can use the conversion to amend their comparative share price past performance. This can be done by varying the method used to translate past returns, earned in national currencies, into euros.

- National currencies are all converted into euros at the fixed conversion rates as at 1 January 1999;

- Prices are translated into, say D-mark, and then translated into euros at the fixed conversion rate;

- Prices are converted into the ECU as a proxy for the euro; or

- Prices are converted using some synthetic euro rate such as a specially-created basket consisting of weights (e.g. by GDP) of 'in' currencies.

A commission advising the Bank of England on this issue advised that past records should be converted to euros using the fixed conversion rates, but investors should be aware of these different methods when analyzing time-series data.

## Systemic risk management

What happens in January 1999 when 10% of *every* (not just one or two) financial market participants' conversion routine fails? What happens when each of these 10% failures is different from all others? What happens when this does not get resolved for two, three or six weeks into 1999? What does this do to the liquidity and credibility of the euro? What resources can the ECB, through the national central banks, call upon and from where should it draw them? The impact of this liquidity squeeze will be felt across the global markets. Contingency funding plans will be all too important.

The aggregated risk across the financial markets in this scenario is hugely significant, but more importantly, real. Operational failure and liquidity risk have been the most common cause of bank failure. Look at the demise of Barings or BCCI to see how easy it is to bring a bank down.

Lending banks may begin to pull lines on other banks experiencing conversion difficulties, though it will be very difficult to determine who has successfully converted and who hasn't. Unsuccessful banks will begin to emerge and their ability to remain liquid will be endangered if lending banks pull lines for fear of operational failure. Difficult credit decisions will be required as it will be difficult to differentiate between fails resulting from operational failure and actual defaults.

The market needs clarification over the role of national central banks and the ECB would have as lenders of last resort during a crisis. Will national central banks continue their lender of last resort operations at their own choice and on their own account? Is there a need for the ECB to preserve European-wide systemic stability?

When responsibility is not clearly allocated, there is a risk that a crisis will be exacerbated by delays in the provision of assistance. Such delays may be due to misunderstandings and disputes among potential lenders of last resort about who is responsible.

Dirk Schoenmaker, an economist at the Bank of England, provides a hypothetical example. A large French company issues commercial paper in London which is bought by the London branch of a Portuguese bank. Suppose the French company faces financial problems and cannot repay its debt at maturity. The implications include uncertainty in the London market and doubts about the solvency of the Portuguese bank. The question then becomes which central bank – the Bank of England, the Banque de France or the Banco de Portugal – should intervene. This type of problem will become a common issue as cross-border mergers and acquisitions in Europe continue.

Most analysts have concluded that official intervention should depend on the scale of the problem. Support for individual banks can still be given at the local level by national central banks on their own account. But problems affecting EMU-wide markets will require ECB intervention. The primary worry is what happens when local problems become cross-border headaches.

Even now there is some considerable ambiguity about the mechanisms for resolving crises involving the flows across the European payments system and about the co-ordination of systemic risk management functions. The Maastricht Treaty is silent about lender-of-last-resort responsibilities. Article 105 of the Treaty does not provide for a general, direct involvement of the ECB in the supervision of financial intermediaries or institutions, and the subsidiarity principle applies, with national supervisors remaining fully competent.

In addition, Article 105 (5) envisions only a supporting role for the ECB in ensuring the smooth functioning of European financial markets, and it empowers the ESCB to promote the smooth operation of the European payments system. EMU national supervisory bodies, only in some cases the national central banks, will continue to have a mandate for enforcing EU directives on capital adequacy, accounting standards, disclosure standards, risk management practices, regulation and market surveillance. However, there is no central authority with the explicit mandate to ensure stability over the EMU financial system in its entirety.

During a fast-breaking crisis, a central authority – usually the central bank – would require immediate access to information for assessing the financial condition of its counterparties, and in particular their liquidity and solvency. Consequently, the ECB will need to ensure close co-operation within the ESCB and the relevant supervisors in order for it to be able to act decisively and quickly.

In a situation where an institution is experiencing difficulties in settling its payments obligations, or is liquidity-constrained or fundamentally insolvent, the central bank usually has a choice: it can provide access to lender-of-last-resort facilities or it can deny access to the payments system, in effect allowing it to fold. In recent years, the latter has been the preferred option. But what happens when a large number of institutions are simultaneously experiencing operational difficulties, including the central bank itself? The challenge in Europe is to create a clear and easily implemented crisis management mechanism, with clearly assigned co-ordination and responsibilities.

ISMA doubts that the existing mechanism for repo operations implemented indirectly through national central banks can be smoothly co-ordinated, particularly in a crisis. The fact that the ECB will not undertake the function of lender of last resort raises more concern as it is not quite clear who will co-ordinate the management of euro liquidity in a crisis if it is not the ECB.

Central banks have a long tradition of working together during such crises and there is no reason to suppose they would not do so in managing the euro. However, there is a key difference from the management of national currencies by the national central bank: namely, the absence of a single government to whom the central bank can turn for support in managing the crisis. As one participant pointed out:

> 'What happens if the support involves some element of subsidy? Technically, that would have to be cleared with DG IV of the European Commission – and they are hardly notorious for moving quickly in a crisis.'

Also, as the collapse of Barings vividly illustrated, cross-border crises are much more complex to manage. Some might argue that the absence of a central government will make euro crises easier to manage, and this cynical view may be correct. However, it does mean that crisis management in the euro may work out differently than in the past, particularly bearing in mind that it would involve a number of central banks whose 'home currency' is involved. They may take different views about the inflationary implications of extra liquidity, or about the relative desirability of permitting a given institution to fail, particularly if it is a 'national champion'.

Central banks do more than set monetary policy. They often have vital roles in overseeing entire banking systems, whether that involves the conduct of banks, the efficiency of their networks, or the level of understanding by senior staff of financial products. In terms of regulation, the Maastricht Treaty provides greater powers to national authorities. At present, nine of the 15 national central banks in the EU are directly responsible for banking supervision. The remaining six are indirectly involved. Events such as the collapse of British bank Barings or the string of derivatives-based corporate disasters throughout the 1990s have underlined the need for market-savvy regulators.

But the regulation and safeguarding of banks under EMU is an unresolved issue. Unlike the federal reserve in the US, which has wide authority over banks, the ECB's mandate will give it more of an advisory role. Its diminished authority stems largely from the Maastricht Treaty, which gives greater weight to national monetary authorities and finance ministers.

The treaty says EU finance ministers have authority:

> 'acting unanimously on a proposal from the Commission and after consulting the ECB and after receiving the assent of the European parliament, (to) confer upon the ECB specific tasks concerning policies relating to the prudential supervision of credit institutions and other financial institutions.'

This heavily hedged statement is complicated further by EU rules. A bank in one country may establish subsidiaries and branches in other EU countries. However, each bank will be subject to home-country supervision. Some see this arrangement as a potential source of trouble. In a system of segmented financial markets, differences in bank regulation can be tolerated. In integrated markets they cannot. Witness the varying stages of implementation of the European Capital Adequacy Directive or the Basle Accord across European countries.

Studies have suggested a variety of approaches towards supervision, with some focusing on the distinction between small and large international banks. A report by the Brussels-based Centre for European Policy Studies argues for a two-tier structure, with national authorities responsible for smaller and medium-sized banks and the ECB in control of big multinationals. Alternatively, EU finance ministers could be given greater powers to oversee banks, particularly since EMU would probably prompt consolidation in the financial industry.

But history tells us that regulatory changes are, at best, slow to implement. Can any of this be done in time for the start of EMU when perhaps it will be most needed? Who is going to monitor what and how? How can regulators determine whether or not a bank is sufficiently prepared when even senior management of the banks do not possess such information? Even if they were aware of the dramatic lack of preparation, what action could they take to remediate the situation?

What could a regulator do if it was able to determine the real state of preparation in the firms it is supposed to oversee? What if an institution was so significantly behind in its preparation that it posed a significant operational and credit risk to its counterparties and clients? What would be the response? This is a particularly gritty issue with respect to multi-national institutions. Separate regulators will continue with independent boards and separate powers. So who does what when multiple organizations and multiple regulators are having difficulties?

Perhaps they could increase capital weightings, but this does nothing to prevent the tide of operational failures. It could even augment the liquidity squeeze as organizations fight desperately to control credit exposures. But, let's face it, how many banks allocate capital on the basis of regulatory capital? Whilst some of the more unsophisticated banks use regulatory capital to determine the level of investment in one business line or another, the majority now use some combination of risk measurement to allocate capital. RAROC (risk-adjusted return on capital) is just one example. The implication is that banks use regulatory capital only to act as a constraint on capital allocation, if at all.

The regulators believe that it is important for regulated firms to recognize that they must continue to meet their ongoing regulatory obligations, notwithstanding the market changes which will result from EMU.

For example, the constituent entities of the UK's Financial Services Authority (FSA) are encouraging all the firms which they regulate to conduct thorough audits of all their business processes and product lines in order to ascertain where these will be affected in any way by the introduction of the euro. Where additional risks arise as a result of this unique event, firms must take steps to mitigate and control these risks, as they would any other new operational risks which are identified as part of normal ongoing risk management and compliance procedures. In short, firms must be in control of their business during and after the advent of the euro, as at all other times.

The FSA constituent regulators have incorporated a review of firms' preparations for EMU into their ongoing surveillance and monitoring procedures during 1998. General guidance has been issued on areas of concern already identified, and the FSA will continue to issue guidance as the EMU process develops. However, firms cannot in general expect their regulators to issue detailed prescriptive guidance on what steps firms should take. The introduction of the euro will affect every firm differently, depending on the nature and scope of its business and the exact control systems used. It is for firms to identify and control any new risks which arise, in order to comply with their ongoing regulatory obligations to organize and control their internal affairs in a responsible manner.

To ensure that sufficient priority is attached to its work preparing for the euro, the Bank of England announced in January 1998 that it had formally established a Euro Preparation Division. Aside from its work helping to prepare the financial infrastructure for the euro, the Bank is interested in the state of preparations by individual firms. For example, it discussed the state of preparations with the Chairmen and Chief Executives of the leading financial institutions operating in London at its second and third symposiums on the euro in January and October 1998 respectively. But how does the Bank of England really determine the state of preparations when firms are unlikely to admit to problems for fear of either repercussions or loss of competitive face?

Nevertheless, the Bank has been reviewing with a representative sample of UK and internationally owned financial institutions their level of preparedness for the introduction of the euro. In the process, the Bank aims to establish whether there are any gaps in the preparation of the infrastructure.

Ultimately, it seems that we are completely dependent upon the ability of each financial market participant to deliver a successful conversion. Should this not be the case we must hope that regulators, notably central banks, can act swiftly and in concert under the auspices of the ECB to prevent a liquidity disaster stemming largely from operational failure. Chapter 7 looks at some of the key components of a successful conversion strategy.

# MANAGING THE RISKS

Whilst there are major implications for the measurement and management of different types of risk, the euro possibly represents the greatest test of an organization's ability to manage operational risk, implicit in its ability to manage its conversion project. An inability to deliver a successful conversion, concurrent with Year 2000 and other programmes such as integrating a merger or acquisition, will inevitably lead to major operational failure.

There has been much talk of implementing firmwide risk management systems, but rarely with respect to successfully delivering a major programme. Nevertheless, we can usefully draw on some of the issues as conversion to the euro is explicitly firmwide. Management's ability to capture and manage the risks of conversion is critical to the success of the conversion weekend and this is, necessarily, across the entire organization.

The exact requirements for a risk management system to meet the needs of the firm, ideally to span continents and time zones, are not easy to define. This is easy to see when you look at the multiplicity of systems and procedures designed to deal with the multiple types of risks (market, credit, liquidity, operational, legal and so on) that arise from dealing in different asset classes (currencies, interest rates, equities, commodities and, more recently, credit) across different time zones (e.g., offices in New York, London and Tokyo).

Whilst companies vary greatly, there are some common themes such as technology infrastructure, assimilating large volumes of reliable data, and producing information that can be used at any level necessary. But knowledge, not information, is power.

The company must also decide who 'owns the risk': who takes responsibility for measuring, limiting and allocating it. Various frameworks are possible: the most promising, which deliver risk information to the most senior levels of management, require the evolution of new measurement techniques.

The scope of risk management must fall across all risk types, as well as individual businesses. A measure of risk which captured only a few of the major risk types – market, credit, liquidity, operational and legal – would be missing crucial elements of the bigger picture. As many observers have noted, credit risk has brought down more banks than its better understood cousin, market risk, and the Barings, Daiwa and Sumitomo fiascos can all be read as the results of operational risk. While the integration of market and credit risk is well under way, there is some distance to go before other risks are brought into the fold. Nonetheless there are still ways to classify such risks and the controls necessary to manage them.

As Clifford Smout, head of the banking supervisory policy division at the Bank of England, told a conference on regulation early in 1996: 'Risk management is somewhat like apple pie: we're all in favour of it so long as someone else does all the cooking and it comes free. But risk management is not a free lunch: and the more elaborate the pie, the more expensive it is.' Richard Farrant, then chief executive of the UK SFA, told the same conference: 'Evidence emerges constantly that firms are not only inconsistent in their risk management practices but even have difficulty maintaining their standards and practices across their group.'

Risk management systems today by and large handle market, credit and liquidity risks. Operational risks and legal risks are only just beginning to be formally recognized by the industry. In the words of a US house trader, 'the guys in operations are able to lose money faster than my traders can.' But risks inherent in delivering large-scale change programmes are understood even less. Even where they are actively managed, it is very rare to find two firms that measure and/or manage these risks in the same way. This makes it extremely difficult to assess the state of preparation between firms, further complicated by the non-standard implementation of the euro in each firm.

One problem with creating a process to manage these risks is that there is no common way to measure them – but without a way to quantify the risk, it cannot be managed efficiently, if at all. Other forms of risk that banks are more used to managing, such as market and credit risk calculations, are often based on the same building blocks. One of the most significant of these is revaluation. Once a transaction has been revalued, it can be aggregated with others, either by transaction type or portfolio, for market risk analyses, or by customer, for credit risk analyses. It would, therefore, be more efficient to carry out these valuations once and share them between the credit risk system and the market risk system. Technology aside, the difficulty will be getting disparate risk organizations (e.g., the credit and market risk managers) to work together and to agree on standard methods for calculating and tracking exposures. The same is true for managing project risk across major programmes.

The biggest challenge facing risk managers is the integration of risk analyses across major programmes. Whilst firms have frequently recognized the need for some form of measurement of euro (or Year 2000) programme risk, very few have tried to integrate risk measures across programmes, such as the euro, Year 2000, and others. Without doing this, banks have little chance of understanding overall implementation risk – that is, the risk of failing to simultaneously deliver projects within major programmes for the same systems and processes using the same resources.

The key to business success lies in a cultural mindset that treats risk with an attitude of discovery, accepting that change is inextricably linked to risk and change is inevitable. A two-way approach is often best.

- *Project level up* – an organization needs a consistent and disciplined approach to viewing risk across the organization from as close to the project level detail as possible.

- *Strategic level down* – risk tolerance levels need to be based on shareholder and board of director preferences. However, tolerance levels around euro conversion will have to be significantly raised in order to avoid operational meltdown.

Such a two-way approach needs to be designed in a way that can be pro-actively managed across the entire firm. There are four principal different models for the firmwide risk management function.

- *Virtual model.* This is the holy grail where comprehensive information is accessible to all involved in risky activities, thus distributing responsibility across the organization.

- *Centralized model.* The remoteness of the risk function in this case is both a virtue and a weakness, in that it allows objectivity but may be too far distant from the front line staff to appreciate their concerns and the risks inherent in their business and projects.

- *Decentralized model.* This is perhaps the most commonly used where a small amount of critical risk information is simply passed to senior management.

- *Hybrid model.* Centralized systems do not work well for organizations with global and disparate operations; for these a 'near-firmwide' decentralized treatment, with risk management at the local level and independent oversight at the global level, is more likely to be useful.

Regardless of what system is used, the quality of data always remains a problem. Even those organizations that have built comprehensive data warehouses still have data reliability issues. This is not just due to data management limitations, but also because many of an organization's dependencies are likely to be external. Despite the best efforts of all concerned, that data is not guaranteed to be 100% reliable, consistent and useful.

The exchanges and the vendors are taking steps to master the volume of data but what actions are they taking to master its quality? Almost everyone in the data supply chain now claims to be moving to improve quality – either by preventing errors entering the system or by catching and correcting them en route.

For example, Liffe applies entry check points, tailored for each different contract traded on the exchange. Inevitably some errors do slip through the system, either due to in-house errors, or errors further along the data chain. It also has a set of correction routines, messages that it sends to delete a particular price and give the correct price. But it's a broadcast feed – it works for some vendors but some don't recognize the error routines.

The vendors, such as Dow Jones, Telerate, Knight-Ridder and Reuters, take the output from the exchanges as well as from other sources, such as brokers and market makers, and apply another layer of quality checks.

Among the methods used are filter techniques that trap suspect prices which fall outside pre-set ranges (either the actual price range or the price differential). These are put into error logs for further investigation. All the filter values are based on market norms and are reviewed on a regular basis. Much of the filtering is dynamically controlled on a manual basis, so filters can be widened in the event of volatile market conditions.

Reuters has developed a software product called Intelligent Quality Toolkit (IQT) which uses artificial intelligence techniques to check real-time data for suspect items. The rules for assessing data can be tailored to individual instruments.

Many organizations take feeds from several vendors and cross-check their data. The Bank of England recommends that a bank's back office takes its data from a different source to its front office. An alternative is to accumulate data from all external sources into a data warehouse and apply checks and cleaning techniques, to create a single consistent source of high quality data that all applications across the organization will use. But how realistic is this, certainly in the short-term?

As all organizations in the data supply chain will be simultaneously and independently converting the same data, the opportunities for error are huge. The problem with many attempts at quality control is that they are under-resourced and therefore neither comprehensive nor quick in their response when errors or omissions are detected.

Some suppliers provide their data both electronically and as hard copy. This gives users the opportunity to cross-check, which frequently throws up discrepancies. But manual checking and correction is becoming impossible. With some banks now dealing or tracking over 4000 instruments, manual monitoring of data is now impossible. It requires some kind of automation, but with the speed and sophistication to deal with the idiosyncrasies of many different and often exotic instruments. The relatively crude threshold-based methods of most data filters that are currently employed are likely to be inadequate.

To compound the problem, many organizations are now putting data out over the Internet. This data is usually both historical and free. Exchanges are putting their prices on the World Wide Web, after a delay so as not to conflict with their real-time price services.

Organizations need to get the data right at the source, to get it input right first time. The most important thing is to get the process right, to get the quality fixed at source. But if the quality of the data is outside your direct control, then it has to be a market-wide effort to improve the quality.

It seems probable that when these operational risks are quantified, banks will discover that losses from conversion failure will be as large, if not greater, than in other, more actively managed risks. This was certainly true for UK's Big Bang in 1986 as losses due to operational mistakes announced in 1987 demonstrated, notably with respect to the quality of data conversion.

Assuming financial markets survive the conversion weekend, notwithstanding the likely collapse of a number of institutions, banks then have to cope with the complexities of the three-year transition period.

Banking associations were uneasy about the EU's decision to rule out the 'Big Bang' option of enforcing a complete switch to euros at the start of 1999. The EU has opted instead to launch the euro only in the wholesale markets. By comparison with clearing banks, the wholesale market handles a small number of transactions in very large amounts, so in theory the back offices of investment banks and securities houses should be better placed to sort out any transitional problems individually. However, we have already seen the enormous difficulties that the wholesale sector has been experiencing in making the transition. Further, the phased transition also means that these institutions will have to be able simultaneously to do business in euros among themselves and to deal with their clients using the old national currencies.

These retail clients will still be buying and selling their goods and services using the notes and coins of the old national currencies. But these notes and coins will each be worth a fixed euro amount, and retail clients will have the option of switching their book-keeping and their bank accounts to euros at any point between 1999 and 2002. No one can tell how many will choose to do so. If the euro establishes its credibility early on, many big corporations will rush to switch their accounts to the single currency. That could pressurize their suppliers to make an early switch, too, with a knock-on effect right down the business ladder. Or major companies might seek to pay their employees in euros, or their dividends in euros, which would spread the currency to tens of thousands of retail bank accounts. The EU might welcome that, but it would put heavy logistical pressure on clearing banks, which could only handle the demand if their information technology systems were fully prepared for it.

If, on the other hand, the euro has a more traumatic birth, non-financial companies will prefer to stick to the old national currencies for as long as possible. The sheer scale and complexity of the potential risks that we have already discussed is mind-boggling. So much so that it has merited very little open debate. Conferences and roadshows by EMU participants have been shy of examining what might go wrong. Often those commentators that appear to be concerned about the risks have been sidelined as 'non-believers'.

Either way, the euro is here to stay. However, given the scale of work and the risks we have seen this represents, perhaps we should ask the question as to whether it was sensible to pursue such an aggressive deadline. Whilst the financial markets are renowned for their ability to take on Herculean tasks and succeed, is this one step too far too soon? It is notable that the Maastricht Treaty was signed at a time when Year 2000 was not recognized as such a major issue. Perhaps a different timetable may have been decided with this in mind.

> if, on the other hand, the euro has a traumatic birth, non-financial companies will prefer to stick to the old national currencies for as long as possible

This view is far from isolated. However, the will of the political élite has set in motion a euro train that was unlikely to be stopped, even delayed? Views have been mixed on this issue as the following sample of quotes demonstrates.

'It will be difficult to win this race against time even if modern management methods are applied and all participants co-operate unbureaucratically.' *Bundesbank council member Helmut Schieber, March 1996.*

'A postponement of the introduction of the euro would be the safest way to doom it to failure.' *EU Commissioner Yves-Thibault de Silguy, February 1996.*

'For the Bank of France things are simple. There is a treaty which imposes a timetable. We will apply it.' *Bank of France governor Jean-Claude Trichet, January 1996.*

'A start date on 1 January 1999 is not a question of war and peace; to threaten an end to currency union, or disastrous consequences for European integration, if there is a delay is a crass exaggeration.' *Bundesbank council member Reimut Jochimsen, November 1996.*

'The currency union, once set in motion, cannot be allowed to derail. If necessary, a delay is less problematic than a later derailment.' *Bundesbank President Hans Tietmayer, February 1996.*

'Anyone who demands a delay in the start of the project is clearly not aware of the consequences.' *Bundesbank council member Hans-Jürgen Krupp, November 1996.*

With the benefit of hindsight pragmatic project management would have told us that introducing the euro on 1 January 1999 was not the best plan, particularly with the millennium just one year later. The strain on resources has been and will continue to be immense, not least the problems associated with uncertainty and inconsistency. Therefore we must be prepared for the consequences of considerable problems over the conversion weekend and beyond and the possible implications for the success of EMU caused largely by lack of preparation, in turn largely the result of political uncertainty.

# CHAPTER 5

# So, how prepared are you?

A study by MORI at the end of 1996 found just over half of the companies in the survey had undertaken any specific action to prepare for EMU; 28% had formed a steering committee, varying from 59% in Germany to 8% in Spain; while one in six had implemented conversion projects, ranging from 36% in Germany to 7% in Italy. Since then, as uncertainty has been replaced with certainty, the figures have increased but not as much as you would expect.

A similar survey of 302 European companies by KPMG towards the end of 1997 found companies better prepared: 81% of those companies surveyed had carried out at least some form of review, though 32% had no plans to conduct a thorough strategic analysis. Whilst 50% of companies had put EMU towards the top of the corporate priority list, only 2% had completed the implementation of their action plan, if they had one.

Britain's smaller businesses, which account for nearly half of private sector jobs, are comprehensively failing to prepare for Europe's single currency, according to a UK Treasury report published in August 1998. Only 11% of small and medium-sized enterprises were aware that the euro's launch date was 1 January 1999. Whilst 31% felt they should make preparations, only 5% had done so. The report is the first in a series of six-monthly bulletins to be produced by the Treasury on the state of preparations for the euro.

All surveys looking at the state of preparations for the euro have the same message – that many companies have not been sufficiently preparing. In some cases this is due to a lack of awareness, in others it is a lack of resources, whilst for some it is simply not considered a priority. But we have seen how the euro affects companies within and outside the euro-zone. Multinational companies operating in participating countries – countries that form part of the first wave of the EMU – are fully impacted by the introduction of and changeover to the euro.

Domestic enterprises typically operating within a single participating country without exporting or importing generally do not have any foreign currency transactions. As a result these enterprises have never needed to perform a currency translation before, because it was simply not necessary. With the introduction of the euro, these enterprises need to get used to another currency. Although the problems of the changeover might be slightly less complex in these enterprises, it will still be a major exercise that needs to be properly planned for. This is most immediate for companies operating with the first-wave EMU zone, but domestic enterprises in the rest of Europe should be gearing up for potential entry in a second or later wave.

In addition to internal pressures, the changeover process will soon become market-led. A number of companies plan to switch over to the euro in 1999, for all or part of their operations. Arbed, Philips, Siemens, Solvay, Daimler-Benz are some of the examples. This will probably have an accelerating effect as companies will want to be seen as leaders rather than followers in the changeover process. The end-consumer will also dictate the pace of change by demanding that transactions are made in euro, facilitated by the expansion of Internet, electronic banking, and pre-paid cards, forcing businesses to follow suit.

As we have seen, EMU is not simply about the introduction of an alternative currency, but about accelerating the development of the single market in Europe. This means that companies must fundamentally review, not just their IT systems, but also products, marketing, supply chains, location of operations, international organization, business processes, as well as the needs and responses of customers and competitors. The key to success lies in the timely completion of a thorough strategic analysis and plan, followed by a rigorous and fully resourced implementation programme.

The questions in Table 5.1 will help you to assess the state of your euro preparations as well as providing a high level checklist of the actions required to address the challenge of the euro. This list is a generic one, based upon the work and activities of the more prepared companies but should nonetheless highlight the areas that you should at least have covered in your euro preparations. Generally, the more positive answers you provide to the questions below, the further advanced are your preparations. You can use the questions to highlight areas which need further attention, but note that not all activities will be relevant to all companies.

| *Preparatory steps* | Not relevant | Not yet started | Under way | Completed |
|---|---|---|---|---|
| **Management structure and resourcing** | | | | |
| Have you set up a euro steering committee? | ☐ | ☐ | ☐ | ☐ |
| Have you appointed a euro project manager with sufficient seniority to have an overview of the enterprise and to get things done? | ☐ | ☐ | ☐ | ☐ |
| Have you obtained sponsorship of the project by executive management? | ☐ | ☐ | ☐ | ☐ |
| Have you established a project team with representatives from all departments affected by the changeover? | ☐ | ☐ | ☐ | ☐ |
| Have you established working groups for each business line and function? | ☐ | ☐ | ☐ | ☐ |
| Have you ensured that arrangements are in place to enable the enterprise/euro project team to respond quickly? | ☐ | ☐ | ☐ | ☐ |
| Have you allocated responsibility clearly for implementation of the necessary measures within the framework of project management? | ☐ | ☐ | ☐ | ☐ |
| Have you analyzed the need for external problem solvers/services such as consultants, software companies and contractors? | ☐ | ☐ | ☐ | ☐ |
| Have you estimated the cost and manpower requirements for your euro preparations? | ☐ | ☐ | ☐ | ☐ |
| Have you allocated a budget for your euro preparations? | ☐ | ☐ | ☐ | ☐ |
| Do you know the impact on your other investment plans? | ☐ | ☐ | ☐ | ☐ |
| **Management controls** | | | | |
| Have you installed a reporting system providing you with a steady flow of information on the state of preparations including risk management? | ☐ | ☐ | ☐ | ☐ |
| Are you taking the opportunity to harmonize your controlling and reporting procedures throughout the company? | ☐ | ☐ | ☐ | ☐ |

*Preparatory steps*

| | Not relevant | Not yet started | Under way | Completed |
|---|---|---|---|---|

**Strategic analysis and planning**

Have you started collecting relevant information on the euro and the impact of the changeover to the euro, both within and outside your company?

Have you spoken to your advisors about the euro, including your bank, accountant/auditor and major software suppliers?

Have you prepared an analysis of your current situation and identified areas which will require changes, i.e., operational impacts for all the functions and departments of the enterprise?

Have you identified the business benefits from reduced exposure to currency fluctuation, reduced transaction costs, easier price comparisons, improved access to capital markets and funding, etc.?

Have you assessed the impact on prices, wages and profitability?

Have you analyzed the impact on your current production and operational strategy, including location of operations?

Have you identified new product/market opportunities?

Have you reviewed your strategic alliances?

Have you reviewed your relationship with associates/subsidiaries?

Have you considered implications for long-term decisions, including any acquisition plans?

Have you undertaken a business (SWOT) analysis including an industry/competitor analysis?

Have you considered the implications for major stakeholders, including shareholders, investors, public administrations, suppliers, customers, employees and the general public?

▶

| *Preparatory steps* | Not relevant | Not yet started | Under way | Completed |
|---|---|---|---|---|
| Have you talked to your major suppliers and major customers? Will they force you to move over to the euro early? | ☐ | ☐ | ☐ | ☐ |
| Have you assessed the impact on your marketing strategy and pricing policy, particularly with respect to the issue of price transparency? | ☐ | ☐ | ☐ | ☐ |

**Organization and business line strategy**

| | Not relevant | Not yet started | Under way | Completed |
|---|---|---|---|---|
| Have you defined a strategy for the euro for your organization and each of your business lines? | ☐ | ☐ | ☐ | ☐ |
| Have you defined your strategic objectives? | ☐ | ☐ | ☐ | ☐ |
| Have you considered the impact the changes may have on your overall strategy. Would you possibly combine these changes with other strategic changes? | ☐ | ☐ | ☐ | ☐ |
| Have you reviewed both strategic and operational measures in the various divisions or functions within your company? For example, pricing policy, marketing strategy, management structure, investment plans, production operational strategy, financial strategy, market/product opportunities, business processes, accounting procedures. | ☐ | ☐ | ☐ | ☐ |
| Have you identified all euro-related projects including a timetable and priority for each individual project? | ☐ | ☐ | ☐ | ☐ |
| Have you defined euro requirements for changes to business processes? | ☐ | ☐ | ☐ | ☐ |
| Have you defined business requirements for changes to IT systems? | ☐ | ☐ | ☐ | ☐ |

**Conversion strategy**

| | Not relevant | Not yet started | Under way | Completed |
|---|---|---|---|---|
| Has a decision already been made on the optimal time for your company to convert to the euro? | ☐ | ☐ | ☐ | ☐ |
| Have you defined your changeover strategy, including timetable and budget? | ☐ | ☐ | ☐ | ☐ |

## Preparatory steps

|  | Not relevant | Not yet started | Under way | Completed |
|---|---|---|---|---|

Have you prepared a communication plan addressing customers, shareholders, public/press, employees and other stakeholders?

Have you prepared a training plan to ensure your staff can understand and deal with the euro?

Have you prepared training material for your staff?

Have you prepared information for your staff concerning changes to wages, pensions, contracts, insurance, etc.?

Have you co-ordinated all conversions within individual divisions or functions in order to minimize duplication of effort and ensure there are no gaps?

Have you defined how you will convert to the euro in terms of manual and automated processes, 'Big Bang' conversion, gradual changeover, etc.?

### Marketing and pricing

Have you assessed each of your markets to identify the way in which they will operate after the euro is introduced?

Have you studied the possible consequences of the introduction of the euro for your competitive position? For example, be aware that price discrimination between various export markets will be more difficult after the introduction of the euro as price differentials will become transparent. Are you going to simply convert export prices into euro or are you going to adjust them to reflect changes in translation, currency and transaction risks created by the common currency?

Have you reviewed your pricing strategy, because it may not be possible to maintain price differentials between existing national markets?

Have you decided whether you are going to set the same prices in all inner countries (consider local competition, transportation costs, marketing costs, etc., which will still differ per country)?

## Preparatory steps

|  | Not relevant | Not yet started | Under way | Completed |
|---|---|---|---|---|

Have you assessed whether you can lower prices for the inner countries to reflect the removal of the currency risk aspect in your past pricing strategy?

Have you assessed the need to change your prices for the pre-inner countries given the rounding/adjustment you may make for the inner countries?

Have you considered how your competitors will react?

Have you established your customers' attitudes towards the introduction of the euro?

Have you considered informing your customers when you are able to handle sales/orders in euros?

Have you ascertained the preferences of your customers regarding euro pricing and dual pricing? Note also that there could be a difference between having price lists in euro and national currency units (they could be different in real terms) and the dual display of prices (where exact counter values are displayed).

Have you ascertained whether there are any legal requirements in respect of price changes resulting from the introduction of the euro?

Have you decided to use dual pricing and if so for what period?

Have you ascertained whether there are any guidelines from your government for those products that are subject to price control(s)?

Have you assessed the implications for promotional material – price lists, folders, etc., which refer to prices in national currency or other currencies that are likely to become part of the EMU? For example, have you decided for which ones you want to use dual currency, which ones you want to adopt the euro? Following your pricing decision for the pre-inner countries, have you created a special mailing to them?

*Preparatory steps*

|  | Not relevant | Not yet started | Under way | Completed |
|---|---|---|---|---|
| Have you decided how to change price lists to euro by using the fixed rate or decided on what rounding should be made to arrive at round prices or 0.99 prices? |  |  |  |  |
| Are you working with your customers to agree a switch to euro purchasing and your switch to euro pricing? |  |  |  |  |
| Are you actively ensuring that your customers notice you are gearing up for the euro? |  |  |  |  |
| Have you found out when your suppliers wish to change to euro pricing? |  |  |  |  |
| Have you prepared for the impact of the euro on purchases and supplies? |  |  |  |  |
| Have you considered the impact of euro on lease contracts? |  |  |  |  |

**Operations**

|  | Not relevant | Not yet started | Under way | Completed |
|---|---|---|---|---|
| Have you considered whether you need to centralize your operations further given the EMU wide transparency of prices? |  |  |  |  |
| Have you considered relocation of operations? |  |  |  |  |
| Have you considered rationalization of your supply chain to take advantage of the single currency? |  |  |  |  |
| Have you considered whether you should outsource more functions? |  |  |  |  |
| Have you assessed whether you need to change production processes to cater for the new pricing strategy? |  |  |  |  |

**Finance and accounting**

|  | Not relevant | Not yet started | Under way | Completed |
|---|---|---|---|---|
| Have you decided when to prepare your annual and consolidated accounts in euro either in addition to the national currency or instead of the national currency? |  |  |  |  |
| Have you identified when national and local governments will accept returns in euro? |  |  |  |  |

▶

## Preparatory steps

Not relevant | Not yet started | Under way | Completed

Have you enquired whether there will be any changes in official reporting requirements, e.g., statistical returns to government departments that will necessitate additional changes in the accounting system and related software?

Have you decided the date on which you will change your internal reporting to euro (relationship with external reporting and competitive position)?

Have you considered whether you wish all your subsidiaries to report in euro, and by what date?

Have you considered to what extent and when you want to introduce a dual currency system in your accounting system?

Have you decided when to change over your internal accounting to the euro?

Have you considered and prepared planning and budgeting in the euro, including comparative figures, historical data and standard costing system?

Have you considered whether your (standard) costing system needs to be adapted (all costing information will no longer be comparable)? In a number of cases, costings will be filed all over the place, with different bases, duplicating or even contradicting each other.

Have you considered the accounting treatment including publication of accounts, treatment of historical information, and internal reporting including treatment of permanent exchange differences, foreign currency contract and non-monetary assets, rounding differences and liabilities in foreign currency?

Have you enquired whether it is possible to create provisions for the conversion costs (statutory accounts and accounts for tax purposes where they are different) or to capitalize these costs (the preferred accounting method is to write these off through the profit and loss account)?

Have you considered the impact of accounting gains and losses on conversion?

## Preparatory steps

*Not relevant*  *Not yet started*  *Under way*  *Completed*

Have you considered how to treat foreign currency operations (subsidiaries and branches) in EMU countries in consolidation, including the treatment of exchange differences arising from the consolidation?

Have you co-ordinated the changes in accounting procedures if you have subsidiaries in different countries, so that you will be able to operate the same systems for payroll, accounts payable and receivable, etc., in all countries adopting the euro?

Has tax treatment of introduction of the euro been considered both for company tax and VAT, including filing of tax returns in euro?

Have you decided when to change your payroll to euro?

Has preparation for payroll activities and pensions in euro, including informing staff and consultation with Workers' Council, been started?

Have you reviewed and confirmed your agreements with insurance undertakings?

### Treasury and banking

Have you reviewed and confirmed your contracts and agreements with banks?

Have you carried out a financial review of your existing treasury contracts?

Have you arranged for confirmation of amounts, interest rates, due dates, etc., with banks, enterprises and other financial institutions (change to euro, and date at which it will take place may depend on the counterparty in the case of swaps, options, futures and other derivatives)?

## Preparatory steps

Not relevant   Not yet started   Under way   Completed

Have you investigated your banks' euro facilities, including conversion of accounts in EMU currencies to euro and conversion charges? Will accounts in EMU currencies and in euro be offset or will they be considered separately for purposes of minimum balance and interest calculation, making/receiving euro payments without a euro account, replacement of cheques and bank transfer forms, etc.?

Have you considered rationalizing your banking relationships, e.g., can you reduce the number of accounts and/or banks?

Have you ensured that your investment decisions take account of the euro, including products, amounts and interest rates?

Have you considered how the euro will affect your balance sheet and currency management?

Have you decided whether electronic payments in euros are acceptable or desirable? Weigh the costs of working in euros and the national currency against the wishes of customers.

Have you decided if and/or when to redenominate your debt and equity and considered how and in what currency you want to make coupon and dividend payments?

Have you decided what changes, if any, to treasury management are being made arising from the reduced number of dealing currencies and from cross-border pooling of balances? For example, combining any treasury functions currently being operated in different countries ?

### Legal issues

Have you investigated contract continuity, particularly outside the EU?

Have you reviewed contract terms and conditions to see that the euro is adequately covered?

Have you considered changes to your staff employment contracts and pension arrangements?

## Preparatory steps

Not relevant | Not yet started | Under way | Completed

Have you reviewed new and revised legal provisions affecting internal and external accounting, contract law, company law and marketing requirements?

Have you sought legal opinion with respect to your existing financial contracts?

### IT

Have you completed a review of your IT strategy and systems, including the business criticality of each system?

Have you identified existing systems to be changed to deal with the euro?

Have you confirmed each impacted system can cope with conversion, including triangulation and rounding rules?

Have you ensured that your information systems are well-documented (so that you know where you need to insert the conversion factor)?

Have you listed all software that will need to be modified and detailed the changes required?

Have you considered whether you should use the modifications required for the euro as an opportunity for a total upgrade of your information systems and whether this is feasible in the time available?

Have you introduced proper procedures for safeguarding the updating of databases, in particular where a dual currency system will be in place?

Have you redesigned as many reports (including costs and turnover reports) as possible into a form which makes them easy to convert from national currency (and other currencies participating in the EMU) into euro (use worksheets or spreadsheets or simple text files)?

Have you reviewed and defined changes to all end-user computing applications such as spreadsheets and databases?

▶

## Preparatory steps

Not relevant    Not yet started    Under way    Completed

Have you identified all system interfaces, particularly with external parties such as EDI, and ensure these parties are compatible with both your and their changes?

☐ ☐ ☐ ☐

Have you asked your software supplier about the possibility of building in euro modules and check whether the modifications needed fall within the terms of the maintenance contract (most standard accounting software packages offer facilities to make conversions between denominations)? Will there be any bottlenecks and if so how can they be resolved? Should you consider buying a new application package?

☐ ☐ ☐ ☐

If you use software that was developed in-house, have you prepared plans for the changeover to the euro, including which systems, at what dates, dual currencies and have you included contingencies for possible bottlenecks when it comes to reprogramming?

☐ ☐ ☐ ☐

Have you planned the installation of euro modules? These modules need to be able to generate dual-currency invoices and price lists as well as to convert purchases, sales and salary slips automatically into euros or national currency as appropriate.

☐ ☐ ☐ ☐

Have you reviewed the need for new systems?

☐ ☐ ☐ ☐

Have you identified suitable packages that meet your needs if you intend to purchase?

☐ ☐ ☐ ☐

Have you studied the implications for various payment systems including cash registers, credit cards and electronic payments?

☐ ☐ ☐ ☐

Have you decided if and when you will accept payments in euro (linked to price and cash register decisions)?

☐ ☐ ☐ ☐

Have you made arrangements with credit card undertakings, banks or providers regarding change to dual currency system if applicable, final change to euro, and ascertained who will pay for the costs of the modification?

☐ ☐ ☐ ☐

## Preparatory steps

| | Not relevant | Not yet started | Under way | Completed |
|---|---|---|---|---|

Have you identified whether your current equipment can handle dual currency? Have you contacted your service provider to see how they will support you in handling the changeover and to find out who will bear any induced costs?

Have you made arrangements to amend your invoicing software to reflect your chosen pricing strategy (i.e., dual pricing or direct transition from national currency to euro)?

Have you obtained appropriate IT resources and considered the implications for staffing euro, Year 2000 and other major IT projects?

Have you prepared a training plan to ensure that personnel receive training in the use of the euro modules?

Have you prepared functional specifications for all systems to incorporate your euro business and conversion requirements?

Have you designed, built and tested systems that have been changed, enhanced or upgraded for the euro?

**TABLE 5.2**

**Assessing the euro importance of your enterprise**

| 1 = does not apply at all ; 5 = strongly applies | 1 | 2 | 3 | 4 | 5 |
|---|---|---|---|---|---|
| We are an enterprise with exports in many currencies. | | | | | |
| We belong to a inner-country. | | | | | |
| We make heavy use of European bank-transactions. | | | | | |
| Our customers are primarily end-users. | | | | | |
| We make extensive use of price-differentiation within EU. | | | | | |
| Our IT system cannot handle extended numbers of price/currency items and decimals. | | | | | |
| We consider the improved access and transparency of the euro-market as important to our future strategy. | | | | | |
| Our customers/vendors plan to changeover to the euro very soon. | | | | | |
| Our competitors will be ready for the euro. | | | | | |
| We have a major calculation problem because of international procurement. | | | | | |
| We do financing in EMU currencies (ECU). | | | | | |

# Best practice management actions, tools and techniques

# CHAPTER 6

# Strategic
# analysis

# STRATEGY

For most of the time, a company's strategy is just reviewed and updated. From time to time, however, organizations realize that they have a need for a fundamental appraisal of where the business is going. Upon recognizing this need for fundamental change or validation, management embarks upon a significant strategic initiative, requiring a shift from the annual strategic (or business planning) cycle into a more structured strategic process (*see* Figure 6.1). There are two main catalysts to this shift:

- competitive pressure forces a company to analyze its goals and objectives;
- a fundamental environmental shift that significantly alters opportunities and threats.

These catalysts are not always mutually exclusive. In many cases, the second is a pre-cursor to the first. This is certainly the case with the euro, which probably represents the most significant economic change in Europe this century. The knock-on effect to the competitive landscape is huge, most obviously in financial services, but so too in many other sectors, particularly those where structural barriers to entry are low.

The competitive pressure that price transparency will bring is significant. And not just within Europe. Those companies which are simply watching their European counterparts should take heed that EMU is also a major opportunity for non-Europeans. Taking a continental view of Europe rather than a country/sector view has long been the approach of some major US corporations. Greater competition, resulting from markets increasingly operating at a pan-European level, may well alter the structure of markets, possibly via more cross-border mergers and alliances. More immediately, though, pricing problems are one of the largest EMU headaches for many businesses as this is where customer service pressures will be most acute. When a company starts to show prices in euros, its trading partners, and possibly end consumers, are likely to be affected.

The competitive positions of companies can no longer be overturned by exchange-rate movements but will reflect productivity, inflation and cost differentials across euro-zone countries. This greater transparency should permit a better allocation of capital and available resources. The greater transparency of conditions of competition should also facilitate the international comparison of balance sheets (notwithstanding differences in accounting treatment), the transparency of export prices, mergers, acquisitions and alliances and, more generally, company development strategies.

The elimination of exchange rate instability and the associated costs will

**FIGURE 6.1**

**From the strategic cycle to the strategic process**

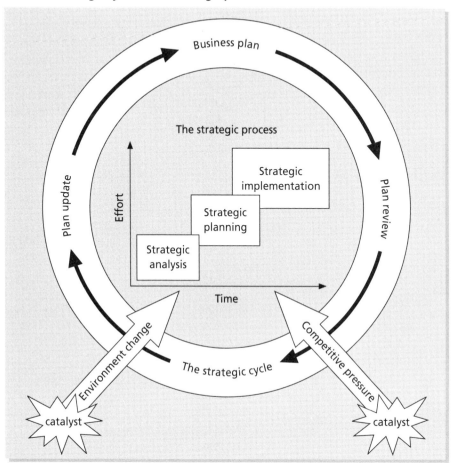

encourage greater cross-border trade and investment and enable companies to better exploit the opportunities of the single market. Further, the introduction of the euro will lead to a more unified, deeper and more liquid market in public and private debt. Firms can expect to see this translated into reduced financing costs as banks and other financial institutions seek to increase their lending opportunities.

Trade with euro zone members will increasingly be denominated in euros as opposed to NCUs. Indeed, this may be the preference of US and Asian trade partners who would prefer to deal in a single currency. Many multinational companies have stated that they will invoice in euros during the transition period to suppliers in both participating and non-participating countries alike. Public

> the competitive positions of companies can no longer be overturned by exchange-rate movements but will reflect productivity, inflation and cost differentials across euro-zone countries

procurement contracts of participating governments, as well as contracts with European institutions may be denominated in euros any time from 1 January 1999.

We are also likely to see some seepage of the euro into the retail sector. For example, SMEs may be asked to invoice in euros by dominant suppliers; tourists from the euro zone, and indeed from other countries such as the US, may wish to use the euro in hotels and at popular tourist destinations.

A company's ability to respond to these changes, perhaps defined as its ability to maintain above average long-term profitability, is predominantly centred upon two variables:

- flexibility, or the potential for altering strategy at short notice in a rapidly changing environment; and
- implementability, or the ability of an organization to accept a strategy in view of its culture.

It is essential that companies bear in mind these two variables when responding to the strategic challenges posed by the euro, including:

- *When to start using the euro:* this decision depends on factors such as the degree of international exposure and whether the company has branches and subsidiaries throughout the EU, as well as demands from customers, suppliers and investors.

- *Benefiting from the euro in financial markets:* managers should at least ensure that relevant contracts (derivatives, swaps, etc.) take due account of the introduction of the euro, and finance/treasury departments may need reorganizing. Further, companies should be looking at how to benefit from the newly emerging euro markets, in terms of balance sheet management, funding and costs.

- *Converting prices to euro:* prices must be set at convenient levels which are effective from a marketing standpoint and, inevitably, some prices may need to be adjusted in real terms. It will be necessary to explain such price changes to customers who will invariably be suspicious about hidden price increases. Information to consumers (be it in the form of dual price displays, extra personnel to explain the changeover, calculators or other aids) is likely to become an important marketing tool.

- *IT strategy:* the euro, in addition to the Year 2000 problem, has stimulated many companies to re-think their IT strategies, choosing to replace ageing legacy systems rather than attempt to fix them for both the euro and Year 2000. Banks are having the added problem that technology is changing the rules of doing business. A recent IBM report noted that 'technology has reduced both the role and value of financial intermediaries, collapsing margins in many banking businesses, including brokerage, corporate lending and global custody'. At the same time, growth of electronic banking, research on the Internet and electronic exchange markets, plus the growth in competition from the 'non-bank' sector has fundamentally changed the structure of the market. Aside from M&A activity within the industry, the competitive landscape is changing rapidly. In the US, companies such as AT&T and General Motors have grown a substantial share of the credit card market. Similarly in the UK, Marks & Spencer, Sainsbury, Tesco and Virgin have all entered the financial services market since 1996.

- *Staff training:* the most immediate group of staff who need information is those who have to plan the changeover to the euro, especially where operations in the euro will begin early. Eventually, all staff will have to be trained so that they can continue to fulfil their professional responsibilities. Particular attention should be given to staff who are in direct contact with the general public: they will need to be able to explain conversion calculations and other implications of the euro to customers. Finally, companies will need to explain the implications of the euro on wages, social security, pensions, etc.

Companies need to prepare if the move is to be achieved in an orderly cost-effective manner. Early preparation ensures that companies are able to exploit potential opportunities to use the euro from its introduction on 1 January 1999. Moreover, investment costs could be lowered if euro specifications have been incorporated into the ongoing capital replacement schedules of companies. In addition, early preparation could avoid the logistical bottlenecks due to lack of skilled personnel in-house or among outside contractors.

Early preparation is equally important for companies located outside the euro-zone since the use of the euro will not be confined within the zone. It is likely to be used extensively for some transactions as of 1 January 1999, in both 'pre-in' Member States and in third countries. Banks, corporates and public administrations in 'pre-in' countries who will use the euro therefore need to make similar preparations to their counterparts in participating Member States.

Large multinational organizations with complex trading, currency, fiscal and general financial management arrangements need to be able to satisfy shareholders and markets that they have taken appropriate prudential steps to budget for the inevitable costs and that they have put in place properly resourced action programmes to meet the challenges.

Financial institutions stand to make – or lose – the most from EMU, but there is mounting concern many will find themselves unprepared for the biggest event to hit the financial markets this century. The British Bankers Association (BBA) said it estimated the necessary information technology changes alone would take about three years, but many financial institutions did not start preparing until late 1997, even early 1998 in some cases, leaving just one year before the start of EMU. Whilst most companies have a greater degree of choice about when to change over, financial institutions must be ready by 1 January 1999 if they are to survive the 'Big Bang' transition to the euro.

In December 1996, British management consultant firm KPMG released a survey showing most top European companies had made no attempt to estimate the cost of EMU to their business. Of 301 major European firms questioned for the poll, carried out in July and August, only 8% quoted a figure for the cost of the changeover.

While almost three-quarters said they expected to benefit from EMU, two-thirds of them said they had no strategy for coping with it, although half were in the process of developing one. German-based firms were best-prepared, with 52% saying they had a strategy already in place. Only 19% of British-based companies and 25% of Italian-based organizations had a working plan. More than a third of companies surveyed across Europe had not yet started looking at IT preparations. By December 1997, this picture had improved somewhat: 81% of companies surveyed had carried out some form of review, though 32% had no plans to conduct a thorough strategic analysis.

> early preparation is equally important for companies located outside the euro-zone since the use of the euro will not be confined within the zone

Whilst 50% of companies had put EMU towards the top of the corporate priority list, only 2% had completed the implementation of their action plan, if they had one.

Outside of Europe, preparations have been even less advanced. Many in the US started by ignoring developments, slowly yielding to a scepticism that EMU could actually work. These experts argued that monetary union based on the US dollar took many years to evolve, and is supported by labour mobility and fiscal transfer mechanisms that are hardly developed in Europe. With so much doubt in the air, it is no surprise that US companies have largely ignored the developments taking place in Europe.

But this view may be changing. There are hopes that Europe could become an easier, more 'American' market in which to operate – the same sort of anticipation that was prevalent in the US and Japan in the run-up to the 1992 introduction of the single market. But those expectations were only partly met. Although the single market programme resulted in single national corporate entities in the main European countries, some of the potential efficiencies of operating across the continent never materialized. Perhaps the euro will stimulate further reorganization of corporate activities into less fragmented operations.

No-one doubts the potential revolutionary impact of a single currency across Europe. Unfortunately, it's tricky for investors trying to work out specific winners and losers, or indeed which companies will survive at all. At one end of the spectrum, some organizations are trying to capitalize on the commercial opportunities presented by the advent of the euro. Strategic planning and the investment of capital has allowed these organizations to create a competitive advantage to make the most of the opportunities and deal with the threats.

At the other end of the spectrum, applicable to the majority, organizations are following a euro-survival strategy – that is, do the minimum necessary to make the transition to the euro – if they have a strategy at all. In many ways, the euro is seen as an inconvenience to business as usual rather than a major catalyst for change. Most EMU impact assessments have focused on the costs of defining and making minimum changes rather than realizing business opportunities or dealing with potential threats. A more thorough strategic process has been postponed to some later date though, inevitably, it will be required well before 2002.

If companies are to enhance their profitability when prices are pushed down and wages up, they will have to rethink their fundamental strategies. The longer this process is left, the harder it is to implement strategic changes as the timescale to achieve it gets shorter as does the window of opportunity. Whilst 1999 sees the introduction of the euro in wholesale markets, euro notes and coins will be introduced in 2002, where the changeover will impact all corners of the participating economies.

Whatever decisions are made, it is better to make them within a structured strategic process. This provides a consistent framework to assist and justify the decision-making process particularly where large-scale change is expected, whilst supporting a downstream cross-functional implementation programme. A strategic process can be broken down into a number of distinct, yet overlapping phases as shown earlier in Figure 6.1:

- strategic analysis
- strategic planning
- strategic implementation.

By merging the phases and emphasizing improvements or changes to products, markets, customers, production costs, distribution channels or other courses of action, an organization can begin implementation without waiting for the completion of the entire process. This approach frequently offers a better chance of success, though the dynamics of change must allow for a degree of pragmatism and stability.

> **increasing the level of effort devoted to strategic planning and, more importantly, to strategic implementation can dramatically increase your chances of success**

Too often resources are misallocated in the strategy process. So much effort goes into the analysis stage that strategic planning and implementation receive less overall effort. Successful strategies are the ones that are implemented, not the glossy brochures that sit on the shelf.

Therefore, increasing the level of effort devoted to strategic planning and, more importantly, to strategic implementation can dramatically increase your chances of success. There are a huge number of strategic plans that have failed to be fully implemented, often due to a simple lack of investment in this phase. Management's ability to create an environment and a strategic process to allow it to succeed is fundamental.

# STRATEGIC ANALYSIS

A strategic analysis, or impact assessment, should provide management with a high-level understanding of the impact of a changing environment on their business. It should identify the resource implications of these changes and the likely level of investment in alternative options. This information provides a crucial input to the strategic planning phase.

There are many different ways to conduct an impact assessment, the approach largely depending upon the nature of the environmental change. The complexity of the euro, particularly the pervasive all-encompassing nature of its impact, necessitates a more detailed and thorough analysis as many of the impacts are not immediately obvious. Further, the level of investment required to simply survive the changes in some markets may fundamentally alter the business strategy and as such you cannot avoid or skimp on your analysis. Just as you would conduct a thorough 'due diligence' study of a potential acquisition, or assess the level of IT investment to solve the Year 2000 problem, you need to conduct a thorough euro impact assessment.

Due to the impact on the business, there are some fundamental decisions that must be made. An impact assessment should not try to answer all of these decisions as some key decisions cannot be made until you have the results of the assessment. In place of actual decisions being made, you should state clearly any assumptions that you make, but be wary of leaving key decisions until too late, as this may fundamentally affect your ability to implement your desired strategy in the time available.

The smartest approach also looks forward to implementation. You can save a lot of time and effort if your analysis provides a framework for actually making any changes to your business, operations or systems. Analyses, or impact assessments, that have been too complex and detailed have added little extra value to a high-level study, as much of the detailed work has to be repeated during the implementation phase.

Figure 6.2 highlights the key components of a strategic analysis of the impact of the euro on your business. I shall look at these in more detail as each component is required to complete a successful strategic analysis.

Firstly, you need to create the analytical framework for your current position and markets, including an understanding of the resources at your disposal, and

**FIGURE 6.2**

**A strategic analysis framework**

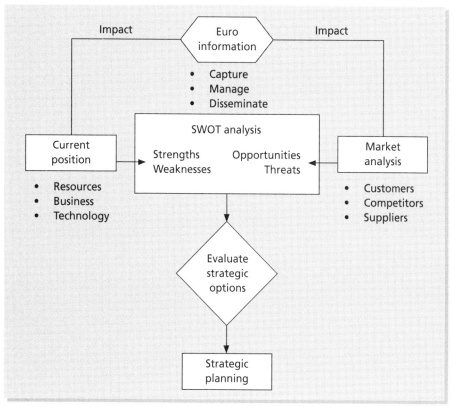

a model of your business and technology environment upon which to base an impact assessment. Secondly, you need to understand the euro and its impact on your current position and markets. This means that you have to capture and document knowledge about the euro in a way that is useful to your analysis. Thirdly, you need to combine the strengths and weaknesses of your current position with the opportunities and threats from your market analysis to perform some form of SWOT analysis. This provides the basis from which you can identify and evaluate your alternative strategic options.

In order to conduct a strategic analysis you therefore have, as a pre-requisite, the requirement for knowledge, either internally of your business, or externally, of what is going on in the marketplace. Your ability to successfully conduct any form of strategic analysis is thus centred upon your ability to acquire and use information to create knowledge. It is important to recognize the difference between information and knowledge. Information, no matter how interesting or useful, doesn't add value unless your employees apply that information to their work – that is knowledge.

But what knowledge do you need? In the case of your current position, most of this knowledge should already exist internally, but in what form? Can you immediately access the information and use it to conduct an impact analysis? SWOT analysis is fundamentally a comparative study between your organization and your competitors – this inevitably requires a mixture of internal and external information. So too with a euro impact assessment, which necessitates a combined understanding of the external environmental changes that are happening with a detailed understanding of your business, not just internally, but also in relation to your supply chain, stakeholders, competitors and customers.

Those organizations more likely to sustain competitive advantage are those that are able to learn faster than their competition. Knowledge creation, retention and management is key to this success. So too is the right choice of infrastructure to support this process. With so much information floating around about the euro, how do you filter it, capture it, manage it, disseminate it and use it to the benefit of your customers? There is the daunting problem of how to manage euro 'information overload'.

The competitive advantage of any organization is most often the knowledge of its staff. That gives tremendous power to employees, who can take their knowledge and go elsewhere. Whilst this may prevent some organizations from investing in training and knowledge-building of their people, it is ultimately up to the organization to either retain that knowledge, or capture it in some way, or preferably both.

Once you know what knowledge and skills you need, you must acquire it. There are three basic options: buy, rent or develop (*see* Table 6.1). Most likely, you will use some combination of all three.

Developing knowledge, rather than buying or renting it, is a better investment if skills and knowledge are needed by employees in the long term. Firstly you have to allocate an individual or team to research all there is to know about the euro. Secondly, you have to filter relevant information, document and store it in a way that is useful to your analysis and the ongoing support of your euro changeover programme. Whilst you can control exactly the format and content of this research, it takes a considerable amount of time to accumulate. Thirdly, you have to disseminate this information to everyone that will be involved in the analysis and definition of business requirements in the first instance, and the rest of the workforce later.

There are many ways to disseminate knowledge, from formal training programmes to self-development media. Formal training programmes can be set-up by sending employees to external trainers or by setting up internal programmes. For euro awareness training, it may be better to combine these two approaches by bringing external trainers in-house. In addition, to help facilitate learning, the

**TABLE 6.1**

**Key methods of acquiring euro knowledge**

| BUY | RENT | DEVELOP |
|---|---|---|
| Hire people who have the knowledge and skills you need | Hire a consultant | In-house research |
| Form a partnership with an organization that has the required knowledge and skills | Subcontract work | External training courses |
| Outsource a function to another organization that has the knowledge and skills you seek | Obtain assistance from customers, suppliers, training courses, professional associations, market bodies, accountants, etc | In-house training programmes |

company must provide the technology to help employees access and re-access learning – spreading the knowledge. You must know when and how to use all forms of media, from CD-ROMs and videos to presentations and workshops to e-mail and databases.

Most importantly, don't forget that often the best learning results arise from learning in a team. A cross-functional project team enables employees to learn about different parts of the company from teammates and from other functions and departments. Use this cross-functionality to your advantage.

The advantage of buying knowledge is that you are fully able to control how it will be used. Hiring talent is a good strategy if your company needs an immediate infusion of new skills, ideas and knowledge. However, is this sustainable or even tenable in current market conditions?

Renting is an effective strategy for companies that need short-term knowledge that can't be filled by existing employees. Someone with a wider base of experience can also validate an approach a company wants to take. But be careful to ensure that the knowledge is customized, not a consultant's one-size-fits-all approach.

Whichever way you choose to source euro information, there are some key factors, shown in Table 6.2, critical to success in organizing, processing and sharing knowledge.

TABLE 6.2

**Key factors for euro knowledge management**

| Organization | Processes | Technology |
|---|---|---|
| • Reduce duplication of effort | • Distributing and using information | • Application of intranet and data warehousing solutions |
| • Enable sharing of ideas and solutions and overcoming cultural barriers to sharing | • Support global/ distributed organizations | • Construct warehouse, databases, knowledge servers, document management |
| • Mobilizing the organization to share know-how and best practice | • Integrating information and business processes | • Harness expert systems, desktop tools, business applications |
| • Corporate-wide deployment | • Structured information for use by business lines and functions | • Establish information dissemination mechanisms including Internet, intranet, e-mail |
| • Common language/formats | • Access to knowledge | • Infrastructure |
| • Ownership/accountability | • Update, feedback and change control mechanism | |

## Current position

Any strategic analysis must begin by a thorough understanding of your current position. Without this knowledge it is very difficult to begin to plan or implement, even if you know your desired future position, as you will not know your starting point. If you have been thorough in managing your strategy cycle, you should be able to pull out the most recently updated business plan which should contain the most recent data. Otherwise you will have to dust off an outdated one and methodically update it.

### Resources

There a number of key factors in analyzing the resources you have at your disposal. These include the actual tangible resources, but also the intangible resource including experience, control, leadership and ideas. You should develop and document an understanding of what financial facilities are available, the adequacy of current physical assets and your staff, and the strength of existing products. You should also have a realistic view of your intangible resources, though it is often more difficult to gather the requisite information. Nevertheless, examples of areas you should look at are shown in Table 6.3.

> any strategic analysis must begin by a thorough understanding of your current position

**TABLE 6.3**

**Identifying tangible and intangible resources**

| Tangible resources | Intangible resources |
|---|---|
| • Liquidity and availability of finance | • *Experience* – of borrowing; product development; different markets; external agents; moving location; and managing growth (either organically or through acquisition). |
| • Technology | |
| • Physical assets | |
| • Labour quality, skills, age, attitude, flexibility | • *Control* – including the adequacy of information and control systems; the degree of professionalism and responsibility of the management team; the adequacy of planning and budgeting; and the degree of delegation. |
| • Product range and life | |
| • Managerial resources | |
| • Customer base and loyalty | • *Leadership* – what is the ownership structure; the personal capabilities and ambitions of senior and middle management; the management style; and the attitude to change. |
| • Supplier base and quality | |
| | • *Ideas* – including research and development capability; the degree of development and/or testing of these ideas; and the degree of market planning of these ideas. |

## *Business modelling*

In order to conduct a euro impact assessment, it is very useful to have a good picture, or model, of your company upon which to base the assessment. The definition of your firm's business that seems best for giving focus and direction to the company generally embraces a number of factors:

- customer targets
- markets and/or geographical location
- products
- business functions and processes
- technology employed.

As the euro may affect all of these factors, it is implicit that you include each of these factors in the strategic analysis of your business. In order to analyze the impact of the euro, it is easier to decompose the company into its constituent business lines (defined as some combination of products, customers and markets) and business functions (such as marketing, treasury and accounting which generally support all business lines).

By combining a thorough understanding of the processes that support each business line and function with a detailed map of the technology that supports each process, you can use the model for two purposes:

- firstly to understand the impact of the euro on your business; and
- secondly to provide a framework to define business requirements, or changes to technology as a result of your euro strategy.

Process modelling is a tool that provides a means of communicating complex business functions in a form more easily understandable by people, in particular the nature in which processes dynamically work with data (*see* Figure 6.3). Business processes are effectively a set of logically related tasks performed to achieve a defined business result. Rarely do they exist in isolation as processes require information from other processes, and they in turn provide information to other processes. Therefore it is important to analyze and model dependencies to provide further understanding of the interaction between process and data, just as it is important to analyze the interfaces between IT systems.

Some processes may be event-driven, typically executed due to the arrival of some information or the passing of some point in time. For example, one of the most obvious and critical temporal events in planning for the euro changeover is end-of-period event. For 'Big Bang' conversions, it is important that you understand the end-of-period processes which must be completed before any conversion tasks can be performed before the next start-of-day process begins.

The level of decomposition of a business function into processes and the rigour applied to the analysis depends on the purpose and scope of the project. Analysis of the impact of the euro generally requires considerable detail as it combines both changes to the process itself and changes to the underlying technology. You should aim to identify product or country-specific variations and to associate each process with the departments carrying it out and the systems being used, comprising computer applications, information sources, procedure

**FIGURE 6.3**

**Process structure**

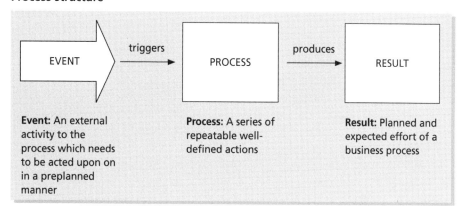

manuals, etc. Volumetric data can also be collected for each process to support the quantification of impacts. However, too much quantity can detract from the quality of the model.

The technology department should build a full list of components of the current and proposed applications and how they are maintained. This can be used to cross-reference against the process-based analysis described above to ensure completeness and consistency, whilst any planned business or system changes are identified. For each system identified, you should aim to understand and document the system owner, the business lines/functions which use it, the main constituent sub-systems, maintenance responsibility, change control/approval mechanisms, relevant service agreements, lead times for changes, charging arrangements for changes and current change plans.

## Market analysis

Once you have a general understanding of EMU, you will need to assess how it will impact:

- how you do business with your customers;
- the products/services you sell;
- how you do business with your suppliers;
- existing and potential competition.

An initial impact study should highlight the key areas that require more detailed analysis of the issues involved and the practical implications of EMU for your business. Try to identify the characteristics of relevance to your company and bear in mind the strategic opportunities and threats for your SWOT analysis. You can use the framework of issues set out in Chapter 2 to conduct this initial impact focusing on customers, suppliers, competitors, internal organization and other stakeholders, even build a simple diagrammatic illustration such as that in Figure 6.4.

Whilst you can delegate this process to individual business lines, it is important to acknowledge the interdependencies between a firm's various business lines and functions. This calls for some degree of central analysis.

When you enter a market or market segment, the objective is growth. If you remain in a market, you may have to turn the business around, subsequently or concurrently seeking growth, although at some point you may be content simply to hold and defend market share. In each situation, however, your objective may be frustrated by competition. The competitor's offering is the standard against which our own offering is compared. In analyzing your existing and potential competition, you should consider both market parameters and your relative

## FIGURE 6.4
### Initial business impact analysis

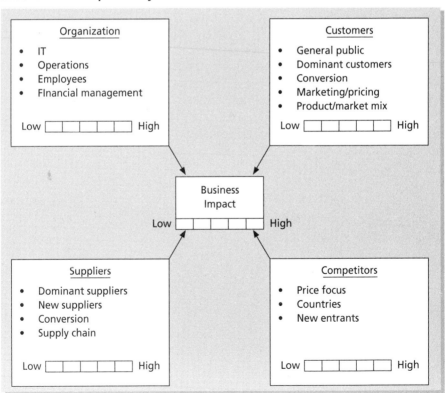

*Source:* Bank of England.

position in that market. Examples of factors that you should consider are shown in Table 6.4.

**TABLE 6.4**

**Market analysis considerations**

| Market parameters | Business position |
|---|---|
| Size | Market share |
| Growth | Share trend |
| Profitability | Relative profitability |
| Cyclicality | Relative competitive position |
| Pricing flexibility | Leadership – quality, technology, manufacturing, marketing |

In any exchange relationship, buyers consider what else might have been bought instead. A necessary condition in a free market is to have a sufficient number of buyers perceiving rival offerings as inferior to your own. If this condition is to be achieved, it must be actively sought through attempting to stay ahead of the competition. Consequently you will need to consider two factors in your competitor analysis:

- defining your company's competition and assessing the capabilities and intentions of competitors; and
- collecting and analyzing information on competition.

A firm's competition is traditionally defined as those firms competing in the same market. However, rivals are not restricted to firms in the same business, as competition involves all those catering for the same needs, either in the form of substitute products or potential new entrants. However, there is a limit to the relevance of the analysis and consequently most competitor studies will focus on key competitors and potential new sources of competition.

Competitive intelligence is knowledge and the analysis of competitor capabilities and intentions, in the form of goals, current strategies and beliefs, should be designed to assist in strategy formulation, including:

- developing competitive strategies;
- comparing relative strengths and weaknesses *vis-à-vis* competitors;
- monitoring competitor activities; and
- warning management of rival moves whether actual or contemplated.

## *SWOT Analysis*

SWOT, or Strengths, Weaknesses, Opportunities and Threats, is simply a useful way of summing up the factors affecting strategic analysis. Strengths and weaknesses represent the key characteristics of the organization when compared to its competitors. Characteristics may include such factors as people, organization, systems, communications, products, finance, credibility and knowledge. Opportunities and threats should highlight the key dynamics of the environment in which an organization is operating. This includes market dynamics, technology, the economy, society and legislation. Importantly, you should consider the wider dynamics of the market in which you are operating, not just those that the euro will directly impact.

Often companies find it easier to use a building block approach to this analysis. This means that mini SWOTs are prepared for each product, geographical location or business line, before being aggregated into a SWOT for the entire organization.

The most common method for identifying strengths and weaknesses, or opportunities and threats, is brainstorming by reasonably small groups, say between six and 12, of senior managers. Once the key factors have been identified, more detailed objective analysis is required. One of the most important components of this detailed work is validation. It is all too easy for managers to believe their own propaganda – is your SWOT analysis realistic in the light of your baseline resources? Is it backed up by quantitative market research, or by detailed reviews or surveys of technology, staff and customers?

Objectivity is critical in this process as plans that stem from it will have little chance of success if you are not realistic. This is why consultants are often employed to facilitate the process and provide independent objectivity, as well as for their knowledge and experience of the process. Equally, external advisers may be employed to provide market or technical expertise when analyzing opportunities and threats. There is no harm in using 'outsiders' providing you know exactly what you want them to do for you. Remember, getting through the analysis quickly and efficiently means that you can get into the more crucial planning and implementation phases.

Whilst SWOT provides the basic framework for analysis, there is a plethora of tools and techniques to assist its individual components – balanced business scorecard, benchmarking, product life cycles, entry and exit barrier analysis, competitor analysis, statistical forecasting, the Boston matrix and risk analysis to name but a few. The detail of these techniques is outside the scope of this book but, as always, pick the right tool for the right job. Further, the tool is simply giving some structure to your decision-making, not making the decisions for you.

## Business process changes

Once you have developed an understanding of how EMU is likely to affect your business you will need to focus on the detailed changes required for each of your key business functions and processes such as marketing, purchasing, treasury and accounting. You may choose to define euro requirements according to your main business functions and processes. Some examples include:

### *Marketing, sales and distribution*
- New customer/market requirements
- Price transparency
- New price points and displays
- Distribution channels
- Dual pricing and invoicing
- Payment handling
- Customer service and communication.

### *Production, product development and purchasing*
- Product adaptations/development
- Supplier relationships and links
- Purchasing mechanisms
- New price markings.

### *Accounting and finance*
- Financial reporting
- Accounting issues
- Taxation
- Interest and exchange rate conversion
- Banking relationships
- Funding and investment processes
- Budgeting process.

### *Human resources*
- Training
- Communication mechanisms
- Structures and staffing.

Throughout this process it is useful to capture and document your likely euro requirements for each business line, function or process. There are generally three levels of euro requirement as indicated in Figure 6.5, one flowing from the other. Strategic decisions should drive the framework for developing more specific requirements for changes to business processes and information technology.

**FIGURE 6.5**

**Levels of euro requirement**

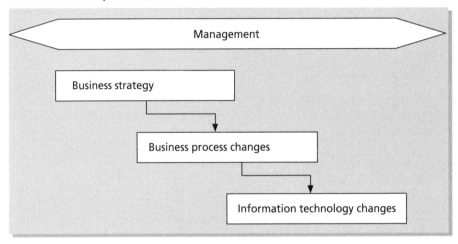

Enterprises should use the introduction of the euro to examine their business processes in detail with a view to identifying how revisions in the manner in which they do business can lead to longer-term advantage. Changes in the business environment, such as the introduction of the euro, can change the functionality that is expected from information systems. In deciding on additional functionality enterprises need to take into account that the most flexible approach will often be the most expensive in terms of administrative overheads and modifications of information systems.

All the data gathered about the business together with the identified euro requirements can be used to pinpoint and quantify the impacts of the new environment and its regulations. These requirements can form the basis for your information technology impact analysis, solution design, conversion and implementation. Your business model should help you fit euro requirements to the IT systems which support each business process. The results of the impact analysis should tell you the extent of resources required to adapt existing systems.

Having completed the analysis, it is worthwhile considering whether it is preferable to 'fix or buy'. It may be a good time to purchase new software that will incorporate euro features, as well as Year 2000 compliance and other functionality, rather than upgrade an existing system. This decision will be based upon the costs of adapting or buying, future business needs, as well as ongoing operating and maintenance costs. For some larger organizations, it may also be worth considering the further option of outsourcing or contracting out IT facilities.

## Evaluate strategic options

In an ideal world, all possible courses of action would be set out for you. In strategy, however, there is no preset list of options. These have to be developed and some creative thinking is needed to come up with a good list of alternatives. It is always worthwhile to include the 'do-nothing' option – can the company prosper in the long-term if no changes are made to the way it operates? Whilst standing still is rarely a successful strategy, it is a useful option to include, as the evaluation process usually gives significant impetus and commitment to the other options. As Figure 6.6 illustrates, strategic options generally fall into three categories:

- improvement strategies
- expansion strategies
- diversification strategies.

The availability of options is fundamentally dependent upon the current position and baseline of the company. If a company is operating with a 60% market share and generating a return on investment of 30%, there would appear to be little scope for expansion or improvement within its current environment. On the other hand, a company with a low market share has considerable scope for growth.

A company experiencing difficulties, such as making considerable losses, may have limited cashflow for growth until it can raise its profitability through improvement. However, strategies based upon improvement alone may still suffer from the problem that sooner or later markets will change, products will lose appeal and competitive forces will erode market share. Improvement alone simply postpones the do-nothing option. Nevertheless, the basic form of improvement, survival (or defending market share), is a key strategic consideration as all firms are to a greater or lesser extent vulnerable to internal and external influences such as competition, economic trends, technological innovation, human resource issues and inefficiency.

Expansion can take two guises: either you expand the range of products or services being offered for sale within the existing market; or you sell the existing range into new markets. Diversification is perhaps a third type of expansion strategy as it means doing something different, not in place of existing products and services, but in addition. Whether the goal is to protect or to advance market share, the company must decide whether to:

- *Move before competition.* Should the firm act ahead of competition? Such a

**FIGURE 6.6**

**Strategic options**

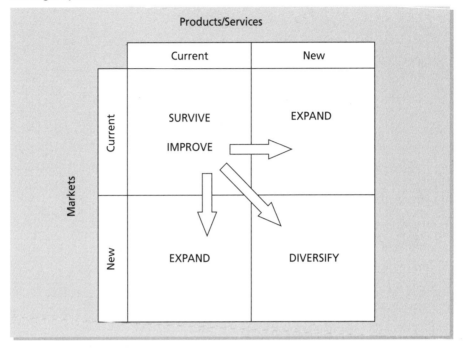

leadership role is not a matter of taste but depends on the firm's ability to adopt such a role.

- *Move with competition.* If a firm moves with competition, it reacts immediately to competitive moves. Such a strategy is appropriate when a firm lacks the capability to act ahead of rivals but possesses the flexibility to respond.

- *Move away from competition.* A firm may decide not to meet competition 'head on' but to seek its goals in a more roundabout way or to seek other goals.

Each option needs to be analyzed in detail, using all known facts about each option. On top of the facts, you will need to know the chances of each option realizing its potential value. Unfortunately in business strategy, the odds for each alternative are not easily calculated and indeed 'facts' may be no more than intelligent guesswork. However, the options should be placed on some form of scale, such as that shown in Figure 6.7.

You should be able to combine your business line, business function and IT analyses to determine the business case for alternative implementation options. Whereas the business line drives the strategic response and appropriate investment, IT determines build, buy and outsource options with associated costs,

**FIGURE 6.7**

Selecting strategic options

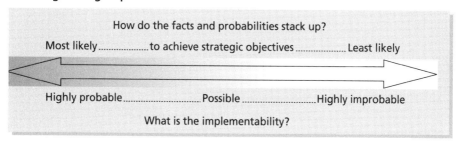

benefits and risks. Good option evaluation considers all the relevant factors, including both quantitative factors such as cost and man-day effort and qualitative factors such as competitor behaviour and impact on employees.

## Estimate implementation impact

The quantification of impacts and likely changes, carried out by the appropriate business managers and IT system owners, should identify the resources, effort and costs, and likely end date or dependency date, for the solutions required to satisfy your euro requirements. Quantification data can be captured and validated in a variety of ways, though the more specific you can be about the requirements for each potential strategic response to the euro, the easier it is to quantify the potential cost.

Your business line analysis should identify organization and business line strategic requirements which may include a combination of mandatory requirements, such as conforming to dual pricing regulations and market-driven requirements, such as responding to your customer or supplier euro requirements, as well as requirements for strategic change, such as product/market diversification. This should also consist of expenditure necessary for individual business lines to plan, manage and co-ordinate their response to EMU.

Your business functional analysis should identify the basic adaptations which will have to be undertaken for each possible changeover strategy, such as reviews and change management initiatives to detail the exact EMU impacts and to develop changes including business processes, controls, staff roles and documentation. You should also consider the training and communication costs for each strategy.

All of these strategic and functional changes to your business will obviously impact your IT environment. Your IT analysis should include a review of your current IT strategy, IT environment adaptability, effectiveness of current application development environment, hardware and software capacity, resource capacity, use of code scanning tools, as well as the interaction with other projects such as Year 2000. If you have a well-developed business process model that allows you to map changes to business processes to those systems that will be impacted, it is easier to estimate the man-day effort, in terms of functional specification, development and testing, involved in the implementation of your euro requirements. You should also consider the cost of running a 'central programme office' to manage and co-ordinate the significant change programme that you will need to ensure the delivery of your euro strategy.

Arguably the hardest part of decision-making is actually choosing the course of action to take. Sometimes it is obvious, but often the choice is between options which are not perfect. The decision in strategy planning can be taken by following a set of decision rules. Ideally, all the options are gradually sifted, so that in the end the action taken is the best action, having regard to your strategic objectives. Decision criteria frequently include:

- strategic fit with objectives;
- degree of risk;
- management values;
- portfolio balance or strategic combinations of alternatives;
- investment requirement;
- practical feasibility and/or capability;
- potential payout; and
- minimization of competitive retaliation.

The choice of strategy(ies) depends partly upon the size of the gap between current and future position and partly on the strengths and weaknesses of the company, and the threats and opportunities which may arise in the business environment. It also depends on the risk appetite of the company and the availability of investment funds, but most importantly on 'implementability'. Can it be done – do you have the resources such as time, skills, experience, and is it realistic? You will need to ensure that the changes are capable of practical implementation in the time envisaged, and that these changes will produce the desired results. This applies not only to IT system changes, but also to changes in operating processes – from price list conversions to handling customer payments to dealing with employee queries.

The snag is that all this takes time and if care is not taken, the decision may be too late – or if left too long – some of the options get eliminated by external factors and not by choice. This can often be the case in a decision to build or acquire. Dithering over decision has left more favourable acquisitions to competitors. Ultimately, the best strategists use analysis to stimulate the creative and decision process or to test the ideas that emerge through brainstorming.

Analysis in itself does not always provide the answer. Equally, you should recognize that the development and specification of requirements for the euro is generally an iterative process. Your analysis should try to identify the various options that you have and select a course of action. The success of your implementation will in many ways depend upon your ability to continue to refine and update your requirements as you progress.

# Strategic planning

There is a need in any firm for business-wide strategic planning following the collective evaluation of the company's products and businesses. Planning for the euro is particularly important in order to provide co-ordination among business lines and functions. This helps prevent business lines from acting as independent entities when business functions and processes are interdependent.

There is of course no one logical objective approach to planning. Strategic analysis, characterized by free discussion to produce ideas and commitments, should produce the basic input for planning in conjunction with suitable procedures that fit the firm's way of working. The plan provides the platform for understanding, communicating and gaining the support of those concerned with its implementation. Rarely can planning be conducted in isolation from those that will be responsible for its implementation as it should be recognized right from the start that those with the power to frustrate whatever is suggested must buy-in to the process and to the plan.

Many strategic plans can easily become too complicated. The best plans readily convey the linkages between the various steps in the strategic process, whilst highlighting the principal actions which will allow the milestones to be reached and therefore the goals to be achieved. They should set the objectives for each department or business line across the organization and become the prime input to the development of detailed business plans and budgets during the implementation phase. At the same time it also provides a management control framework to ensure successful implementation including structure, reporting, risk management and communications.

## Handy hints

### Strategic planning

- A real strategy looks at both short-term and long-term goals and results. If you don't survive the short-term, who cares about the long-term? If you only focus on the short-term, you've got no direction or strategy.

- Think SMART (specific, measurable, achievable, realistic, time-specific) when defining your strategic objectives.

- Commit to a continuous strategic process with plenty of room for change. A good strategy breathes new life every day. Don't expect to follow a 10-year vision precisely.

- Three years is a good time for planning. Know, for each product category or business line, what you are going to do in the next three years. Once you know this, set short-term goals.

- Remember that creating or planning the strategy is only half the story. Failure most often results from failure to implement. And when implementing, don't try to find the perfect solution or fit. An 80% solution implemented today is better than a 100% solution that is never implemented.

## Contents of the plan

For the euro, similar to other major change initiatives, there are a number of major components to your strategic plan. Each of these components should draw extensively on the analysis that you have already done and should interlink with each other.

1. Strategic objectives
2. Organization and business line strategy
3. Conversion strategy
4. Communication strategy
5. Management structure and resourcing
6. Management controls.

# STRATEGIC OBJECTIVES

## Mission

This identifies the long-term aims of the company, the company's *raison d'être*, and encapsulates your vision. It should be easily understood and should define the business the company wants to be in, be measurable, differentiate the company from competition, be relevant to everyone, and be stimulating and exciting. The mission is an important statement as it is a key means of communicating the strategy to the workforce. You should avoid financial aims – this is a by-product of a successful strategy.

## Goals

These should elaborate the key elements of the mission and summarize the key objectives of your strategic response to the euro. Depending upon your strategy, these may range from simply protecting existing market share to the development of new products, expansion into new markets or growth through acquisition. For example, your objective may simply be to ensure the company can operate in a single currency environment, or to minimize the costs of implementation, or to minimize the commercial risks of EMU. Alternatively, your objectives may be to identify/exploit new European market opportunities. Whether offensive or defensive, examples of different types of goal include:

- *Distinctive capabilities* – these identify what the company can do which set it apart. The factors that differentiate it from its competitors. Your strategic analysis should succintly demonstrate this.
- *Products/markets* – these cover the various sectors of the business and define the range of activities the company wishes to be occupied in, including geographical boundaries.
- *Position* – this describes what the company wishes to achieve in terms of market share and physical size.
- *Profitability* – this describes the financial objectives of key stakeholders as well as the commitment to long-term investment. They are generally described as some form of return on capital.
- *Values* – these describe the shared values and beliefs of the company towards which managers and employees can direct their policies and actions. Values should not be 'woolly' statements, but rather firm commitments that translate into real investment, for example, into training and development, communications, and knowledge management.

Strictly, organizations have no goals, only people do. Members of an organization have different and often conflicting goals. Management has a responsibility to clarify organizational goals and to attempt to integrate personal goals with the overall objectives of the organization. Goals are translated into objectives and policy. Objectives set out more specifically the goals of the organization, the aims to be achieved, and the desired end-results. Objectives and policy, together, provide corporate guidelines for the operation and management of the organization.

Management should recognize the realistic timeframe over which goals can be achieved and set standards of achievement and targets along the way. Milestones should be reviewed, and possibly amended, as activities progress along the plan.

## ORGANIZATION AND BUSINESS LINE STRATEGY

Companies can choose whether to make the minimum preparations necessary for EMU – or whether in addition to work to obtain advantages from the market changes which will follow. As far as the latter is concerned, companies should at the very least define the basic strategic framework around the euro. Depending upon the quality of your strategic analysis, you should be able to include:

- *future vision* of how to operate in a euro environment, including changes to operations;
- *major opportunities and threats* for each business line and country of operation, including analyses of cost savings, penetration of the euro market, European product, process and system integration, potential mergers and alliances, as well as the technical cost of the changeover;
- *a framework* to link the main features of your euro strategy including management structure, conversion strategy and communication strategy (each of which should also have a separate section);
- *business line plans* including human resource plans, customer communications and business requirements for IT: these business requirements will need to be translated into IT functional specifications during the implementation phase with particular emphasis on testing, migration and data conversion; and
- *assumptions* underlying the strategy and plans.

Some companies have created a high-level organization strategy allowing detailed business line strategies to be developed at the business line level as the first stage in implementation. The larger your organization, the better it is to do this as it places responsibility for the euro distinctly within each business line. In conditions where a firm has diverse products catering to distinct markets, particularly across national boundaries, each with its own requirements for success and demanding separate strategies and programmes, an approach focusing purely on business functions will have drawbacks. Business line ownership and buy in to the process and plans is critical. The extent to which this happens will directly influence your organization's ability to successfully address the challenge of the euro.

Business line strategies should detail the approach being taken to respond to the challenge of EMU. The strategies will then be used to facilitate the definition and development of business, operations and technology projects to deliver the required business changes. You should always capture your assumptions in the plan as these often have a significant bearing during and after the strategy formulation stage. During this process, major cross business issues should be identified as well as a mechanism for resolving them. This is important as the whole process is inherently iterative as interdependencies and EMU issues will continually be identified, most of which require resolution in order to proceed through the implementation phase.

Much of the content of this section should simply be output from your strategic analysis as you have evaluated the various options and selected an appropriate strategy for your organization and the business lines within it. Monitoring the assumptions underlying the strategy provides a check on its continuing validity. When assumptions are no longer valid, plans need to be revised to take this into account. Your management control framework should also allow this change to take place as smoothly as possible within your implementation programme.

## CONVERSION STRATEGY

The introduction of the euro has already been described as a unique event in history. It is this uniqueness that causes most of the problems. The introduction of the euro is unprecedented in the following respects.

- During the transition period two different currency units will be used within the same Member State.
- Enterprises will be faced with situations in which they receive financial information in both euro and the national currency units.
- Enterprises may be required to produce financial information either in euro or the national currency unit or in both.
- It may not be possible to change all information systems over to the euro at the same time. This means that information systems working in the national currency unit will have to communicate with systems working in euro.

Irrespective of your organization and/or business line strategies, at a certain point in time organizations in participating countries will have to switch over to the euro completely. Both current and historical financial information, denominated in the national currency unit, that an enterprise still needs after the changeover to the euro, must be converted to the euro unit. As such, your conversion strategy represents a minimum response to the euro even if you do nothing else.

There are two fundamental conversion decisions that you need to take. Firstly, you need to decide when to change over; and secondly, how to change over. For both decisions, you will need to take into account all aspects of your environment, factoring in ties with customers, suppliers, European operations, capital markets, as well as the internal constraints of your IT environment. You could opt for a 'Big Bang' conversion approach where you combine all conversions at one single point in time. You will need to weigh up the pros and cons of each approach, and consider how those areas subject to external constraints can be factored in to your overall conversion strategy.

> there are two fundamental conversion decisions that you need to take. Firstly, you need to decide when to change over; and secondly, how to change over

Timing of conversion may be further restricted by your customers' requirements. Organizations with a small number of major customers are likely to find that the timing of the changeover process to euro pricing and transaction processing is dictated by their customers' own timetables. Table 7.1 gives some arguments for early and late conversion.

The timing of detailed preparatory steps will be determined by your preferred changeover date and process, as well as the extent of the changes required. For organizations who plan to convert to the euro early – whether by choice or by pressure from customers, competitors or suppliers – there is an immediate need for detailed preparations. Indeed, it takes a considerable amount of time to fully specify, design and implement IT functionality and process changes. The length of the transition period does appear to provide some flexibility but the realistic timetable available to complete preparations may be much shorter than at first thought.

It has been estimated that, for a medium-sized company with a single site installation, conversion will take approximately 9–12 months. For a multi-site large company the estimate is 18–24 months, and for large banks and very large corporations the estimate is 36–48 months. However, these are simply estimates. The timetable for IT conversion to the euro will vary considerably from company to company and will depend on other factors such as:

- the complexity of systems;
- the age of existing systems and the programming language in which the software is written;
- whether applications are custom designed or packaged solutions; and
- the data structure.

**TABLE 7.1**

**Optimal time for conversion**

|  | Early conversion | Late conversion |
| --- | --- | --- |
| Typical companies: | • Cross-border trade relations within and outside the EU<br>• International distribution and production companies<br>• Associated companies in EMU countries | • Primarily regional sales and procurement markets<br>• Small ties with big companies<br>• High cash turnover |
| Arguments: | • Fewer currencies to process<br>• Standardization of accounting and controlling<br>• Simplification of payments business within EMU zone<br>• Greater price and cost transparency<br>• Competitive advantage with customers and suppliers<br>• Avoid bottleneck with conversion-related products and services | • Waiting for definitive national regulations<br>• Avoid start-up mistakes of others, wait for practical experience and external problem solutions<br>• Keep in step with public financial administrations<br>• Delaying conversion costs |

You may consider flexibility as a facility that could simplify your conversion to the euro, by diluting its effect over a longer horizon, or as a proposition that could effectively add value to your clients, and form some competitive advantage. Alternatively, you may be in a position, because of the scarcity of resources, where you prefer to limit the changes to your systems to mandatory requirements. However, deferring the conversion of the bulk of your business (cash account, currency of trading and reporting) is unlikely to put you in a stronger position compared to your peers. Furthermore, developing and running a flexible environment to accommodate the different needs for you and/or your customer base will prove to be costly and cumbersome to manage.

An important part of the conversion strategy of any organization is reducing the number of instances where it has to deal with two different currency units. For example, you can take several actions to reduce possible changeover problems.

- Try to change over to the euro at the same time as suppliers and customers. However, trying to force suppliers and customers to use the euro is not possible within the legal framework for the euro.

- Ensure that within a large enterprise all branches or sites change over to the euro at the same time.

- Change over to the euro when the national authorities are ready to accept payments, tax returns and statistical data in euro.

Companies need to decide which conversion strategy is most appropriate – a 'Big Bang' conversion, a gradual conversion or implementation of new information systems. In a 'Big Bang' approach, the organization prepares for a changeover of all its information systems at the same time. This approach avoids the problems of working with mixed systems (some euro and some national currency unit). This can only be done by carefully analyzing both the impacts and overall feasibility of completing all necessary euro conversion tasks within a fixed time period.

Planning, testing and managing a 'Big Bang' conversion necessarily involves the mobilization of the entire organization and a detailed hour-by-hour understanding of who does what and when. As a minimum, an organization must understand the conversion critical path and the resources required to make it happen. For this, the enterprise will need well-trained and well-prepared staff. Furthermore, it is important to take into account the time necessary to convert all historical data from the national currency unit to the euro. Where the conversion of historical data is expected to take a long time, for instance a week or longer, additional hardware could be necessary or a gradual conversion approach could be more appropriate.

Under the gradual approach the systems would change over to the euro on an 'as-necessary' basis or 'when-ready' basis. This avoids some of the risks associated with a 'Big Bang' approach. A disadvantage of this method is that some systems use euro while others continue to use the national currency unit. This means that special interfaces between these systems need to be built, to convert data from one currency unit to the other.

Such interfaces have a very short useful life and may therefore be relatively expensive. An additional risk is that of data pollution where users inadvertently combine financial data denominated in different currency units. The gradual approach requires extensive internal co-ordination in order to keep your staff fully on track. It calls for a high level of concentration over an extended period, which is inherently difficult.

Some enterprises may not be able to modify their information systems for the use of the euro, or their software supplier may not offer a 'euro-proof' upgrade of the system. In these cases the enterprise might consider switching over to an entirely new system. This new system should then offer all the euro functionality that the enterprise needs. Selecting the right software package, developing custom-made modules or even configuring the parameters of standard software requires a significant amount of lead time. In addition, the enterprise will have to plan for the data migration from the old to the new system, and will need to decide in which form it wants to keep its historical data.

This section of the plan will need to address the following aspects that will form a part of your conversion approach decision.

- *Defining the scope and nature of the changeover problem* – Describing the existing systems and determining the quality of those systems.

- *Determining priorities* – In setting priorities the importance of the information systems and their complexity must both be taken into account. Where systems are essential for the operations of the enterprise they need to get a higher priority. Modifying complex systems requires more time and effort.

- *Dependency on third party software* – Enterprises that rely on third party software have little control over the functionality, timing, quality and price of the 'euro compliant' software. Therefore, they must reduce the associated risks to acceptable levels.

- *Designing and testing conversion processes* – Changeover to the euro will inevitably combine automated and manual procedures and routines. It is vital that you design and test the integrity of each routine as well as the interfaces between routines and the outside world.

- *Identifying methodologies and tools* – Some software companies have already developed tools to help businesses establish a diagnosis, including switches, database converters, scanning tools and tests.

You also need to consider the quality, structure and organization of your IT environment when planning for the introduction of the euro. In many cases the existing IT infrastructure of enterprises is far from perfect. For example a company that has acquired several other enterprises over the past ten years may have many different information systems in use that perform more or less the same tasks. Preparing for the euro changeover could mean that this enterprise has to make similar modifications to, for example, five or six information systems that perform the same tasks. Such a duplication of efforts can be both inefficient and expensive.

A modification of all existing information systems may well not be an automatic choice as the most attractive changeover strategy. There may be an underlying need to improve the IT environment; the euro changeover (in combination with the Year 2000 problem) may act as a catalyst to make more fundamental changes to your IT environments. For example, an organization that has been using an information system for the past 15 years may, as a result of the changing business environment and new functionality demands by users, become obsolete. Normally, the system would be used for an additional four or five years before replacement. However, the prospect of a potentially expensive upgrade to deal with the euro changeover might be reason to opt for an early replacement.

A phased changeover to the euro at first sight seems easier for IT managers to implement since individual systems can be adapted to handle the euro on an 'as needed' basis. But one disadvantage of this gradual approach is that interfaces need to be built between systems still using national currencies and those working in euros. The gradual approach also requires extensive internal co-ordination. However, whilst it avoids the problems of working with mixed systems, the 'Big Bang' approach is more risky and requires meticulous planning and testing if disasters are to be avoided.

> a modification of all existing information systems may well not be an automatic choice as the most attractive changeover strategy

An additional complication associated with a 'Big Bang' approach is related to the fact that in many information systems the transactions are assigned to a financial period. For example, a financial year runs from 1 January until 31 December. From the start of the new financial year all new transactions are recorded in the financial period January. However, the financial period December is not 'closed' yet because the enterprise still needs to make year-end closing entries and corrections. The financial period December will only be 'closed' somewhere between January and April. A 'Big Bang' approach would be complicated in this case because the financial period December is in a 'national currency unit' year, while the financial period January is in the first 'euro unit' year. Year-end processing requirements have to be carefully documented in order to understand when conversion could actually take place.

Ideally, companies should seek wherever possible to use existing application processes to minimize the complexity and risk of conversion, including tried and tested channels of communication. However, new functionality will be required to process many conversions and this should be built and tested as early as possible. There is no one solution as it very much depends on the internal systems and applications processes of each institution.

Converting financial information poses a significant problem for virtually all financial information systems, even those that have a 'foreign currency' module. This is because multiplying or dividing balances, particularly historical balances, by a fixed conversion rate is not often a built-in option. The following options are available to convert financial data.

- *Manual conversion* – This requires that all data is manually translated into euro and then input into the financial information system. This solution has the disadvantage that it is very susceptible to errors and is labour intensive. Nevertheless, in the case of small financial information systems that keep little historical data it may be the most cost-efficient alternative. Enterprises may also want to take this opportunity to implement a new financial information system.

- *Conversion utility* – Financial information can also be converted automatically, but this requires the development of a special one-off conversion utility. Developing such a conversion utility can be fairly easy when the financial information system is based on a standard (relational) database management system. However, in the case of proprietary data formats, developing a conversion utility may not be a trivial exercise. Furthermore, the conversion may require some extra processing time and hence will need an associated review of processing capacity.

- *Modify information systems* – In this case the conversion utility is built into the financial information system and forms part of the added 'euro functionality' of the system. This method probably offers the most flexibility to the user of the financial information system but it comes at a cost.

- *Encapsulation* – All financial information continues to be stored in the original national currency unit, but all input and output are converted to and from the euro unit. Encapsulation can only be a temporary solution because converting all input and output is burdensome; and the information systems will tend to generate rounding differences. In the UK, some companies adopted this approach for decimalization, whereby financial information was stored in pounds, shillings and pence and inputs and outputs in pounds and pence converted accordingly. Where these systems were not subsequently upgraded, significant problems occurred. In one notable banking example, resulting rounding differences actually led to a significant loss of business.

For each of the possible strategies noted above the matter of testing (at individual module, application and system level) should receive sufficient attention, in addition to the need for good version control and configuration management. For the Year 2000 the testing and integration efforts are judged to be the single most substantial activity (that is, approximately 50% of all costs), and this is likely to be similar for the euro. Some key considerations for determining your conversion processing routines include:

- **Complexity** – The degree of complexity involved will be determined by the data structures within existing application systems. This includes conversion of any static data. Conversion routines, whether manual or automated, should provide the facility to generate conversion audit reports to reconcile pre- and post-converted data. You should also try and identify critical success factors for each conversion process. For example, do they need to be reversible and repeatable?

- **Triangulation** – The conversion process, known as triangulation, can be a complicated problem for many systems, and most software providers still do not have a solution. You should be sure when to and when not to use it. A commission paper issued at the start of May 1998 confirmed that UK firms will not have to use the official six-figure euro conversion rate when changing between sterling and the euro-11 currencies. This will not be the case, however, if and when the UK participates.

- **Rounding** – Particular legal rules will come into force in relation to the rounding of euro amounts arising out of the conversion process. The adaptation of application systems will need to ensure that the 'rounding rules' will be accommodated, for example, converting customer balances to euro will need to follow a defined formula. You will also need to determine adjustments to P&L caused by any conversion process.

- **End of period processing (e.g., year-end)** – Whatever time you convert, you need to complete any normal end of period (such as end of day, week, month or year) processing before starting conversion. This may include the completion of batch processing, backups/archives, reconciliations/adjustments and period-end reports (such as year-end reports). When is end of year complete? When can conversion start? Should you provide one checkpoint for all systems or different checkpoints for each system?

- **Back-ups** – Ensure back-ups, both pre- and post-conversion, are available in case of an emergency system restore is required. This will cover situations such as difficulties arising in the conversion of data to euro or if the transition to new systems software does not proceed as planned.

- **Contingency** – Plan sufficient time for investigation, roll-back/restores, repeat/re-run, additional batches and invocation of pre-planned contingencies

- **Post-conversion** – Check the conversion has worked properly including scrutinizing any conversion audit reports and making reconciliations and/or adjustments. You then need to get ready for 'business as usual' including starting all on-line systems and final sign-off. You will need to ensure that appropriate sign-offs are obtained both pre- and post-conversion. Consideration should be given to conducting a post-implementation review of IT systems to ensure that they are functioning in the intended manner.

- **Systems documentation** – Comprehensive user and system related documentation should be made available. This will assist in training and support.

- **Training** – Users will require training to enable them to operate and make use of the adapted (or new) systems. This training will need to be scheduled so as to minimize disruption and enable a smooth changeover process.

Once you have designed suitable conversion processes for all your systems and processes, you will need to test them. This is particularly important where you are considering a 'Big Bang' approach to conversion as you must test the interdependencies between conversions across all of your systems. The dilemma is that conversion planning will require a significant number of multiple tests to enable an organization to have sufficient confidence in the workability of its plans before conversion itself. But it cannot engage in full-scale testing as rarely do organizations have a test environment that completely replicates the production environment. Therefore, there needs to be a mechanism whereby the organization can conduct sufficient testing to ensure confidence in its plans without a full test environment.

This can be achieved in a modelling environment where multiple tests can be performed and the conversion process simulated. The major constraining factors in developing such a model include:

- the time, commitment and resources it would take to populate the model;
- determining the stable environment as at the time planned for conversion, i.e., taking account of Year 2000, euro functionality changes, integration plans, other development work, system replacement plans, etc.;
- understanding and documenting the batch and time period (end-of-day, month-end, year-end, etc.) parameters of each system/process;
- understanding and documenting the conversion requirements for each system/process; and
- understanding and documenting external constraints.

In Figure 7.1, the conversion of System 2 would be delayed if it required a data feed from System 1. The times that year-end batch jobs finish may be known

## FIGURE 7.1

**Mapping dependencies between systems**

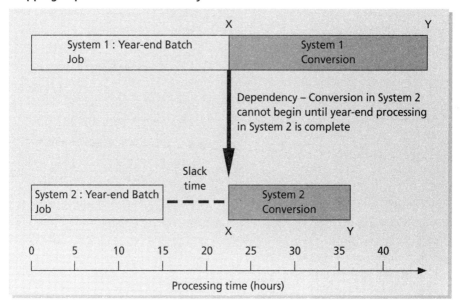

from previous years. If it is not known or the times have changed significantly due to changes in either systems or data volumes (company mergers) then the times will need to be determined. The first step in determining where year-end jobs finish is to determine how long all the job suites take. This can be done in three ways.

- If good data is held from previous years, it can be scaled to account for volume changes with estimates made for any system modifications.
- If no data is held for previous years, then test runs may need to be held.
- If no data is held and it is not possible to carry out tests, estimates can be made based on other batch runs (e.g., month-end jobs) and scaled for volume. Clearly this method may lead to less accurate estimates.

When all job completion times are known, then dependencies between the batch jobs need to be defined and the data captured. This should give the time for point X.

Conversion tasks and requirements, including static data, transaction data, position data and account data would then need to be added to each system/process in order to understand the interdependencies and critical path required to successfully complete conversion in the time available. The duration of conversion tasks will need to be estimated by:

- running test conversion jobs and scaling the results;
- modelling the times from known performance (clearly this method may lead to less accurate estimates).

When the duration for each job is known, then dependencies between jobs need to be defined and the data captured. This should give the time at point Y.

Having determined point X and point Y for each system/process and the interdependencies between systems, processes and interfaces, you can work out the critical path for conversion. By conducting multiple iterations and what-if analysis, you can test the total time taken and stress test the critical path. You may need to take action to alleviate conflict within the critical path and provide contingencies where appropriate.

In addition, you should plan 'stop and wait' signals to allow intermediate reconciliations, checks and audit trails to be carried out followed by 'green light' signals to allow each system/process conversion routines to start or continue. These 'green light' and 'stop and wait' signals should be assigned to individuals within a mechanism that allows signals to be passed between individuals.

Organizations considering a 'Big Bang' approach to conversion should ideally have completed at least two full dress rehearsals of their systems, procedures and processes before undertaking conversion itself. The term 'dress rehearsal' is used to describe a full simulation of the conversion process. A dress rehearsal should provide assurance that the complexity, timescales and interdependencies for actual conversion can be achieved. The objectives of a dress rehearsal should be to demonstrate that:

- all preparatory work for the conversion weekend has been completed (for example, conversion processes have been technically proven);
- all activities required for a successful conversion can be achieved in the available timeframe; and
- adequate capacity and resources have been allocated and contingency plans exist in the event of systems failure or processing delays.

The dress rehearsal should focus on testing infrastructure capacity; timing and scheduling; technical and human logistics; internal and external dependencies; procedures for resolving problems; internal and external communications; and contingency plans. For those firms with offices in more than one country, the dress rehearsal should also test the ability to communicate and reconcile across regional boundaries.

Other key conversion planning considerations include:

- agreeing timetable for testing with customers, third parties, vendors and suppliers as appropriate, as well as internal testing teams across functions;
- logistics planning to ensure that factors such as building access, transportation for staff, accommodation, information packs and disaster recovery have been taken into account;
- ensuring resources are available to test and run the conversion routines during the time available;
- assigning clear roles and responsibilities to perform conversion tasks and lines of decision-making authority: for example, responsibilities for requirements, reconciliations before, during and after conversion and review and sign-off of conversion processes during conversion;
- creating and testing contingency plans, including invocation criteria: for example, to deal with non-compliant suppliers, or a system failure during conversion;
- ensuring any customer requirements for conversion are received and addressed;
- preparing, agreeing and testing communication strategy with customers and suppliers, including features such as a business helpline and contact points.

If you use purchased packages, find out if the supplier of each package is going to provide a 'euro upgrade' to accommodate your required changes. When will these changes be available and at what cost? If you are planning to buy new software you will need to assess which package best suits your needs.

For bespoke software systems, it will be necessary to specify the changes required to meet the needs of the various user groups. Companies will also need to identify all spreadsheets affected by the conversion to euro and put plans in place to make appropriate changes to the formulae and historical data. Spreadsheets by their nature are often used to plug gaps in existing systems or to help integrate the information flow between different systems. Therefore, they need careful review to ensure that they are individually modified to cope with the euro. Unlike software application systems themselves, you will not be able to rely on software house test procedures to ensure that they will be able to cope with the changeover.

## COMMUNICATION STRATEGY

Your communication strategy has two essential components. Firstly, it should be outward-looking by determining the way in which you will communicate your euro strategy to the marketplace, notably your customers, but also other stakeholders such as suppliers and investors. This is particularly important where your customer base is the general public.

Secondly, it should be inward-looking, focusing on gaining support for the strategy and implementation process as well as determining your staff awareness and training plan. Designing a potentially effective strategy is not enough. It is necessary to carry others along with you either because they have the right to veto your proposals and/or because you seek their support for successful implementation.

If you are advocating a change in strategy, you may have many battles to win – from getting your change position recognized as a legitimate topic for discussion, to getting agreement on a new strategy and the requisite funds allocated, to winning commitment on all the stages of implementation. Defenders of the current position, or *status quo*, need only succeed in preventing the issue from coming up on the agenda for adequate discussion by displacing it with 'more relevant issues', by arguing that it would be too disruptive. It is important that you ensure that such self-imposed constraints do not prevent a successful implementation. Training and education is often the most effective method of obtaining support because it can clear up any misunderstandings and convince others of the need and the rationale for change.

The training of employees is extremely important when changing over to the euro. The euro changeover will require that all employees adapt to a new system of references, to a new language. It is therefore fundamental to obtain the full understanding and commitment of the entire staff so that they can properly implement the necessary internal changes and that they are able to explain them to customers. This will require appropriate communication and training.

It is important to give employees a top-down message of commitment. Staff should be informed of the actions being undertaken and invited to make suggestions and play an active role. Employees will have to deal with a number of issues for which they should be well-prepared.

- The introduction of the euro in combination with other programmes may cause a shortage of IT staff. It can be worthwhile to give users of information systems additional training so they can assist the IT department in the work related to the euro.

- In many cases the functionality of the existing systems will need to be increased. Employees should receive sufficient training so they can make full use of the new features included in the systems.

- Manual currency conversions are notorious for causing clerical errors. Employees should be well-trained so that they can avoid making these errors and that they are able to recognize when others have made these errors.

- It will require some time before people grow accustomed to another currency. For as long as they have not grown used to the new currency, there is an increased ongoing risk of currency-related errors (such as conversion errors, mixing up of currency units and data input errors).

Training is particularly important where you combine elements of your inward-looking strategy with elements of your outward-looking strategy, notably where you are using front-line staff to communicate to your customers.

Increasingly, companies and the general public are being informed about the euro and its consequences. In addition to European Commission campaigns, all Member States have been urged to launch information campaigns. This application of the principle of subsidiarity makes sense: to be credible and effective, communications must be shaped by the culture, language and concerns of the citizen. The Commission's role will be to supply information, to stimulate and to co-ordinate. It will make available to Member States a variety of communications instruments including technical reports, question-and-answer texts for the general public and videos.

The Commission does stress that social partners, companies and non-governmental organizations all have important roles to play. Schools, too, have not escaped attention. A group of experts set up by the Commission was charged with examining the role of the education system in disseminating knowledge and information about EMU. The group says that the need to teach the euro in schools is inescapable because of the wide impact it will have on daily life. Importantly, the group stresses the need to provide teachers with basic information on the euro prior to the event, but this seems unlikely.

All this official communication, in addition to extended media coverage, means that your customers are likely to ask you questions about your own euro preparations as they become more aware themselves. It is far better to be pro-active in your communications with your customers (and other stakeholders) than to be unable to answer such queries.

One question is when to start the communication campaign. This depends on the type of business; for companies, it depends of the degree of contact with the end consumer: companies dealing with large, corporate customers can probably delay contact, though these run competitive risks if these customers request early conversion to the euro. Those dealing directly with consumers should probably start early, due to the lead times required, and inform personnel and consumers of the decisions which are being made. Companies could actually seize the opportunity to increase their market share.

> it is far better to be pro-active in your communications with your customers (and other stakeholders) than to be unable to answer such queries

However, timing is a difficult issue. The euro will only be physically available for the general public as of 1 January 2002, but people will start to read and hear about it long before then. Long-term macro-economic benefits such as price stability or improving economic competitiveness may not be appealing enough for the general public. It is very important to point out concrete factual arguments in support of your euro strategy. This applies to other stakeholders. Communication with shareholders should not be neglected.

Fortunately for most companies, the majority of buyers have to acquire knowledge – about features, brands, prices, service – in order to compare the alternatives before making a decision. This gives the seller an opportunity to influence the decision-making process.

Traditionally, however, many salespeople often see sales from a unitary perspective – their own. They think in terms of how to approach buyers, make presentations, and use various forms of closing techniques to get the sale. Today's buyers, though, tend to be more sophisticated and prefer the buying process to revolve around their needs and concerns. This is particularly important when companies are reinforcing messages or creating new messages in response to a market-wide change such as the euro. Key considerations include the following.

- *Determine a need* – study the changes affecting your customers, and find opportunities to add value.

- *Find the best solution* – research the alternatives and design buying criteria that meet the need.

- *Gain commitment to buy* – try and open a relationship rather than close a sale, whilst resolving potential concerns.

- *Achieve lasting value* – buyers have immediate expectations about the results of the purchase. Ensure you set realistic expectations that you can meet, or preferably, exceed.

As one of the various instruments which will help users to familiarize themselves with the euro, dual price displays will play a key role for consumers, retailers and service providers. They must therefore form part of a global strategy. Given the diversity of ways used to display prices, it is important to show flexibility in their use so that each retailer can select the most suitable technical solution for his particular circumstances. This approach will keep down the cost of dual price displays, part of which will be borne by consumers in the form of price increases.

In order to give you enough time to adapt and plan your investments, it is important that you ensure you clarify the regulatory framework for dual price displays. In addition there are some basic rules to assist with these displays, including:

- the use of definitive conversion rates for calculating the counter-value;
- no obligation to accept payments in euros for retailers who use dual price displays during the transition period;
- a clear distinction between the reference unit and the counter-value; and
- the use of existing formats and designs.

Decimalization in the UK – which replaced 240 old pennies with 100 pence to the pound – was perceived as one of the greatest organized inflations of the century. Significantly, rounding tended to be on the upside with the consequent impact on shop prices. This was equally true of metrication in the UK, where consumers worried that unscrupulous shopowners used confusion over the new weights and volumes to introduce price rises. Consumers will also worry that the transition to the euro will also provide an opportunity for companies to make hidden price rises: therefore you should be positive and clear in the messages you give your customers.

## Handy hints

### Communication strategy

Keep it simple, complete and direct
Use metaphors and analogy to keep it interesting
Use many different forums to spread the word
Integrate the different capacities of employees and customers
Repeat, repeat, repeat
Lead by example
Explicitly address inconsistencies
Listen and be listened to
Tell them how it is
Give the big picture

# Developing a communication strategy

Communication can take a number of different formats. Most communication strategies will incorporate a number of different media depending upon what is being communicated and to whom. Figure 7.2 identifies some of the major communication channels and styles that should be considered and matched to the needs of each type of audience.

**FIGURE 7.2**

**Communication channels and styles**

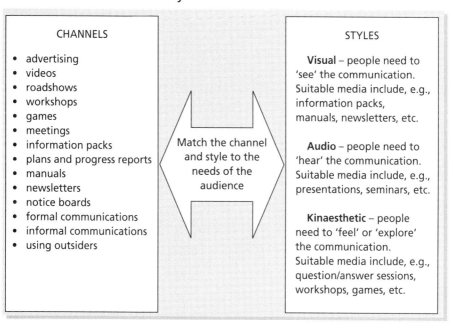

CHANNELS

- advertising
- videos
- roadshows
- workshops
- games
- meetings
- information packs
- plans and progress reports
- manuals
- newsletters
- notice boards
- formal communications
- informal communications
- using outsiders

Match the channel and style to the needs of the audience

STYLES

**Visual** – people need to 'see' the communication. Suitable media include, e.g., information packs, manuals, newsletters, etc.

**Audio** – people need to 'hear' the communication. Suitable media include, e.g., presentations, seminars, etc.

**Kinaesthetic** – people need to 'feel' or 'explore' the communication. Suitable media include, e.g., question/answer sessions, workshops, games, etc.

Think carefully about the type and style of communication that you want to become a feature of your strategy and use this wherever practical. Traditional methods of communication in your organization may not be best during the changeover to the euro – think about the message and what you are trying to achieve.

The strategy itself will normally take the form of a written document detailing the media, audience and messages for each stage of the implementation process together with the person(s) responsible for taking the action and planned time scales. It is also useful to include metrics to establish the effectiveness of different forms of communication.

Change situations such as the euro are generally characterized by high levels of ambiguity and uncertainty. This creates the need for rich information to change people's attitudes and understanding in a relatively short period of time.

People generally want as much information as soon as possible, therefore you should try and ensure full and early communication of intentions, possibilities and overall direction to minimize the shock of change. Try and communicate as much as possible as soon as possible – tell them more than once and in a variety of different ways – ensure that the behaviour and actions of senior managers are consistent with and support the message.

There may not be an ideal time to communicate so it is not wise to wait until you have the whole story before communicating. The longer you leave your communications, the less time that customers and employees have to absorb, understand and adjust to the content of the changes taking place.

You should also be aware of the need to control potentially harmful rumours – the grapevine will be extremely active in times of change. Whilst this can be used to the organization's advantage, in general the aim should be to minimize the opportunities for employees to hear of intentions outside of formal channels. In most cases, people listen to their managers – make sure that they have the information they need to communicate and that they are all singing from the same hymn sheet.

Simply 'telling them' is rarely sufficient – you need to provide opportunities to absorb and explore the meaning of the changes and encourage participation. The more personal the message the better. Cascading information encourages owner-ship, but be careful about timing, and the way in which the message is put across.

Planned communication will never be enough, therefore the strategy needs to be continually monitored to assess effectiveness and continuing appropriateness (change situations are by definition dynamic in nature). Revisions should be made and incorporated as appropriate.

## MANAGEMENT STRUCTURE AND RESOURCING

Management structure is the pattern of relationships among positions in the organization and among members of the organization. The purpose of structure is the division of work among members of the organization, and the co-ordina-tion of their activities so they are directed towards achieving the goals and objec-tives of the organization. The structure defines tasks and responsibilities, work roles and relationships, and channels of communication. Structure makes possi-ble the application of the process of management and creates a framework of order and command through which the activities of the organization can be planned, organized, directed and controlled.

Good organization structure does not itself produce good performance. But a poor organization structure makes good performance impossible, no matter how good the individual managers may be. Consequently, organizational issues also embrace functioning and performance. More specifically, organization covers:

- The structure of the organization:
  - grouping tasks to form individual jobs;
  - grouping jobs into sections, departments and teams;
  - delegating authority, allocating responsibility and determining the number of levels in the managerial hierarchy;
  - the various systems and procedures used in communication and control.
- The functioning and performance of the organization:
  - providing an organizational climate that motivates people;
  - designing communication and information systems for effective decision-making, control and co-ordination;
  - building an overall organization that is responsive and adapative to change.

The structure of the organization often constrains the availability of or terms under which resources become available to the project. Whilst functional organizations have projects, the perceived scope of the project is generally limited to the boundaries of the function. This is fundamentally different from the scope of the euro project team where the functional organization has to create a special project team which includes staff from different functional departments. In addition, there is a need for it to create its own set of operating procedures and it may have to operate outside the standard, formalized reporting structure.

The euro changeover is a totally new challenge for businesses. It is far more complex than the adjustment of the computer calendar to the new millennium or other currency reforms, such as decimalization in the UK, reunification in Germany, or the recent currency reforms in Brazil and Poland.

The introduction of the euro should be viewed by companies as a major project and managed as such. The euro changeover of information systems is a complicated process that should not be underestimated. Therefore, all but the smallest enterprises need to set up a euro project team that can guide the organization through the changeover process. Naturally, the adjustment of businesses will depend on a number of internal and external factors.

- *Internal* – the size of the company, its fields of activity, its international exposure and degree of contact with the general public.
- *External* – the country of origin, the strategy of competitors, the strategy of customers and the preparation of public administrations.

Depending on the size of your enterprise you could set up a euro project team with members of the departments affected. The euro focal point should not be a junior (or a middle manager in a larger enterprise), but someone with the seniority to view the enterprise as a whole and the authority to get things done. It is essential that the process of preparing the organization for EMU receives demonstrated commitment and support from senior management. Without this, a significant risk exists that the issue of EMU will not be given the degree of priority it requires across the organization. On a day-to-day basis, the best results are likely to be achieved by involving managers from each business line, function and/or regional area affected. This multi-disciplinary team must be led by an individual with a broad understanding of the business and a clear mandate to make this project a priority. At a more detailed level, project subgroups can be established so that practical implications can be addressed thoroughly and in a co-ordinated fashion.

It is also important that key business partners such as customers, suppliers and bankers are involved, to learn their approach and knowledge, but also to understand their preferences and priorities arising out of EMU. This is particularly important, as it is likely that your key customers or suppliers will have a significant bearing on when you change over to the euro. Equally, you should consider the involvement of external business organizations in your workplans in order to minimize the duplication of effort and to share knowledge on key issues and how to address them.

**it is essential that the process of preparing the organization for EMU receives demonstrated commitment and support from senior management**

You will need to plan, arrange and conduct planning sessions with steering groups and key managers to define how the EMU implementation programme should be structured. The defined approach will need to balance EMU and other business imperatives and support each of the individual projects identified in your organization and business line strategies. The design of an effective structure – including the allocation of work and the network of jobs – should allow you to achieve your strategic objectives.

Having created your strategy and designed an effective structure, you need a system of manpower planning which provides the link between objectives and organization structure as well as a framework within which personnel policies, including a systematic approach to recruitment and selection, are planned and operated. This way you can develop a series of measures to ensure that the required staffing resources are available as and when required as shown in Figure 7.3.

The concepts and methods of manpower planning are relatively straightforward, though some more sophisticated statistical and quantitative techniques have been developed. Whilst helpful, you must always consider the amount of detail and accuracy required and suit the proceeds to the needs of the organization. Whatever approach you take, you should at least consider the following five factors:

- An analysis of existing staffing resources;
- An estimate of likely changes in resources by the target dates;
- A forecast of staffing requirements, including skill sets;

**FIGURE 7.3**

**Manpower planning**

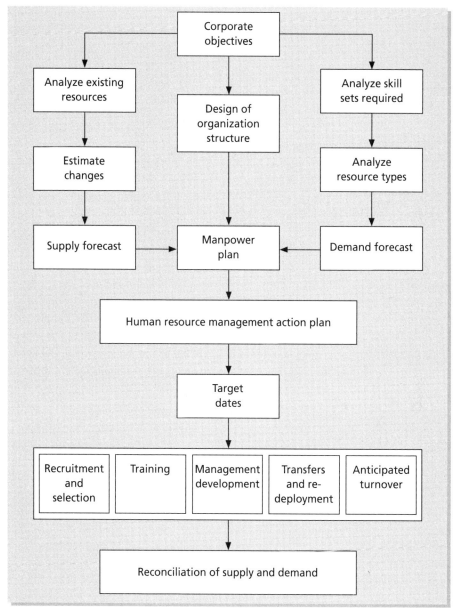

- An understanding of resource types and supply, including permanent staff, contractors and consultants;
- An identification of likely bottlenecks which should be addressed at an early stage and/or which will require external assistance.

It is important that you are clear about the resources you require because if you are unsure about what you are looking for, how will you recognize a suitable person when you see one? Equally, the recruitment and selection process should consider not just technical competence but also, the cultural and social fit with the organization and in the context of the overall manpower plan.

Staff retention is equally critical as recruitment. The costs of staff turnover cannot be ignored, particularly at a time when a detailed understanding of the organization and its systems is required. These costs are not just the direct costs of recruiting replacement staff, but also the more intangible costs of the disruptive effect on managerial time as well as the loss of in-house skills and knowledge.

The introduction of the euro more or less coincides with the Year 2000. From an information technology point of view this means that a substantial amount of work needs to be done in a relatively short period. The current IT departments of enterprises may not be able to modify the information systems, in time for the euro and the Year 2000, without additional staff. Therefore, an enterprise will need to train and hire additional IT staff and must make an effort not to lose valuable IT specialists, who were involved in developing and building the enterprise's existing systems, to other enterprises that also have a temporary shortage of IT staff.

## MANAGEMENT CONTROLS

The euro is the mother of all projects. Consequently, quality project management skills are required throughout the organization. But project management does not come naturally to most people. Since most organizations are built around ongoing operations, and the skill set and techniques required to run a project are quite different from those that are required for managing an operation, firms are often left with a serious lack of project management resource.

For this reason, as well as the need to provide a consistent and co-ordinated framework for implementation, it is useful to provide guidelines for project management including planning and reporting, risk management and contingency planning. A dedicated programme office can be used to provide this co-ordination function as well as a source of project templates, milestones and standards. A programme is a group of projects managed in a way to obtain benefits not available from managing them individually. Typical EMU programmes among investment banks have included anywhere from 250 to over a thousand individual business, operational and technology projects, with each of these further subdivided. In a programme environment, each resource needs to understand what work they are expected to perform and also needs to report back actual achievement.

The absence of disciplined project management and structure typically results in a resource drain, loss of focus for the organization, and serious slippage in productivity. Valid planning implies not only that objectives are attained but that such attainment is the result of planning. This means that attention must be directed not simply at minimizing deviations from plans, but also at detecting errors and the effectiveness of plans.

# CHAPTER 8

# Strategic implementation

# THE MANAGEMENT OF CHANGE

You've now completed a thorough strategic analysis and you've prepared a comprehensive strategic plan. Now you have to implement – you have to gain commitment, motivate and mobilize the organization, prepare detailed plans, create an efficient management structure, manage the change programme and achieve your objectives. Some of the key success factors in making your strategic plan work include:

- Management committed to implementing the plan, constantly reinforced by their actions, with priorities consistently applied and demonstrated;
- An appropriate management structure – an inappropriate structure can seriously undermine the implementation process;
- Communicating the plan to all staff – everybody doesn't need to know all of the detail, but should at least be informed of the essence so that they can play their part – a common sense of purpose can dramatically improve your chance of success; and
- Management information that reflects what you are trying to achieve and regular reviews of progress.

In many ways, your strategic plan is like a story or a script for a movie. However good the script, the actual production of the movie, the skill of the actors, producers and directors, etc., is essential to success. We are all aware of how different movies of the same book can vary from outstanding success to dismal failure. Similarly, just as a substandard plot can be a successful movie through proficient execution, so a suboptimal strategy may be successful through skilful execution. An implementation is successful if it achieves the predicted consequences, or objectives, within acceptable limits. However, the unexpected does occur, so there is a need for some flexibility or, if alternative futures can be set out, you should have contingency plans drawn up.

A euro project is a change process, a process that changes people's working environment as well as their understanding of the organization of which they are part. As such, both the organization and the work towards goals are complex as the end result is a product which is not purely technical but a composite. It combines technical solutions and new strategies, as well as developing people with new knowledge and an organization that operates successfully in a new environment. This presents a number of management problems.

Firstly, particularly in businesses that are not accustomed to working with projects, it is difficult to achieve an understanding of the resources required for a successful project. There are several reasons why line organizations are reluctant to commit resources.

- They hope that staff can participate in project work on top of their regular job, without any reduction in their original responsibilities.

- They do not understand why the project should take such a long time.

- They do not understand that a reduction in resources means a reduction in quality.

> a euro project is a change process, a process that changes people's working environment as well as their understanding of the organization of which they are part

Secondly, even if there is a real understanding of the need for resources, there are often problems releasing the required people at the required time. Usually people in the organization are committed on a full-time basis to other tasks and cannot participate in the project unless these other tasks are covered one way or another.

Thirdly, a project includes people from different backgrounds having different skills and experience. That a project brings together people with different skills is precisely the point of project management; project tasks are solved by precisely this method. However, these people with different skills probably have not worked together previously and this is the challenge of the project manager. Their varied backgrounds, expectations and ambitions can impede the success of a project if no effort is made to form a 'team'. Time must be devoted to providing opportunities for project members to get to know each other, enabling them to draw on each other's strengths later on.

The euro problem is complex with many sections of the organization involved. The required change and development can be a difficult and unfamiliar concept to many line managers. All-round expertise is required. At the same time problems must be resolved within a relatively short time span if the organization is not to be weakened competitively or criticized by the public. In some cases, the quality of customer operations and the survival of companies will depend on how well they manage their projects.

As long as people are involved, there are four vital ingredients which underpin the successful management of change including: leadership, commitment, involvement and recognition. These four ingredients should focus on delivering success *through* people and not inflicting change *on* people. Consequently, processes designed to co-ordinate the euro changeover effort across the organization should be designed to support the actions of people.

Good leaders appreciate how important it is for them to be role models because they appreciate that change starts at the top – or it doesn't start. They understand that behavioural practice, not just intellectual knowledge, is the catalyst to trigger the transformation process. If senior management are espousing one thing and doing another the process of change will soon falter. Poor leadership undermines the development of trust, and if left unchecked soon generates widespread cynicism – the quickest way to halt change.

But success doesn't just rest on the most senior people. Leadership needs to extend down throughout all levels of the organization. Any individual who manages people is a leader and the creation of followership amongst their people is equally important. The challenge is often getting them to embrace this leadership role.

Without widespread and genuine commitment any change effort is doomed to failure as it gets strangled by existing systems, structures and procedures, supported by people who are committed to keeping their heads down and doing everything to maintain the *status quo*. The project can simply be choked by the lack of necessary resources and decisions. As such you should try to create a 'community' where there is a strong sense of 'team' and a genuine desire to work towards a common project goal.

Given the pervasive nature of the euro problem, issues can often go undetected. By encouraging people at all levels to become actively involved in the implementation process, you can reduce the inevitable resistance to change and help ensure that you address all the issues. Involvement can also become part of your awareness and training plan as staff actively seek to acquire greater knowledge and understanding of EMU and the euro. Encouraging the transfer of knowledge between people involved can substantially add to any formal EMU training programmes that you may develop.

Managers must be sufficiently hands-on to give active support, but sufficiently hands-off to give teams the space to solve and implement their own solutions. Changeover to the euro requires continuing involvement and commitment over extended periods of time. Without recognizing the efforts of your staff, both formally and informally, it is difficult to create an environment in which people remain motivated and committed. The loss of key players during the process of change can seriously undermine your implementation efforts, therefore it is important to recognize the work of those involved. This should be a continuous process constantly reminding people that they are valued.

Change in organizations, whether it involves re-engineering, restructuring, merging, introducing the euro or Year 2000, is complex, dynamic, messy and scary – and, often, unsuccessful. John Potter, writing for the Harvard Business School Press, identifies the major mistakes made by organizations implementing major change programmes.

- **Too much complacency.** A sense of urgency is required for change. It is vital to muster the necessary effort and commitment. *Did you have to fight to get your euro project on your organization's map?*

- **No powerful guiding coalition.** Change requires a coalition of people who, through position, expertise, reputations and relationships, have the power to make change happen. *Who is in charge of your euro project – is it the CEO, a business line manager, an operations manager or an IT manager? Do they have the power to make it happen?*

- **No vision.** Without vision, change efforts dissolve into a list of confusing, incompatible and time-consuming projects going in different directions – or nowhere at all. Without a documented strategic plan it is difficult to disseminate the objectives and strategy of the organization.

- **No communication of the vision.** Major change often requires people to make short-term sacrifices. But people won't make those sacrifices unless they understand why they are required.

- **Obstacles that block the vision.** Major change demands action from a large number of people. Many initiatives fail because obstacles are placed in the path of these people. Two common obstacles: the bureaucracy of the company or an influential saboteur.

- **No short-term wins.** Complex efforts to change strategies or restructure businesses lose momentum if there are no short-term goals to meet and celebrate. Without short-term wins, people give up – or join the resistance.

- **Victory declared too soon.** After working hard on a change programme, people can be tempted to declare victory too soon. Then their concentration and commitment lag and the company regresses. *How many project managers spend ages creating the project plan then fail to get it implemented?*

Managerial mindset is behind many of these mistakes. For example, the job of managers is to make sure the organization keeps humming along smoothly. Therefore, they're used to avoiding urgency rather than creating it. This means that you must ensure that all your staff understand that the effective and timely management of change to the euro is not optional, it is an organizational imperative.

A lack of empowerment is frequently one of the major barriers to successful implementation, primarily as it can create a serious bottleneck that makes it impossible to implement a major change programme such as the euro which requires continuous multi-level decision-making. A corporate structure that undermines employees' attempts at change is making a rod for its own back. This is particularly the case for cross-functional project teams. A structure based on rigid functional 'silos' that rarely co-operate with each other often creates conflict within the project team. The cross-functional team is often hindered at every turn by managers jealously guarding their functional turf. An organization's rigidity can prove to be more powerful than top management's commitment to change.

The ability to delegate, according to surveys of successful managers, surpasses even administrative, organizational, marketing and accounting know-how. Poor delegating, not just the job, but also the responsibility, the authority, the feedback, the coaching and the support, is ineffective management. Sooner or later, your team begins to work down to your expectations. Top performers consistently demonstrate that there are common elements to successfully dealing with the one constant in our lives: change. In fact, they go one step further and use change positively to succeed.

# THE NATURE OF PROJECTS

Projects and project management operate in an environment broader than that of the project itself. The project management team must understand this broader context – managing the day-to-day activities of the project is necessary for success but not sufficient – hence the importance of the strategic plan.

> because projects are unique undertakings, they involve a degree of uncertainty

Project stakeholders are individuals and organizations who are actively involved in the project, or whose interests may be positively or negatively affected as a result of project execution or successful project completion. The project management team must identify these stakeholders, determine what their needs and expectations are, and then manage and influence those expectations to ensure a successful project. In general, differences between or among stakeholders should be resolved in favour of the customer. This does not, however, mean that the needs and expectations of other stakeholders can or should be disregarded. Finding appropriate resolutions to such differences can be one of the major challenges of project management.

Because projects are unique undertakings, they involve a degree of uncertainty. Organizations performing projects will usually divide each project, or group of projects, into several project phases to provide better management control and appropriate links to the ongoing operations of the organization. Each project phase normally includes a set of defined products designed to establish the desired level of management control. The majority of these items are related to the primary phase deliverable, and the phases typically take their names from these items: requirements definition, design, build, test, integration and others as appropriate. An example sequence of phases for implementation of your euro strategy might be:

1. *Plan* – the scoping and development of detailed plans for individual projects necessary to implement the required euro strategy;

2. *Design* – the specification of requirements and solutions necessary to ensure the organization's staff, customers, processes and systems are ready for the euro;

3. *Build* – the development of the changes to systems and processes necessary to deliver euro changes, and the ongoing commitment to, and training of, staff and customers;

4. *Integrate* – the integration of systems and processes to ensure end-to-end integrity of euro changes, and to test the conversion processes work in an integrated way;

5. *Change over* – the actual conversion of the organization's customers, staff, processes and systems to the euro, and the transfer of ongoing responsibility to the line organization.

You may also want to include your strategic analysis and planning as additional phases prior to the implementation phases. Some organizations have also included a specific mobilization phase, recognizing that a significant amount of time is required to get a large programme up and running.

Within each phase of a project, there are a number of clearly identified processes which each project manager will have to design and implement. According to the Project Management Institute there are five main groups of processes, as Figure 8.1 shows.

- *Initiating processes* – recognizing that a project or phase should begin and committing to do so;

- *Planning processes* – devising and maintaining a workable scheme to accomplish the business need that the project was undertaken to address;

**FIGURE 8.1**

**Project management processes**

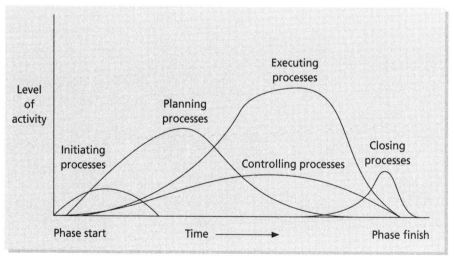

*Source:* Project Management Institute.

- *Executing processes* – co-ordinating people and other resources to carry out the project;
- *Controlling processes* – ensuring that project objectives are met by monitoring and measuring progress and taking corrective action where necessary; and
- *Closing processes* – formalizing acceptance of the project or phase and bringing it to an orderly end.

These process groups are linked by the results they produce – the result or outcome of one becomes an input to another. Among the central process groups, the links are iterated – planning provides executing with a documented project plan early on, and then provides documented updates to the plan as the project progresses.

However you divide your programme into phases, most project life cycles share a number of common characteristics.

- Cost and staffing levels are low at the start, higher towards the end, and drop rapidly as the project draws to a conclusion.
- The probability of successfully completing the project is lowest, and hence risk and uncertainty are highest, at the start of the project. The probability of successful completion generally gets progressively higher as the project continues.
- The ability of stakeholders to influence the final characteristics of the project product and the final cost of the project is highest at the start and gets progressively lower as the project continues. A major contributor to this phenomenon is that the cost of changes and error correction generally increases as the project continues.

Non-project-based organizations, such as manufacturing companies and financial services firms, seldom have formalized management systems or processes designed to support project needs efficiently and effectively. The absence of project-orientated systems usually makes project management more difficult and so the project management team should be acutely aware of how the organization's systems affect the project.

As more and more organizations engage in work which spans national boundaries, more and more projects span national boundaries as well. In addition to the traditional concerns of scope, cost, time and quality, the project management team must also consider the effect of time zone differences, national and regional holidays, travel requirements for face-to-face meetings, the logistics of teleconferencing, and often volatile political differences.

# PROJECT MANAGEMENT GUIDELINES

Project members may not all work by the same rules and procedures, or work may be documented in different ways. This weakens co-operation and reduces the potential for project members to benefit from each other's experience. It will also reduce the project manager's flexibility, as it will be hard to transfer people from one activity to another. Further, it makes it difficult to introduce new staff, as they must be trained in a variety of procedures.

Consequently, it makes life a lot easier at programme level if all the projects that comprise your euro programme are documented and managed in similar ways: in particular a common set of rules and procedures to be used by people while working on each individual project. This provides consistency for planning, reporting and risk management purposes, whilst providing guidance to some managers, who may be inexperienced at running complex, inter-connecting projects.

A programme is therefore a group of projects managed in a co-ordinated way to obtain benefits not available from managing them individually. However, such standardization must always be weighed against the downside of bureaucracy which often results from enforcing lengthy, often unnecessary, procedures. Although many of the projects that comprise your euro programme will have similar characteristics with similar deliverables, few are identical. Therefore it is important to recognize that standard templates for project management have to balance the need for co-ordination against the needs of individual projects.

Well-defined principles and policies for project work create the climate which ensures that a project functions well. Questions that should be answered in the general project guidelines include the following.

- What is the corporate and line management's responsibility for the project work?
- Who is responsible for committing resources?
- What are the tools and methods to be used for the management of the project?
- How are co-ordination and co-operation to be achieved?
- What are the policies for project work, in other words the fundamental guidelines for directing each project?
- What are the procedures and documentation requirements for project work?

A document describing these foundations for all project work should apply to the whole organization – line management, line members, project management and project members – and also to external collaborating parties. It is the common basis for project work and also expresses how project quality will be assured within the organization. If these general guidelines for project work are not defined in advance, valuable project time will be lost discussing principles that should have been clarified at the outset, which will reduce the project's momentum. If you decide to create standard templates for any of these processes, try and keep them simple. The more complex they are, the less likely they will be used, so defeating their own object.

## Handy hints

### Project management

Business is not complicated. Keeping it simple will always be better than making it complex

Set major goals that make a difference and that can be attained (but don't be soft – most people relish a challenge)

Don't let people stray from these goals; hold them accountable at all times

Focus on your goals. If you set too many, you'll fail

Focus on the solutions, not the problems. Do not let managers spend all their time telling you why something can't be done

Avoid large meetings for making decisions. Usually the result of a large meeting is 'let's have another meeting'! Put a few people round a table, make sure they all contribute, and make a decision

Create opportunities to develop your people. The euro offers a fantastic opportunity for staff to learn about project management, other areas of the organization, as well as getting involved

Accept mistakes. The only bad mistake is not to learn from the mistakes you do make. As a manager, if you treat someone like a loser because an idea won't work, you've instantly killed the motivation to come up with other ideas

Feedback. Provide regular positive feedback so that staff feel their contributions are noticed and appreciated

# PROJECT TEAM

Each organization is structurally tailor-made for the type of production or activity in which it engages. This means that each member of staff has set tasks, many of which are repetitive in nature. The introduction of the euro represents a series of new tasks which the majority of organizations are not immediately equipped to deal with. Each of these tasks involve many people in the organization, yet they do not belong in any one place in the existing organization. In this situation, a project approach is relevant. It is an alternative to performing the task within the traditional organization structure.

Project teams are fundamentally different to the more traditional permanent forms of structure typical of line functions. The requirement for a high degree of integration across a wide range of functional activities necessitates a more flexible form of structure and the creation of groupings based on project teams and a matrix organization.

Integration describes the quality of the state of collaboration that exists among departments that are required to achieve unity of effort by the demands of the environment. It is the degree of co-ordination and co-operation between different departments with interdependent tasks.

Studies have found that the most successful firms are those with the highest degree of integration, particularly during a diverse and dynamic environmental change such as the euro. Achieving a high level of integration is, however, no mean feat. It may rely purely upon teamwork and mutual co-operation, though out of necessity, more formal approaches are generally required. These may include formal lateral relations, committees and project teams. This project team is more likely to be effective when it has a clear objective, a well-defined task, a definite end-result to be achieved, and the composition of the team is chosen with care.

For most euro projects, a matrix management structure is appropriate (*see* Figure 8.2). Ideally, members of staff from different departments or sections are assigned to the team for the duration of the project. However, it is more likely that project members must divide their time between project work and their normal duties in the organization. The definition of the matrix structure must clarify the lines of communication and the principles of co-operation. It can also be used to resolve conflicts of priority between the project work and the demands of the rest of the organization. The matrix organization is a combination of:

- functional departments which provide a stable base for specialized activities and a permanent location for members of staff; and
- units that integrate various activities of different functional departments on a project team, product, programme, geographical or systems basis.

**FIGURE 8.2**

**Matrix organization**

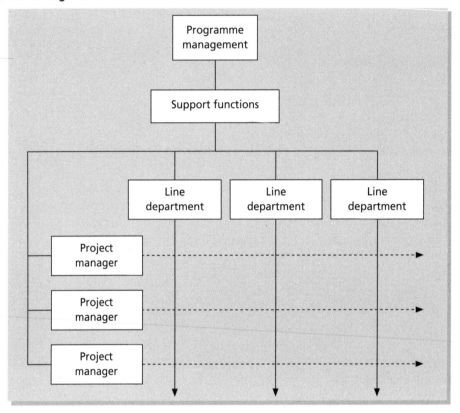

The difficulty with operating a matrix structure is that it sacrifices unity of command and may lead to problems of co-ordination. There may be a limited number of staff reporting directly to the project managers, but assistance is required from other departmental managers who may be required to assign staff to provide help with particular projects.

Given the nature of the euro issue, new problems constantly arise and require actions which cannot be allocated among defined roles in the project structure. However, a fully integrated effective project team should ensure the completion of a task, regardless of who it is allocated to.

Structures which are more fluid in nature are particularly suited to euro programmes which are frequently characterized by:

- the contribution of special knowledge and experience to the tasks of the organization;

- the adjustment and continual redefinition of tasks;
- a network structure of control, authority and communication;
- technical or commercial knowledge located throughout the organization;
- superior knowledge not necessarily coinciding with positional authority;
- a lateral direction of communication, and communication based more on information and advice than instructions and decisions;
- commitment to the common task of the organization;
- the importance and prestige attached to individual contribution.

Within the functional departments authority and responsibility flow vertically down the line, but the authority and responsibility of the project manager flow horizontally across the organization structure, as Figure 8.2 shows. The matrix organization offers the advantage of flexibility, greater security and control of project information and opportunities for staff development. There is, however, the problem of defining the extent of the project manager's authority over the staff from other departments, and of gaining the support of other line managers and their co-operation with the project. This is further complicated when you add contractors and consultants to the project team.

More mechanistic structures, which generally depict daily operations of organizations, tend to follow more established rules, systems and procedures. When you mix these two forms of organization, as is necessary with major programmes, it can be an uneasy mix leading to tension and conflict. It is important that a senior manager is able to act as a bridge between the line and the project team.

However, there is really no alternative to this form of structure and therefore it is important to design and staff it correctly. It is vital to avoid ambiguities between line and project activities, responsibilities and levels of authority. The consequences of structural deficiencies can be disastrous.

- **Low motivation and morale** may result from: apparently inconsistent and arbitrary decisions; insufficient delegation of decision-making; lack of clarity in job definition and assessment of performance; competing pressures from different parts of the organization; and managers and supervisors overloaded through inadequate support systems.
- **Late and inappropriate decisions** may result from: lack of relevant, timely information to the right people; poor co-ordination of decision-makers in different units; and inadequate procedures for evaluating past decisions.
- **Conflict and lack of co-ordination** may result from: conflicting goals and people working at cross-purposes because of lack of clarity on objectives and priorities; failure to bring people together into teams or through lack of liaison and breakdown between planning and actual operational work.

- **Poor response to new opportunities and external change** may result from: failure to establish specialist jobs concerned with forecasting environmental change; failure to give adequate attention to innovation and planning of change as main management activities; inadequate co-ordination between identification of market changes and research into possible technological solutions.

- **Rising costs** may result from: a long hierarchy of authority with a high proportion of senior positions; an excess of administrative work at the expense of productive work; and the presence of some, or all, of the other organizational problems.

It is clear that you need to give full attention to the structure of your programmes. Consideration should be given to both the formal and technological requirements, and to social factors, and the needs and demands of your people. Only this way can you achieve the willing participation of members which lies at the heart of your ability to achieve the task in hand – implementing your euro strategy.

A vital first step, if you have not already taken it, is to set up a cross-functional project team to plan and oversee the implementation of the euro, complemented by a euro steering committee made up of senior management to ensure the wider business strategic issues raised by EMU are addressed. It is clear from the mandate required by the EMU project team that it must be comprised of management from across the organization in order to play a role in:

- gathering information on the introduction of the euro;
- determining the effects of the euro on the enterprise;
- preparing a changeover strategy; and
- managing the implementation of the strategy.

The team should be given sufficient executive power through the steering committee to drive all the organizational and departmental projects towards compliance with your euro strategy and to compel an adequate level of priority throughout the organization. It's vital to avoid the risk that actions required fall between assigned responsibilities or are not prioritized sufficiently. Terms of reference for a typical EMU project team would include:

- identifying the impact of EMU on every department, activity, process, system and interface in the business;
- ensuring timely decisions are made within the line organization;
- preparing an overall EMU programme framework (or master plan) and guidelines to implement the euro strategy;
- creating plans for each individual project within the programme framework and guidelines;

- assigning responsibilities and allocating personnel, resources and budgets accordingly, including the involvement of outside suppliers and agencies;
- receiving reports regularly in order to monitor progress, and reporting progress to the board or whoever has the responsibility for the EMU project;
- taking immediate action to correct missed deadlines or schedule slippages;
- maintaining close scrutiny of political and market developments surrounding EMU, circulating these as appropriate to all relevant departments and staff.

A good project team requires a joint effort from line management, steering committee, project management, elected departmental representatives and anyone who performs a job, large or small, in the project. This interaction is fundamental to the success of your project. Line management will be involved in project work either because they have personnel responsibility for people who do jobs for the project, or because they will participate in or contribute to the professional decision-making processes in the project. In particular, top management and line management must together disseminate information to the staff in the organization on the priorities behind the decisions to back these projects. They must create an understanding of why it is important to implement them.

The usual consequence of failing to clarify responsibilities and the principles of co-operation is that resources are unavailable when required. The key resources are always people with the specialist skills, and they are often the busiest people in a company. Their line managers must agree to release them to the project at the right time. The project manager must use the definition of his or her structure to obtain this agreement. If the line manager is reluctant, the project manager should not accept the situation and try to live with it, as this can simply kill the project. This problem is aggravated if line managers do not arrange cover for key personnel, because then they must do their normal work in their spare time or the project will be delayed.

If the organization has little experience with project work, it is particularly important to give prestige and support to the project and the project manager. This can be achieved to a greater extent by establishing a steering committee than distributing its tasks to a series of individuals. Since the steering committee consists of some or all line managers, it will be perceived as a forum with authority, and its pronouncements will be listened to. The steering committee must:

- ensure the right people are chosen for the project;
- ensure the project is prioritized on the basis of the organization's needs, if circumstances arise in the line organization that create resource problems and individual line managers want to curtail the project;
- contribute to finding solutions if access to resource falters;
- monitor that the decision-making processes in the line organization function

as agreed, guard against decisions made too slowly or too quickly and counteract tendencies among line managers to serve only their own interests;

- approve high-level project (or milestone) plans;
- contribute to motivation and team spirit in the project;
- acknowledge when milestones and project goals are reached – rewards are often in short supply;
- ensure that project management functions at a high level of quality.

It is important to differentiate between a steering committee and a decision-making group as there is a fundamental difference between the two. It is important that key decisions on projects are made within the line and not transferred instead to a group which may be less competent to deal with such matters. The establishment of a steering committee should not conflict with one of the central principles of project work, namely that as far as possible professional decisions follow the normal decision-making process within the organization.

The efficiency of the steering group also depends on the project manager. The way the project manager uses the steering committee determines the results from its work. It is therefore important that the project manager has a clear picture of what constitutes matters for the steering committee. The project manager influences the steering committee's work by laying the foundation upon which the group's discussions are based. He or she must make sure that the steering committee receives documents in good time before a meeting and that each item on the agenda is thoroughly prepared. The project manager must therefore make active contributions toward developing an efficient working style in the steering committee, including:

- setting days for meetings planned at least six months ahead;
- certain permanent items on the agenda;
- minutes with a predetermined structure.

It may seem to be a small practical detail that the steering committee should establish its meeting days for six months at a time, but this is no trivial matter. Participants are often people who are heavily burdened with meetings and missing a meeting can have significant implications for project progress. At every steering committee meeting the project manager must keep the project plan and responsibilities alive by referring to them and relating them to all discussions. It is important that minutes be sent out relatively quickly after each meeting and that they state clearly the actions decided upon and who has been assigned the responsibility for executing them. Late minutes can easily create the impression that 'there is no sense of urgency'. If the steering committee is not disciplined, it cannot expect others to be.

# PROJECT PLAN DEVELOPMENT

There must be a close correlation between the plans for the general development of the business and the development desired from each project. Project plan development should therefore use the output of the strategic planning process, supplemented by pre-agreed project management guidelines, as a framework to create consistent, coherent documents that can be used to guide both project execution and project control across each of the individual projects within your euro programme.

The planning process is almost always iterated several times. For example, the initial draft may include generic resources and undated durations while the final plan reflects specific resources and explicit dates. It is important not to plan any further forward than is practical, but what is practical varies from project to project. In many projects, decisions are made during the initial stages that determine the direction of the project and the activities that will actually be carried out in the later stages. Thus it is not particularly practical to plan the whole project at once, when at the time of planning you do not know what the latter sections of the project will deal with and what types of activity will then be relevant.

The project plan is used to:

- guide project execution;
- document project planning assumptions;
- document project planning decisions regarding alternatives chosen;
- facilitate communication among project stakeholders;
- define key management reviews as to content, extent and timing; and
- provide a baseline for progress measurement and project control.

Given its purpose, the creation of the plan should be a group activity, where the relevant parties work together to solve the task in hand. It is in the execution of the task that people should take individual responsibility. Estimates of cost and time made in isolation of the project members frequently become based on ideal resources and ideal circumstances. However, the knowledge and experience of the staff available, and the time they can devote to the project, may be less than ideal. Hence plans should be formulated to take account of these actual constraints.

Just as important are the motivational and inspirational aspects of planning. They are often neglected in practice, so that planning becomes a tedious chore carried out on the project manager's desk or PC. This results in a lack of ownership of the plan by the parties involved in the project and consequently the plan is never used. It is also important that the various types of expertise required for the project be utilized.

Critical to each project plan is a properly defined scope of the project. Without this, the project may solve the wrong problem, or project members will waste time doing work that is not their responsibility. Euro programme experience frequently uncovers many overlapping projects where effort is being duplicated unnecessarily. Equally, scope management is a useful way to ensure that you have all the bases covered. Project scope management therefore includes the processes required to ensure that the project includes all the work required, and only the work required, to complete the project successfully. Scope definition involves subdividing the major project deliverables into smaller, more manageable components in order to:

> **the creation of the plan should be a group activity**

- improve the accuracy of cost, time and resource estimates;
- define a baseline for performance measurement and control; and
- facilitate clear responsibility assignments.

## Planning levels

It is not practical to use a detailed plan for reporting to senior managers. They are interested in whether or not the project will achieve its goals, and they cannot see this in a mass of detailed activities. They need an overview, or milestone plan, which shows them whether or not the project is on target. If a milestone is missed, then they may want additional information, to show what corrective action has been taken.

Alternatively, a plan that is too broad in scope cannot be used to communicate with project staff. If the tasks are too large, progress cannot be measured at regular intervals. There is a greater chance of misunderstanding and the project members doing the wrong work. Project management therefore requires at least two levels of planning to satisfy the different needs of the various stakeholders in the project. For simplicity, it is suggested that only two levels are used: a milestone plan at the management level; and an activity plan at the project team level.

At each level the tools used for communicating the plan and reporting progress should be on one or two sheets of paper. Managers cannot be expected to comprehend any more in the time available to them. The activities associated with each milestone should also be on one sheet of paper. Project members must be able to see their work easily, and not need to trace a tortuous trail through a network with thousands of activities.

If the plan has to be revised as a consequence of changes in external conditions or because of internal project matters, it is an advantage if not every change requires the total replanning of the project. When revisions are needed, it is beneficial to have planned the project at different levels.

# Milestone planning

In project work, it is quite impractical to operate solely with final goals. It is necessary to have certain checkpoints along the way – these are milestones. It should be easy to ascertain whether or not a milestone has been reached. It is even better if the milestones also provide the company and line managers with useful results. The milestone then becomes both a checkpoint and a deliverable, demonstrating a gradual fulfilment of project goals.

The project does not wait until the last milestone to deliver all the results but aims rather for deliveries in instalments. The milestone plan shows management which end goals and intermediate goals the project should achieve. If the project is broken down into phases, then a milestone plan is required for each phase.

The milestone plan can be looked upon as a contract between the line organization and the project and expresses the commitment undertaken by the project. In one organization, this approach was taken literally such that milestone plans for each euro project were originally referred to as 'contracts'. However, political tensions between the line and the project led to the renaming of these documents to 'charters', as line managers were more comfortable signing a 'charter' as opposed to 'contract'. It is probably wise to avoid the use of legalistic jargon in projects, but the message is still clear. Commitments from the line organization to the project must be precisely described in order to avoid misunderstandings or different interpretations.

> the milestone plan can be looked upon as a contract between the line organization and the project and expresses the commitment undertaken by the project

A milestone plan should be a logical plan. It shows the logical dependencies relevant to the project work. It is therefore important to formulate each milestone in such a way that it describes some form of end point; it must indicate when the work can be considered completed and the result good enough. In general, you do not need to wait until the previous milestone has been reached before starting work on another – as indicated in Figure 8.3.

Earlier I suggested that planning should be a group activity. For group work to function well, physical conditions must be favourable. Everyone must have a fair opportunity to participate actively. One possibility is to use a flip chart. Everyone can see what is written on the large sheets of paper and it is easy to use different colours. Sheets can be torn off when they are covered with text and symbols, and hung up around the room.

Another possibility is that everyone write down a proposal for milestones on Post-it Notes (bits of paper with adhesive strips on the reverse side, so that they can be positioned and then moved about later on). This allows participants to discuss the dependencies between different milestones and their positions in the plan.

**FIGURE 8.3**

**Activities and milestones**

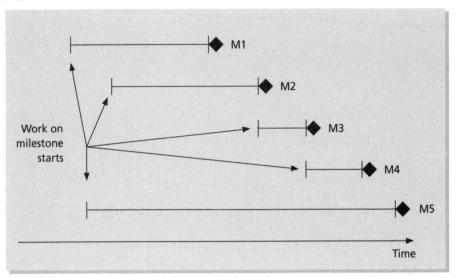

The plan's logical construction should be checked by others rather than those who drew it up. Detailed knowledge of activities should be unnecessary for participating in a review of the plan as it should be easily understood by everyone who needs to be involved in it. Management cannot accept a plan that they cannot understand.

Whilst activities will be unique to each project within your euro programme, it is useful for central consolidation and reporting, to identify those activites common to all projects and assign appropriate and common milestones. You can use project reporting against these common milestones to monitor the ongoing progress of projects and the programme as a whole.

## Milestone scoring

It is possible, providing you use standard milestones across all projects within your programme, to indicate the progress of individual projects at a particular point in time using a system of milestone scoring. A score is allocated to each project on the following basis: the sum of the values of achieved milestones over the total value of milestones to be achieved. (Not all standard milestones will be applicable to each project, so non-applicable milestones can be excluded from the score calculation.)

In general it is recommended that a project is divided up into phases. The point of such a division is that we concentrate on one part of the project at a time, a part into which we can plan with a reasonable degree of certainty. Division into phases makes subsequent time planning more certain. For example, milestones for the design phase of an IT project within your euro programme might include:

1. scope agreed
2. business analysis completed
3. business requirements defined
4. functional specification completed
5. project plan for next phase prepared and agreed.

Taking each milestone in turn, time estimation can be performed in three steps. First you pinpoint the activities which require a great deal of time and resources. Then you estimate the resource requirement for the milestone plan. The resource requirement can be stated in hours, days or weeks of work. Man days are usually used. Thereafter the calendar time is planned and the work is plotted on the time calendar. Therefore, in order to evaluate and set expected times for completion for the different milestones, you need:

- the milestone plan
- an activity overview which supplements the milestone plan and which shows the most time- and resource-consuming activities.

Euro projects have typically been hampered by two time-related factors, both of which you should take into account in your planning. Firstly, if the progress of change is dependent on certain decisions being made within the company, it is common to ignore the political factors underlying the decision, and to under-estimate the time required.

Secondly, whilst most projects have the luxury of purely internal time constraints, the euro has forced schedules upon companies, necessitating in many cases a process of backwards-planning. This means that projects have been given a fixed end-date and schedules have to be created to conform to this finish date. Here managers have started with a fixed end date and then attempted to fit all activities and milestones to that date. The great danger is that the focus is not on estimating the actual time it may take to complete a task but on idealistic goals. These projects have faced serious challenges, as when the actual work is performed the fixed completion date is rarely achievable. Prioritization becomes critical to ensure that those projects falling on the critical path to completion are given sufficient attention and resources to ensure successful implementation.

However, in this instance it is far better to forward estimate and calculate a realistic project completion date. If this is after the imposed completion date, you can then begin to alter the plan in such a way that the two end dates coincide, either by altering the level of resource or the number of activities. It injects a certain amount of realism into the ambitions and objectives of the project, by effectively prioritizing projects in advance.

## Activity planning

Activity planning is the drawing up of a detailed plan to achieve the goals of the milestone plan. It is through activity planning that you work out how to reach the milestones within the time limits and resources allocated. It is important that the planning and organization of individual activities in a project should not be done before it is needed, as detailed plans for activities far in the future are most likely to be wasted. With that said, there are generally four stages to activity planning.

1.  Identify all the activities that must be performed to reach the milestone.
2.  Identify all the people who will be affected by each activity, and determine in which way they should be involved in the work on it.
3.  Estimate the work input necessary for the execution of each activity.
4.  Translate the work on each activity into calendar time.

Euro projects frequently require both technical and procedural change. There is often a tendency in the specification of a project to overemphasize the technical aspects and ignore the organizational aspects. The project manager must therefore maintain a balanced view of these requirements reflected in the activities that are identified for attaining each milestone in the plan.

Because a project is unique, our previous experience cannot tell us in advance all the activities involved. If we attempt at the start to make a list of all the activities, which many people try when they plan at the detail level alone, something is bound to be forgotten. Checklists of activities from previous, similar projects help, but since no two projects are identical they must be used carefully.

Preferably, each activity should not require an unduly large work input (a maximum of 10 man-days) and it should be possible to check that the activity has been completed. These requirements facilitate control. If an activity is very large regarding work input and calendar time, it is difficult to do the controlling job. The reports may for a long time say that everything is going well, and suddenly – the day the activity should be completed, problems arise. The activity is by no means finished, and a considerable amount of work remains. This may also occur with smaller activities, but the point is that here it can be detected much more quickly if the work is not going as planned.

Activities need to be scheduled to ascertain the time it will take to complete the project. Schedule development means determining the start and finish dates for project activities. If the start and finish dates are not realistic, the project is unlikely to be finished as scheduled. The schedule development process must often be iterated (along with the processes that provide inputs, especially duration estimating and cost estimating) prior to determination of the project schedule.

When assigning an activity to calendar time, the fact that a project member seldom spends 100% of his or her time on the project must be taken into consideration. In addition to the project member's other duties, factors such as illness, courses and holidays must be considered.

## Organizational planning

Project work often requires participation by people who are not usually accustomed to this type of work. When they take part in project work, they spend a portion of their working hours on it; that is to say they are not 100% occupied with project activities. Work of this nature and with this type of effort must be organized carefully to ensure that the project work can be completed.

When a project has to be organized, you quickly encounter the following problem. Should people who are to participate in project work be fully released from their other daily duties for as long as the project lasts and be physically relocated to a 'project room'? Or, while they work on the project, should they still occupy their normal work station and divide their time between project work and daily duties? Usually, a combined approach is adopted, with a core team working in a single location, and other project members remaining at their own desks.

Integration of project work into the line organization means that you need to gain acceptance for the fact that project tasks are also an important activity for line staff. When the project is integrated, there is a tendency for people other than the individual project members to become engaged in project problems and progress. Naturally enough, project members discuss their problems and successes with their colleagues, producing increased involvement in the project.

Three important factors must be evaluated before integrating project work into the line organization in this way.

- *The line manager's qualities:* it is especially important to assess whether the line manager will manage to organize his or her department in such a way that project members can be relieved of their normal operational tasks to the extent agreed upon.
- *The project members' qualities:* an assessment must be made as to whether project members will manage to combine their normal tasks and project tasks while giving the agreed priority to the project. There are certain people who need to be supervised constantly; if not, they will always be fully occupied with their normal job instead of project work.

- *The environment in the line organization:* at the outset there must be acceptance in the line of the fact that colleagues will spend a certain amount of time
on project work. In particular, it is a prerequisite that procedures for handling conflicts of priority be clarified and established in advance.

Organizational planning also involves identifying, documenting and assigning
project roles, responsibilities and reporting relationships. On most projects, the
majority of this planning is done as part of the earliest project phases. However,
the results of this process should be reviewed regularly throughout the project to
ensure continued applicability. If the initial organization is no longer effective, it
should be revised promptly.

A quite natural extension of milestone (and activity) planning is the discussion
about who should be responsible for the different milestones. In practice you can
take each milestone in turn and decide upon which parties should play a role in
achieving them, and agree upon the roles of these parties.

It is very useful to create a responsibility assignment matrix, such as that in
Table 8.1, which identifies those people required for each milestone (or activity)
and the level of involvement/responsibility expected. It is important to be organized in such a way that the project has flexibility to acquire different types of
resource at different stages of the project.

The responsibility assignment matrix shows what responsibility the different
parties have for realizing the milestones. Responsibility can thus consist of being
responsible for progress, executing work, making decisions, being available for
consultation or required to review work. A party may well have several roles
simultaneously. It is usual, for example, that the person responsible for progress
also participates in doing actual project work.

## TABLE 8.1

### Responsibility assignment matrix

| PERSON<br>MILESTONE | A | B | C | D | E | F | ... |
|---|---|---|---|---|---|---|---|
| Requirements | S | R | A | P | P | | |
| Functional | S | | A | P | | P | |
| Design | S | | R | A | I | | P |
| Development | | R | S | A | | P | P |
| Testing | | | S | P | I | A | P |

P = Participant   A = Accountable   R = Review required
I = Input required   S = Decision / sign-off required

230

# PROJECT COMMUNICATIONS

Project communications encompass the processes required to ensure timely and appropriate generation, collection, dissemination, storage and ultimate disposition of project information. They provide the critical links among people, ideas and information that are necessary for success. Everyone involved in the project must be prepared to send and receive communications in the project 'language' and must understand how the communications they are involved in as individuals affect the project as a whole.

Key communications processes include:

- *communications planning* – determining the information and communications needs of stakeholders: who needs what information, when will they need it, and how will it be given to them;
- *information distribution* – making needed information available to project stakeholders in a timely manner including the logistics of how many individuals will be involved with the project and at which locations;
- *performance/progress reporting* – collecting and disseminating performance/progress information including status reporting, progress measurement and forecasting;
- *administrative closure* – generating, gathering and disseminating information to formalize phase or project completion.

Communications requirements are defined by combining the type and format of information required with an analysis of the value of that information. Project resources should be expended only on communicating information which contributes to success or where lack of communication can lead to failure. A communications management plan should include:

- a collection and filing structure which details what methods will be used to gather and store various types of information – procedures should also cover collecting and disseminating updates and corrections to previously distributed material;
- a distribution structure which details to whom information (status reports, data, schedule, technical documentation, etc.) will flow, and what methods (written reports, meetings, etc.) will be used to distribute various types of information – this structure must be compatible with the responsibilities and reporting relationships described by the project organization chart;
- a description of the information to be distributed, including format, content, level of detail and conventions/definitions to be used;
- production schedules showing when each type of communication will be produced;

- methods for accessing information between scheduled communications;
- a method for updating and refining the communications management plan as the project progresses and develops.

The euro project, relative to other projects, can be particularly demanding on managers' time due to the need to be fully informed about new events, new decisions (internal and external), and the need to share ideas and formulate solutions. This makes it all the more important to design and implement effective project communications. If you strip away time spent travelling, reading, attending meetings, reporting, the average manager spends probably less than 30% of his or her day actually getting the job done. This is an important factor when designing any form of communication strategy.

Creating effective project communications can save a huge amount of time by cutting out the irrelevant material that managers often spend time reading. E-mail, whilst it has many benefits, is often badly utilized. In many cases, it becomes the only channel of communication. How many irrelevant e-mails do you receive every day? Do you read them, just to check? Or do you delete them, and miss that one important message? How many distribution lists do you really need to be on? One set of managers within the global programme office at a major US investment bank estimated they spent, on average, two hours every day just ploughing through the sea of e-mails. Anything remotely related to the EMU programme was sent to everybody. Quite simply, this was a waste of time for most recipients concerned.

Creating a suitable management structure and planning effective meetings can save a lot of wasted time in meetings. How many irrelevant meetings have you attended recently? Why do you go – manager pressure, peer pressure, you feel you ought to just in case something important is said? Attending a two-hour global meeting for the sake of two minutes' useful information can be quite frustrating. So too, with too much bureaucracy in reporting. How many reports, spreadsheets, project plans have you filled in or created recently that have either been scrapped, binned, changed or seem totally irrelevant?

What about travelling? How much time do you spend, in today's world of global communications, travelling to overseas offices? Is this really necessary? What are the alternatives?

When you add up the time and the cost of ineffective communication, either by attending meetings, travelling, reading or whatever, you can see just how much time, and money, is wasted. As a simple test, log your time spent doing each of these activities for one week and analyze the results – you might be quite surprised.

# PROJECT CONTROLS

Control often has an emotive connotation and is interpreted in a negative manner to suggest direction or command by the giving of orders. Control is not only a function of the formal organization and a hierarchical structure of authority. It is also a function of interpersonal influence. Control systems should have positive effects providing they are designed and implemented in a constructive way. This places emphasis on the exchange of information and feedback and comparison of actual results against planned targets. At the same time, management need to exercise 'control' over the behaviour and actions of staff in order to ensure a satisfactory level of organizational performance.

Control is more than just monitoring and reporting progress. In many projects, control merely means writing a few familiar quotes to the project manager on the current status, or extending some lines on a bar chart to show how far the project has progressed. Perhaps the project manager reads what he gets and then conscientiously files the report, but that is where it ends. Reporting becomes a ritual you do because you are told to, rather than an activity you take seriously. Serious control means evaluating the consequences of deviations from the plan and acting upon them, often referred to as corrective action.

There are five essential elements in a management control system:

- planning what is desired;
- establishing standards of performance;
- monitoring actual performance;
- comparing actual achievement against the planned target; and
- taking corrective action.

With most forms of control, the difficulty lies in generating appropriate criteria for achievement, particularly where project scope is continually changing, and then monitoring the output against target. As organizations, and especially projects, grow in size and technological complexity, a heavy centralized approach becomes increasingly difficult to maintain.

Whatever control mechanisms are employed, for a control system to be meaningful it must be understood by those involved in its operation. Project management must have the ability to make decisions based on the reports they receive, otherwise all reporting is in vain. The level of sophistication should be related to the nature of the activities involved and to the technical competence of the staff. Key characteristics of an effective control system include the following.

- *Decision centres* – The information should enable managers to control their area of responsibility, and should be presented in a form which shows clearly when corrective action is required.

- *Reporting deviations quickly* – whereby project reporting effectively communicates to management where actual performance differs from that planned.
- *Critical activities* – Attention should be drawn to critical success factors. An unnecessary number of controls over relatively unimportant activities can do more harm than good.
- *Flexibility* – As projects are dynamic, so too ought the control systems to be. Whilst you should periodically review your control process, too much change can be damaging, as it is difficult to score when there are moving goal posts.
- *The human factor* – Control often provokes an emotional response from those affected, particularly where corrective action is taken, and the management challenge is to ensure staff remain well-motivated. Motivation is a function of the relationship between the effort expended and how far the outcome is related to reward. Rewards may come in the form of recognition for a satisfactory level of attainment as well as financial rewards.

## Performance reporting

Whilst it is beneficial to have informal conversations on a project, because it aids creative communication, effective control requires that some communication must occur formally, at regular intervals. If not, staff lose respect for the review process and control will be ineffective. It is also important that the reporting and control discussions occur between people who are responsible for the tasks. Performance reporting involves collecting and disseminating performance information in order to provide stakeholders with information about how resources are being used to achieve project objectives. This process includes:

- *Status reporting* – describing where the project now stands;
- *Progress reporting* – describing what the project team has accomplished;
- *Forecasting* – predicting future project status and progress.

The frequency of reporting depends on the level. Reports can be less frequent at the milestone level than at the detailed activity level because of the longer time horizon. It is more important that variances can be detected quickly at detail level so that corrective measures can be introduced before these variances have gone on too long. In general, it is recommended that monthly reporting and control at the milestone level and every 14 days at the activity level is appropriate. Performance reporting should generally provide information on the following matters.

- *Use of resources* – it is important to ascertain whether one has used, or will use, the resources stated in the plan, i.e., actual resources used to the present and outstanding requirement for resources. In general it is easier to give a good estimate of the outstanding requirement than to give a percentage estimate of completion.

- *Time schedule* – this identifies whether the project is on schedule, i.e., whether the activity or milestone will be completed on time.

- *Cost* – this should track project costs versus budget, showing reasons for variances (these are usually a combination of resource, time and scope variances).

- *Quality* – one of the most frequent causes of delays in projects is that the original quality of the work is not good enough. Work may have been executed inaccurately or incompletely, so that it has to be repeated. This is therefore grounds for asking for a report on whether the quality is approved (or signed-off).

- *Project responsibilities* – ideally, you should have a responsibility assignment matrix defining precisely who should perform the various roles in connection with an activity or milestone. It is important that you have a report on whether the work pattern described by the matrix is essentially being followed, or whether there are any variances.

- *Scope changes/additions* – when evaluating the use of resources, cost and project progress, one needs to know whether the work was done according to the original plan, or whether changes or additions were introduced.

- *Special problems (issues)* – this part of the report is generally more free-format allowing the project manager to expand upon issues or problems in the project. However, simply providing a description of the problem is not enough. The project manager should also identify the cause, the consequences and a suggested action.

A simple system to summarize the combined result of these variables to monitor overall progress of your projects could use the following progress assessment indicators:

- RED – project in trouble or unrecoverable within current plan, e.g., deliverable late or missed, over budget, low quality.

- AMBER – caution or recoverable within current plan, e.g., expected to miss deliverables or experiencing problems.

- GREEN – project on track or finished.

Many projects, including the euro, also require information on risk, as we shall see later. It is an important principle that reporting should occur on a document which also shows the actual plan. Each time a report is made, it must subsequently be compared with the plan. This ensures that one keeps to the point. It is better to keep the reports brief since it is generally taken for granted that the report only provides a starting point for a dialogue, where there is a closer examination of what the real problems in the project are. Crucially, the report should provide the person responsible for control with a good basis for further work and/or corrective action.

Whilst the criteria listed above are important for control at the activity level, reporting at the milestone level can be produced at a higher level. The milestone plan is the project's global plan. The milestone report should be a concise account from the project manager to the project sponsor, steering committee and key people in the line organization. The idea is not that they should have a great deal to read, but that they should be able to see at a glance where the project or programme stands. If there are serious problems, they require elaboration in the form of memos and discussions.

## Risk management

Both EMU and Year 2000 programmes are characterized by the need to change a significant number of business processes and systems, a fixed end date, considerable external constraints from regulatory requirements to supplier interfaces, and global impact. These characteristics, coupled with a general lack of major programme management expertise means that programme risk management is essential. How many projects, of considerably smaller scale and complexity, do you know that have failed to deliver on time and on budget? 'Too many', is the likely answer to this question.

Project reporting has often indicated that there is far more work planned to be done than resources, time and management complexity permit. In addition, there is generally a lack of information for managers to prioritize within programmes, let alone across programmes such as EMU and Year 2000. Where there is a high proportion of business-critical applications, this is a significant issue for managers. There is a clear need for risk information to enable decision-making.

It is important that decisions are made within a predefined overall framework, not just on a project by project or application by application basis. This is because an individual project in one location may be tied to many applications with different levels of business risk, and these applications may be in different phases of implementation and have differing levels of implementation risk. It is preferable to use any kind of risk assessment consistently across each major programme where IT applications are involved, e.g., EMU and Year 2000.

Some organizations have created a specific risk management function to support their euro programmes. This function usually takes a pro-active role by ensuring risks are adequately identified, classified, monitored and controlled. Working as a small team, they often help address cross-programme issues such as resourcing and planning, whilst providing recommendations for mitigating actions and contingency plans, including de-scoping or stopping projects, a reallocation of resources and changes to management responsibilities.

Two aspects of risk should be identified and managed within each of the projects that comprise your euro programme. Firstly, business risk which reflects the priority of the project to your organization's business strategy. Secondly, implementation risk which reflects the risk that you will not successfully complete the project. Typical sources of implementation risk include changes in requirements, design errors and omissions, poorly defined or understood roles and responsibilities, poor estimates and insufficiently skilled or numbers of staff.

Whilst the level of business risk often remains fairly static, unless there is a major shift in business strategy, implementation risk is dynamic. There is the opportunity to deliver ahead of schedule (thus minimizing risk), or contingency time in a project's critical path is used (thereby reducing confidence and hence increasing risk). This means that it is important that levels of implementation risk should be periodically reviewed and updated.

## Business risk

Business risk identifies the priority of each application and/or project in your programme relative to the organization's business strategy. A simple classification for IT applications could be as follows:

- *Survival* – systems which directly support core business activities which cannot be undertaken via manual workarounds for even short periods;

- *Critical* – systems which are core to the business or are used extensively by customers where failure could be tolerated for a fixed period without losing control of the business;

- *Desirable* – systems which facilitate operation of key margin or revenue enhancing business operations, but which could not be recovered after a longer term period of manual operation; or systems which are used by and preferred by customers but they are not dependent upon;

- *Other* – systems which are used internally which could be replaced by manual operation for an indefinite period, albeit at increased operational cost, or which could be readily outsourced, or which relate exclusively to marginal non-strategic business.

Whatever classification you choose, it is important that it is agreed at the initiation of the project and maintained in some form of static data source. Business criticality assessments also need to be allocated to projects which do not directly impact IT applications, including:

- *Technology management projects* – for example, base technology upgrades, which could be rated depending on the applications they impact, or have an alternative specific assessment devised for them;

- *Business process projects* – rated either depending upon the IT applications to which the business process relates or according to the priority of the business line to which it relates.

## Implementation risk

It is important to identify the level of implementation risk for each application and/or project within each major programme reflecting the impact of identified implementation risks on each application or project. The intention is to identify the aspects of projects that are particularly exposed to risk, so that the project manager can assess whether he or she wants to take action. When the completion date is an absolute deadline, a risk assessment must be as comprehensive as possible. In addition, the possibilities for reducing the level of ambition along the way should be evaluated, in case you fall behind schedule. Here are some examples of typical implementation risks.

- *The plan itself may have aspects of risk.* Is the progress plan based on a realistic view of resource requirements, access to resources and calendar time? Inadequate planning may lead to gaps in the plan or bravado on the part of a project manager may give rise to excessively optimistic plans. Projects often have a slow start, while the progress plan is based on a fast pace from day one. Has the scope of the project been described in such a way that it will not grow out of control? An ineffective change management process can allow scope and plans to shift without authorization reducing the effectiveness of performance reporting.

- *Technical areas of high risk*, including internal dependencies such as the availability of adequate documentation and IT infrastructure capacity (particularly for testing), and external dependencies such as reliance on third party suppliers.

- *Decisions are often critical for progress.* Which decisions are most important in the project? What happens if these are not made in time or if they must be made again? Can the project live with the decision-making structure and still meet deadlines? Are decisions likely to be communicated as and when they are made and how are inconsistent messages handled? Is there a poor level of management commitment, in terms of visibility, continuity, decision-making and leadership?

- *Resource requirement estimates are always an area of risk.* Which resource estimates are most critical in relation to elapsed time? When assessing risks is it sufficient to concentrate on milestones which require a high level of resource input? It may be necessary to obtain minium and maximum estimates for activities most exposed to risk. This gives an indication of the sensitivity of these activities.

- *Access to appropriate resources and skills.* Review skill sets required (particularly for remediation, implementation and ongoing support of new technologies). Can complete loyalty to the plan from the line be counted on, or will there be resistance? Will the project be regarded as important by key experts, or will they downgrade project work in favour of everyday line work? Are there particular areas that are vulnerable if all the required expertise is not obtained?

A risk assessment should be carried out during the initiation stage of each project and reviewed or redone as each new project phase starts. The identified risks must be assessed and an action plan agreed, including the probability and the impact on the plan or cost if appropriate. During the assessment process for each project you can assign scores to each risk as a way of weighting the level of implementation risk within each project.

A simple method of weighting uses the two variables, probability and impact, such as those shown in Table 8.2. Multiplying the assignment of probability and impact scores gives a priority weighting to that risk. For example, if you deem that, for example, the risk that a project will not have access to a skilled resource is likely (score 3) and the impact of that risk occurring is severe (score 4), then this identified risk has a score of 12.

**TABLE 8.2**

**Weighting levels of implementation risk**

| Score | Probability of occurrence | Impact of occurrence |
|:---:|:---:|:---:|
| 5 | Certain | Catastrophic |
| 4 | Highly likely | Severe |
| 3 | Likely | Medium |
| 2 | Possible | Low |
| 1 | Unlikely | Minor |

Projects should then be given a risk classification based upon the combined effect of the scores of each risk type. A simple classification could be Low, Medium and High. Each category could reflect a range of scores calculated by multiplying relevant scores from each identified risk that impacts the project. Whatever method is used, the level of implementation risk assigned should reflect the overall level of confidence that the deadline for implementation will be met.

The assignment of scores is a necessarily subjective process, but it creates a consistent and logical framework for determining the level of risk within a project. Some organizations have created a standard template of risk types for which scores are assigned to each project in order to consistently determine the project's implementation risk profile, i.e., low, medium or high.

This information can be used in two ways. Firstly to identify projects which may need a greater degree of supervision and/or further action if they are to be completed successfully. Secondly, to identify key programme risks requiring further action. Those risks scoring, say, 16 and above, require specific focus and mitigating action. These key risks may require swift escalation through the management structure to ensure continuing pro-active management of programme risks. This will reduce the implementation risk across all projects.

Responses to risks generally fall into three categories:

- *Avoidance* – eliminating a specific risk usually by eliminating the cause. The project management team can never eliminate all risk, but specific risk events can often be eliminated;

- *Mitigation* – reducing the expected impact of a risk event by reducing the probability of occurrence;

- *Acceptance* – accepting the consequences. Acceptance can be active (e.g., by developing a contingency plan to execute should the risk event occur) or passive (e.g., by accepting a delayed completion date if some activites overrun).

The risk management action plan should document the procedures that will be used to manage risk throughout the project. In addition to documenting the results of the risk identification and risk quantification processes, it should cover who is responsible for managing various areas of risk, how the initial identification and quantification outputs will be maintained, how contingency plans will be implemented, and how risk will be periodically reviewed.

Combining an effective classification of the two types of risk (business and implementation risk) across projects (and even programmes such as EMU and Year 2000) allows you to focus on those projects that have the greatest impact on your business in the event of project failure and identifies the key risks that you need to respond to.

One method used to combine the classification of business risk and implementation risk within each project is to create a risk management matrix, such as the one shown in Table 8.3. As each new project is initiated, classifications of each risk are assigned to the project and logged in the matrix. This allows the programme management team to view and manage the project relative to all other projects underway. Management can focus on those survival and critical projects with high implementation risk (Projects 2 and 4 in Table 8.3), whilst maintaining a watch on medium and low risk and non-critical projects. Contingency plans can be prepared and effort prioritized for business critical projects, with subsequent effort on high risk projects. This tool may also be used to re-

**TABLE 8.3**

**Risk management matrix**

| Implementation risk<br>Business risk | Low | Medium | High |
|---|---|---|---|
| Survival | Project 1 | | Project 2 |
| Critical | | Project 3 | Project 4 |
| Desirable | Project 5 | | |
| Other | Project 6 | Project 7 | |

allocate resources from non-critical projects to critical projects, or from low risk to high risk.

## Change control

Throughout the life of the project plan, change requests are often identified while the work of the project is being done. Frequently, these are due to an error or omission in defining the scope of the project. Overall change control is concerned with (a) influencing the factors which create changes to ensure that changes are beneficial, (b) determining that a change has occurred and (c) managing the actual changes when and as they occur. Overall change control requires maintaining the integrity of the performance measurement baselines – all approved changes should be reflected in the project plan, but only project scope changes will affect the performance measurement baselines.

A change control system is a collection of formal, documented procedures that defines the steps by which official project documents may be changed. It includes the paperwork, tracking systems and approval levels necessary for authorizing changes. In many cases your organization may have a change control system that can be adopted for use by the euro project team. Otherwise the project team will have to create one. An example is shown in Figure 8.4. Key factors to consider include:

- ensuring that changes to any project within the euro programme are fully communicated and understood in terms of impact on other projects and on the overall success of the programme;

- use by everyone involved within the programme who needs to raise, track and monitor changes to projects; and

- recommendations for preserving version control as well as document standards, procedures and responsibilities.

**FIGURE 8.4**

**Change control process**

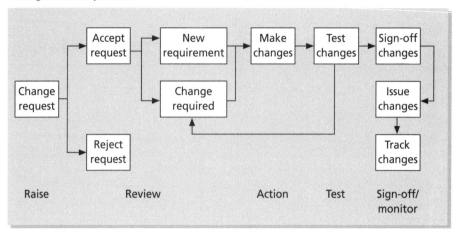

Any changes to a project must be fully understood within the context of the programme so the potential impact on other projects and the programme can be planned, communicated and monitored. Particularly important are changes in scope, plans, budgets and deliverables, all of which may be critical to the success of the programme or dependent projects.

You can use a central programme office as a central repository of information such that the most up-to-date version of all documentation should always be available either on file or stored electronically. Through the change request forms and logs, the programme office ensures that all changes are monitored, actions completed and documents updated and published accordingly.

## Issue management process

Throughout the life of your euro project, you will consistently face a broad range of issues, from requiring knowledge about specific elements of euro regulations to the need for business decisions on strategic requirements. In addition, more mundane issues such as resources, equipment and other logistical factors also have the ability to impact the progress of a project. For example, resource conflicts with your Year 2000 programme may create bottlenecks for testing one or more of your major systems.

All these issues require rapid and effective resolution to ensure that your implementation proceeds to plan. An issue management process, such as the one shown in Figure 8.5, can significantly improve the way in which you log, track and resolve issues. It can also be particularly useful to centralize the process, as

**FIGURE 8.5**

**Issue management process**

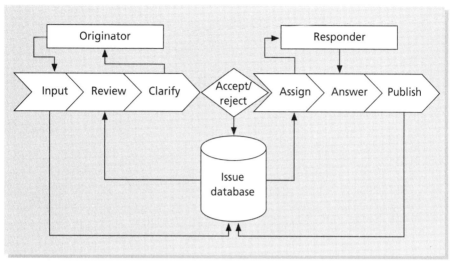

the same issues frequently crop up on more than one occasion, hence reducing the amount of duplication in effort. A programme office function can:

- establish an issues database (this may be accessed via an intranet for example)
- monitor input of issues and provide answers
- present or escalate issues to appropriate decision-makers
- provide guidance on who can provide further information on questions.

# CHAPTER 9

# Integrating mergers and acquisitions

# THE NATURE OF MERGERS AND ACQUISITIONS

Mergers and acquisitions always heat up the management atmosphere. There is so much to do at once and so much at stake, it is crucial to proceed with a clear sense of priorities, and this calls for a carefully structured approach. A merger or acquisition represents a highly charged political climate where people operate with very different personalized agendas. There are so many pressure points (including sagging morale, low level of trust and declining productivity), conflicting points of view (largely due to widespread uncertainty and culture clashes), and management distractions (most frequently centring around personal goals, politics and positioning). Unless you employ a carefully orchestrated project management approach, it is almost impossible to get through the integration without damaging the potential of the deal.

In the same way that the management of your euro programme is the key to euro success, integrating a merger or acquisition is dependent upon the quality of the management process. Strategic analyses of the impact of the euro often include combining forces with other companies as a key strategic option in response to the inevitable transformation of European markets following the introduction of the euro. For both these reasons, this final chapter looks at the key elements of the integration process and provides some guidance. The primary challenge facing managers is to ensure that the integration process is successfully meshed with your euro programme to ensure that both implementations can be completed in the timescale desired.

> **mergers and acquisitions always heat up the management atmosphere**

Whenever a company asks whether it wants to grow or shrink, buy or build, keep or sell, integrate or manage separately, it must always ask the questions 'When?' and 'Where?'. In making these choices, company managers should rely on their collective wisdom and experience, as well as ever-changing information.

Sizing up your targets is important. There are many methods, tools and processes used to identify company strengths and weaknesses and in finding acquisition candidates that can supplement and/or complement your existing business. The detail of each tool is outside of the scope of this book, though it is worth knowing that they are all simply about getting managers to decide on the right company as a merger partner.

There are two fundamental processes required during the premerger phase. Firstly, the acquirer must engage a thorough due diligence review of the target to detect any legal, financial and business risks that the buyer might inherit from the seller. Secondly, there is a strategic review in which the acquirer determines what synergies there are and how it will take advantage of them. Both these reviews

**FIGURE 9.1**

**Merger phases**

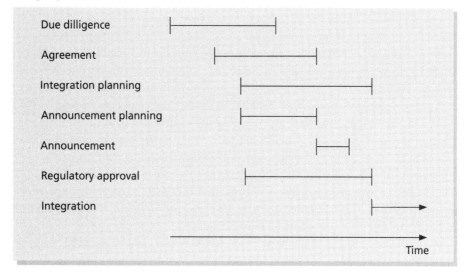

should include the state of euro preparations where appropriate. Eventually, the acquirer (often in consultation with the acquired firm) will have to write up this review in the form of a postmerger integration plan, the subject of the next section.

Identifying synergy can often be a complex process and has often led to unrealistic expectations by management. There are some basic questions, however, that you can ask to determine whether or not you are likely to be successful.

- Does the buyer bring something unique to the deal, so that competitive bids by other companies cannot push the purchase price too high?
- Is the merger or acquisition consistent with sound strategy with respect to diversification and other key issues?
- Has the acquirer attempted to make accurate forecasts of the seller's business? For example, has the buyer assessed the seller's technology?
- Can the acquirer handle an acquisition of the target's size? What proportion of the acquisition can the acquirer fund without issuing new debt or equity?
- Is there good operating and market synergy between buyer and seller?
- Is the new parent committed to sharing capital, markets and technology with the acquired company?
- Do the buyer and seller have reasonably compatible cultures?
- Do the buyer and seller share a clear vision of the newly combined organization, and is this vision based in reality?

- Will the acquirer strive for a rapid pace of integration in implementing the new company's vision?

There are two basic types of merger or acquisition: financial and strategic. A financial-type acquisition rarely requires significant integration to untap the potential available through financial restructuring. Indeed, it may actually be harmful to integrate. Typically the acquired company is treated as a separate entity.

A strategic acquisition, however, where the value-creation opportunities of the deal lie in the synergies between the companies, requires a much greater degree of integration. Here the acquired company often adds value to the acquiring company by integrating with the buyer's existing operations and often involves combinations of companies in the same or related industries, such as banking. Frequently, performance improvement is targeted through reducing costs (usually by reducing headcount) and/or increasing revenues (usually by increasing the customer base).

Strategic acquisitions are generally more demanding on organizations, principally because the integration required to achieve the desired results have a far greater human resource requirement including management skill. And this is at a time where resources, notably from operations and IT, are already stretched to the limit. The euro, and Year 2000, must have a major bearing on your integration strategy. But how do you that?

Strategic acquisitions can also include strategic alliances, where companies agree to share the risks and rewards of a specific project or set of projects. Alliances may be sealed through a contract such as a co-operation agreement to share a resource or funding, through cross-shareholdings, or through shared ownership of an incorporated joint venture. In some cases, alliances may function as a trial 'merger' under controlled conditions, unless the reason for the alliance was a regulatory barrier to merging. Overall, however, the integration requirements are generally lower for alliances than full-blown mergers or acquisitions.

There are three basic types of strategic acquisition:

- *Horizontal* – buying a competitor;
- *Vertical* – buying a current supplier or customer;
- *Diagonal* – buying into a new market, typically a new product or service line that can be marketed through current distribution channels.

Each type of strategic merger or acquisition requires a different integration strategy, though there are common elements to all three. Experience helps enormously. This was the central finding of a 1995 Mercer/*Business Week* study that compared experienced acquirers (an average of six or more deals per year) to relatively inexperienced acquirers (one to five deals per year). The experienced acquirers, which constituted 24% of the acquirer group, did much better than the inexperienced ones at rising above their industry peers in total return to shareholders during the three years following the deal. In the small, experienced group, 72% had returns above industry averages, compared to 55% for the large, inexperienced group.

# INTEGRATION MANAGEMENT

Whilst creating the strategy and preparing the plan is vitally important, most mergers fail to deliver expected results due to ineffective integration management. A review of leading studies from the 1980s to the present, summarized in Table 9.1, shows the many factors affecting postmerger performance. Researchers examined the impact of mergers on the long-run performance of companies (typically three years or

> good integration management is characterized by discipline, focus and dedicated resources

more). The key to value, it seems from the research, lies in postmerger management. This is driven from a realistic, rather than overoptimistic, identification of positive and negative synergies in the pre-merger stage.

Skimping on the investment in the integration effort is often the root cause of poor integration management. Companies often invest heavily in due diligence, then get remarkably stingy in terms of their willingness to spend on the integration effort. The economics argue strongly in favour of allocating sufficient resources to support a sophisticated integration process.

Good integration management is characterized by discipline, focus and dedicated resources. A project group should be formed to manage the transition. This organization needs to be adequately resourced, with people's responsibilities clearly defined. Key management challenges include:

- meeting aggressive deadlines
- achieving tough financial targets
- restructuring quickly with limited information
- merging a variety of systems applications and architectures
- retaining key employees
- maintaining adequate communication
- managing relocations and consolidations.

A large, complex merger takes time to integrate fully – as long as three years in the case of Chase Manhattan and Chemical Banking Corporations. However, it is generally recognized that integration basics should be managed quickly if the merger is to be successful.

**TABLE 9.1**

**Research into the long-term success of mergers and acquisitions**

| Study | Year | Companies | Primary cause of failure, however defined |
|---|---|---|---|
| McKinsey | 1987 | 116 | At least 61% failed to earn back equity capital invested within three years. Primary causes:<br>• weak core business of acquirer<br>• large target size (>10% of acquirer)<br>• overly optimistic appraisal of market potential<br>• overestimation of synergies<br>• overbidding<br>• poor postmerger integration. |
| Bradley et al. | 1988 | 248 | Postmerger gains anticipated by the market may result from:<br>• more efficient management<br>• economies of scale<br>• improved production techniques<br>• combination of complimentary resources<br>• redeployment of assets<br>• exploitation of market power.<br>The ability to realize positive synergies was through effective postmerger integration. |
| PA Consulting | 1989 | 28 banks | 80% of acquisitions have a negative impact on the acquirer's share price. Primary cause of this was deemed to be poor strategy. |
| Chakrabarti | 1990 | 31 | This study found that postmerger performance depended more on postmerger integration than on strategy. His study tracked performance in six areas: sales, profits, return on investment, market share, technological innovation and customer base. |
| Healy et al. | 1992 | 50 | This study showed that the merged firms showed significant improvements in asset productivity relative to their industries, leading to higher operating cashflow. These findings were particularly strong for transactions involving firms in overlapping businesses, suggesting that postmerger integration may play a role in adding postmerger value. |
| Mercer MC/ Business Week | 1995 | 150 | Key causes of postmerger failure:<br>• inadequate due diligence by buyer or seller<br>• lack of compelling strategy<br>• overly optimistic expectations of possible synergies |

**TABLE 9.1**

continued

| Study | Year | Companies | Primary cause of failure, however defined |
|-------|------|-----------|-------------------------------------------|
| | | | • conflicting corporate cultures<br>• slow postmerger integration. |
| Smolowitz/ Hillyer | 1996 | 45 | Key causes of postmerger failure:<br>• cultural incompatibility<br>• clashing management styles and egos<br>• inability to implement change<br>• inability to forecast<br>• excessive optimism with regard to synergy. |
| Mitchell/EIU | 1996 | 150 | This study found that 70% of all acquisitions fail to meet the expectations of their architects. |
| Coopers & Lybrand | 1996 | 125 | This study found that 66% were financially unsuccessful. The study also found a correlation between a slow pace of postmerger transition and low levels of revenue, cashflow and profitability. |
| Loughgran/ Vijh | 1997 | 947 | Companies' stock mergers earned significantly lower returns than cash mergers. Firms that pay in stock tend to have overvalued shares, whereas firms that pay in cash tend to have undervalued shares; during the postmerger period the true valuation of the companies emerges. |
| Sirower | 1997 | 168 | This study found a similar result to the Loughgran study, citing reasons as overpayment, use of stock or debt rather than internally generated cash, and the presence of multiple bidders. Essentially, this boils down to an unreasonable confidence in the positive value of a planned combination. |
| Mercer MC | 1997 | 215 | This study has found that mergers of the 1990s are outperforming those of the 1980s, where 52% in the 1990s are achieving above-industry shareholder returns, versus only 37% of the 1980s deals. The improvement says Mercer, is not related to strategy or price (finding little correlation between premiums paid and value created) but rather to improved postmerger management. |

Whilst integration is generally seen as a postmerger activity, it should not be forgotten that integration cannot be divorced from any of the other phases, including due diligence and agreement. There are important analyses and decisions being made that have an important impact on integration. Notably, the success of a deal is usually predicated on being able to carry out certain integration actions. Whether it is the consolidation of facilities in a particular region, the transfer of technologies needed to get a new product to market, or the enhancement of margins through increased purchasing power, these objectives need to be well documented from the outset. This helps create a common theme throughout all of the major phases – an important step in preparing for the many management challenges still to come.

A successful integration strategy is principally dependent upon the motivation for the merger or acquisition. Typical motives include:

- *Operating synergy* – achieve economies of scale by buying a customer, supplier or competitor;
- *Strategic planning* – accomplish strategic goals more quickly and successfully;
- *Inefficient management* – realize a return on investment by buying a company with less efficient managers and making them more efficient or replacing them;
- *Market power* – increase market share;
- *Financial synergy* – achieve lower cost of capital by smoothing cashflow and increasing debt capacity; obtain a more favourable tax status;
- *Undervaluation* – take advantage of a price that is low in comparison to past share prices and/or estimated future prices, or relative to the organic investment cost.

You should understand these motives and exactly what the integration is setting out to achieve. Whilst high-level expectations will already have been set in the premerger phase, it is at this stage that you can prepare the detailed plans for achieving all those synergies and most importantly account for the other major programmes currently under way in your organization.

The integration will necessarily encompass all the resources, processes, systems and responsibilities of the merger effort, both domestically and globally, ensuring that the integration fits with the company's overall strategy and culture. As with any major change programme, it is important for the entire organization to be involved. The shared sense of purpose can help employees embrace rather than resist the inevitable changes. Your integration strategy may encompass the integration of a wide range of factors including:

- human resources
- financial and tangible resources, e.g., balance sheets

- reputational and other intangible resources, e.g., branding, mission statements
- processes
- management systems – organization structure, controls
- compensation plans
- information technology
- corporate responsibilities
- commitments to customers and suppliers
- commitments to shareholders, bondholders and lenders
- commitments to employees.

Hence the postmerger plan must outline exactly when and how the major resources, assets, processes and commitments of the acquiring and acquired company will be combined in order to achieve the strategic goals of the newly combined company. Although one individual may be assigned to make sure that a plan gets created and respected, the best postmerger plans are ultimately created by groups. These groups should consist of senior managers and key employees from both companies, as well as external advisors including investment bankers, accountants, lawyers and consultants.

It is useful to be aware of the value that different groups of advisors can bring to the table. Often the easiest way to assess the benefits and drawbacks of different groups of advisors is by looking at how they are paid.

If advisors are paid on a contingency basis (a common practice for investment bankers), they may be overly optimistic about how much synergy a deal contains and how easy it will be to achieve. Such advisors may have much valuable expertise to impart when it comes to financing, marketing and structuring a transaction, but their enthusiasm should be taken with caution, especially with respect to the actual implementation process.

> **it is useful to be aware of the value that different groups of advisors can bring to the table**

If advisors are paid on a sliding scale depending on the amount of time a transaction takes, whether or not it ever closes successfully (a common practice when it comes to lawyers, who typically bill by the hour). Such advisors might be tempted to take an overly pessimistic view about a transaction, finding liability exposure under every turned stone.

Consultants are generally immune to these pressures, though there are two common issues that may arise. Firstly, there may be a temptation to overload the company with consultants during the implementation process, which may not be the most cost-effective resourcing alternative; and secondly, consultants may be tempted to take over the decision-making role of managers, which is never good.

Ultimately, managers should use consultants and others to help them make decisions, not to make their decisions for them. In addition, consultants can be particularly useful when acting as an impartial group facilitator. A facilitator essentially acts as an independent third party who helps a group identify problems, find solutions and make decisions. This is most useful in sensitive decision-making which may be subject to dominance or deadlock.

Key considerations for your postmerger or integration plan include the following.

- Are plans consistent with the intrinsic logic of the deal?
- Are the budgets clear and assigned?
- Are there written plans to cover both the short-term and long-term?

> ultimately, managers should use consultants and others to help them make decisions, not to make their decisions for them

- Do short- and long-term plans mesh?
- Has the planning process involved both senior managers and employees most affected by the plans?
- Do the plans take into account the operational and cultural realities of the two companies involved?
- What decisions are being based upon the plans?
- Are the plans supported by appropriate resources?
- Do the plans specify measures and milestones of progress?
- Who is accountable for achieving the plans? Establish clear, well-defined reporting relationships and lines of authority.
- Have the plans been distributed to all appropriate parties?
- Is there a programme for communicating the plans internally and externally?
- Don't underestimate the time and planning effort required in the merger process.
- Be aware of the limitations of your resources, particularly in the acquired company where motivation may decline.
- Communicate more than usual. Keep people informed, as everyone is hungry for information. Remember that mergers and acquisitions cause the communication channel to grow longer, as more people are involved and the distance from decision centres increases.
- Tell them how it is. Don't promise that things will stay the same in either company.

Merging or acquiring has frequently been one of the strategic options which many companies have considered as part of their strategic responses to the euro. Merger deals have become the primary instrument of corporate strategy, principally because strategic change in many of today's industries does not allow time for organic growth. If you want to compete it seems, you have to grow, and to grow, you have to merge or acquire.

But research has shown that the long-term results of combinations are far from convincing. The main killer of value and postmerger results has been poor post-merger management. The impact of two major programmes, EMU and Year 2000, can only weaken organisations' abilities to successfully integrate at this time. However, the business opportunities in some sectors are too strong to turn down. Consequently, managers will be under considerable pressure to deliver successful results across multiple programmes.

# CHAPTER 10

# Conclusion

Eventually all organizations operating in Europe or in European currencies will make the transition to the euro. The impact is most immediate and far-reaching in the financial services sector but it will also stimulate significant competitive realignment in other sectors. Indeed, leading companies are already deriving competitive advantage from their investment in early preparations. However, the majority of companies are only beginning to understand the impact of the euro, in particular the complexity of managing such a significant shift in the environment in which they operate.

All surveys looking at the state of preparations for the euro have the same message – that many companies have not been sufficiently preparing. In some cases, this is due to a lack of awareness; in others it is a lack of resources; whilst for some it is simply not considered a priority. But we have seen how the euro affects companies within and outside the euro-zone. Multinational companies operating in participating countries – countries that form part of the first wave of the EMU – are fully impacted by the introduction of and changeover to the euro.

Domestic enterprises typically operating within a single participating country without exporting or importing generally do not have any foreign currency transactions. As a result these enterprises have never needed to perform a currency translation before, because it was simply not necessary. With the introduction of the euro, these enterprises need to get used to another currency. Although the problems of the changeover might be slightly less complex in these enterprises, it will still be a major exercise that needs to be properly planned for. This is most immediate for companies operating with the first-wave EMU zone, but domestic enterprises in the rest of Europe should be gearing up for potential entry in a second or later wave.

The best we, as managers of organizations of all shapes and sizes, can do is be professional and prepare for the short- and long-term consequences of this historic event in the best way possible. That means we should be thorough in our strategic analysis, meticulous in our planning and realistic in our implementation. This is the only way to respond to a fundamentally changing business environment which we must factor into our long-term strategic objectives.

There is no single project that has been, is currently, or is likely to be more complex and demanding on so many organizations at the same time. There are a huge number of detailed and specific tasks to carry out to ensure that you are adequately prepared for the euro. This is true whether or not your country is in or out, and indeed regardless of whether any of the countries where you operate, sell or source supplies actually are in or out.

There are few absolutely prescriptive answers to many questions posed by the euro. Many require strategic, operational and tactical decision-making, and this takes time. Those that have deliberated frequently realize that the implications of the changeover are broader and deeper than they first thought. Few companies have yet to understand the strategic opportunities and threats, primarily because they have either been too preoccupied by the day-to-day practical issues of changing over, or political uncertainty has prevented practical action.

In addition, you cannot manage the changeover in isolation – your timetable may well be driven by the approach adopted by your key customers, suppliers and competitors. These external drivers may make it necessary for an organization to become euro-compatible earlier rather than later. Whatever you do, do not underestimate the time and effort involved. There are clear competitive, efficiency and cost advantages in getting your strategy for the euro right first time.

IT systems represent a large share of the global euro changeover project; however the switch to the euro cannot be reduced to mere IT problems as it involves major strategic and organizational issues. Therefore, information system experts in all departments should be closely involved in conducting the project, but they should not head the project.

In many cases, companies have focused on the IT issues to the detriment of both the business and IT. This has created significant problems, uncertainty and delay to IT as responding to the euro has to be business-led. Frequently the IT department comes under pressure from the business to prepare for EMU but does not specify its requirements.

As we have seen, EMU is not simply about the introduction of an alternative currency, but about accelerating the development of the single market in Europe. This means you must fundamentally review, not just your IT systems, but also products, marketing, supply chains, location of operations, international organization, business processes, as well as the needs and responses of customers and competitors. The key to success lies in the timely completion of a thorough strategic analysis and plan, followed by a rigorous and fully-resourced implementation programme.

A strategic analysis, or impact assessment, should provide management with a high-level understanding of the impact of a changing environment on your business. It should identify the resource implications of these changes and the likely level of investment in alternative options.

Characterized by free discussion to produce ideas and commitments your strategic analysis should produce the basic input for planning in conjunction with suitable procedures that fit your firm's way of working. The plan provides the platform for understanding, communicating and gaining the support of those concerned with its implementation.

Many strategic plans can easily become too complicated. The best plans readily convey the linkages between the various steps in the strategic process, whilst highlighting the principal actions which will allow the milestones to be reached and therefore the goals to be achieved. They should set the objectives for each department or business line across the organization and become the prime input to the development of detailed business plans and budgets during the implementation phase. At the same time it also provides a management control framework to ensure successful implementation including structure, reporting, risk management and communications.

Having completed a thorough strategic analysis and prepared a comprehensive strategic plan, you have to implement – you have to gain commitment, motivate and mobilize the organization, prepare detailed plans, create an efficient management structure, manage the change programme and achieve your objectives. There is a difference between increasing the level of awareness and doing something about the problem. There is a lot of inertia, particularly in large organizations, to get a big project up and running. Some of the key success factors in making your strategic plan work include:

- Management is committed to implementing the plan, constantly reinforced by their actions. Priorities should be consistently applied and demonstrated.

- An appropriate management structure is established. An inappropriate structure can seriously undermine the implementation process.

- The plan is communicated to all staff. Everybody does not need to know all of the detail, but should at least be informed of the essence so that they can play their part. A common sense of purpose can dramatically improve your chance of success.

- Management information reflects what you are trying to achieve and progress is reviewed regularly.

- The euro is the mother of all projects. Consequently, quality project management skills are required throughout the organization.

It is crucial that good project management is put in place to ensure deadlines and objectives can be met, even if the workload grows beyond budget. Many organizations have fallen foul of a multitude of management issues as far as their euro projects are concerned. Each issue in isolation has caused lengthy delays in projects (up to 18 months in some cases), increased costs and loss of business. The absence of disciplined project management and structure typically results in a resource drain, loss of focus for the organization, and serious slippage in productivity. Valid planning implies not only that objectives are attained but that such attainment is the result of planning. This means that attention must be directed not simply at minimizing deviations from plans but also at detecting errors and the effectiveness of plans.

The challenge of the euro project now sits firmly in your hands and the hands of your fellow managers and there is a great deal of work to be done. The experiences we have and the lessons we learn throughout this process will undoubtedly stand us in good stead for the challenging business issues and projects of the future.

# Index